REDBOOK
Flavor
Rules!

REDBOOK
Flavor Rules!

More than 250 recipes
PLUS hints, tips & tricks for really great food

HEARST BOOKS A Division of Sterling Publishing Co., Inc.
New York

Produced by Rebus, Inc.

Rodney M. Friedman	Publisher
Grace Young	Director, Recipe Development & Photography
Kate Slate	Editorial Director, Food Group
Evie Righter	Project Editor
Bonnie J. Slotnick	Writer
James W. Brown, Jr.	Assistant Editor
Timothy Jeffs	Art Director
Yoheved Gertz	Design Assistant
Sandra Rose Gluck	Senior Recipe Developer
Lisa Koenig	Photographer
Paul S. Grims, Karen Pickus	Food Stylists
Debrah Donahue	Prop Stylist
Hill Nutrition Associates	Nutritionists

The Library of Congress has catalogued the hardcover edition as follows:
Redbooks flavor rules! : more than 250 recipes PLUS hints, tips & tricks for really great food.
p. cm.
Includes index.
ISBN 0-688-16255-X
I. Cookery. I. Redbook.

TX714.R428 1999   98-32091
641.5—dc21

First Paperback Edition 2005

10   9   8   7   6   5   4   3   2   1

Published by Hearst Books
A Division of Sterling Publishing Co., Inc.
387 Park Avenue South, New York, NY 10016

Redbook is a trademark owned by Hearst Magazines Property, Inc., in USA,
and Hearst Communications, Inc., in Canada.
Hearst Books is a trademark owned by Hearst Communications, Inc.

www.redbookmag.com

Distributed in Canada by Sterling Publishing
c/o Canadian Manda Group, 165 Dufferin Street
Toronto, Ontario, Canada M6K 3H6

Distributed in Australia by Capricorn Link (Australia) Pty. Ltd.
P.O. Box 704, Windsor, NSW 2756 Australia

Manufactured in China

ISBN 1-58816-216-8

Contents

Foreword

When's the last time you ate something *incredibly delicious?* We mean something so flavorful and fresh, homemade and hearty that it soothed your soul as it filled your stomach. Has it been a while? Maybe—like many people today—you rely on the ever-popular pizza and grabbed-on-the-run take-out for quick meals. Whether you're working long hours or raising a family (or, like many of us, doing both, and more), you sometimes have to sacrifice flavor for *fast*—because you're home, everyone's hungry, and you need to eat NOW!

Still, there comes a time when you're going to crave some real food—home-cooked, freshly made, from-scratch food that tastes incredibly good. Some sample scenarios: Tucking into a homey supper of steaming soup and freshly baked focaccia; baking up a batch of gooey, peanut-buttery chocolate-chip cookies; surprising your sweetie (when it's *not* a special day) with a classic *coq au vin.* Yes, all these delicious deeds are possible—and they won't require endless hours in the kitchen, months of cooking-school classes—or quitting your day job.

Don't worry if your culinary skills are a little sketchy: We'll bring you up to speed. But rest assured that these recipes are no boring basics. They're inventive, contemporary creations sparked with jazzy stuff like fragrant fresh herbs, savory smoked chilies, zesty citrus, pungent garlic, toasty sesame oil, sweet balsamic vinegar, sharp Parmesan cheese, tangy mango chutney, piquant whole peppercorns—have we got your creative juices flowing? And because there's more to life than three squares a day, we've supplied recipes for easy but impressive desserts, breads, and party foods along with the breakfast, lunch, and dinner offerings.

To keep you on track, we've packed the places over, under, and around the recipes with hints, tips, and inside stuff (which wine to choose for cooking, how to flambé a sauce, why muffin batter should be mixed quickly, how to tell when a cake is done). When words can't tell the whole story, we've got pictures. Lots and lots of pictures. So discover the fun, the challenges, and the rewards of cooking. Discover the Place Where Flavor Rules!

Do you know how to...

SECTION CITRUS FRUIT Peel the fruit with a sharp knife, removing all the white pith, which is bitter. Working over a strainer set in a bowl, slide the knife on either side of each membrane to free the segments. When you've removed all the segments, squeeze every last bit of juice out of the membranes.

GRATE CITRUS ZEST There's a special gadget called a zester that quickly grates fine threads of zest (the thin, colored part of the peel) from citrus fruits. Pull the zester across the fruit, pressing down just enough to remove the zest but not the white pith beneath.

CUT STRIPS OF CITRUS ZEST For larger strips of zest, use a swivel-bladed vegetable peeler, again being careful to remove just the colored portion of the peel. You can also do this with a paring knife if you have a steady hand.

PEEL A FRESH PINEAPPLE Twist off the crown. Peel the pineapple by slicing downward with a heavy knife; just cut deep enough (about ¼ inch) to remove all but the small brown spots called "eyes." To remove the eyes, cut V-shaped grooves around the fruit, following the spiral pattern formed by the eyes.

CORE A PEAR When you want to core a pear but leave it whole (for baking or stuffing), use an apple corer. Insert the corer into the base of the fruit and carefully push it just short of halfway into the pear. Twist the corer to cut out the center of the pear, then remove it.

HULL A STRAWBERRY Hulling a strawberry involves more than just removing the leafy cap. You also need to remove the little "core" on the inside. Use a small knife to remove the small cone-shaped core from the top of each berry. Rinse the berries *before* hulling so they don't get waterlogged.

PEEL A MANGO Hold the fruit vertically and slice off the two "cheeks," leaving the flat pit in a middle section. Score the flesh of each "cheek" into cubes without cutting through the skin. Turn the cubed pieces inside out so you can slice off the flesh. Then cut the flesh from the remaining portion (work around the pit).

PIT AN AVOCADO Cut the avocado lengthwise, slicing all the way up to the pit in the center. Twist the halves apart. Then tap the knife blade into the pit; give the knife a twist (like a giant screwdriver) and the pit will come right out. You can then peel the avocado or scoop the flesh out with a spoon.

SHRED CABBAGE Quarter the head of cabbage through the core and cut a triangular section from the base of each quarter to remove the tough, solid core. Then cut each quarter crosswise into shreds or strips.

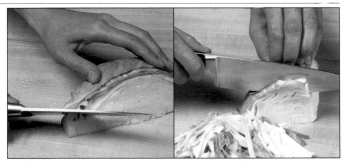

TRIM ASPARAGUS You can simply cut the tough ends from asparagus stalks—or let Nature help you find the right spot: Hold the stalk in both hands, more than halfway down its length. Bend the stalk until the tough portion snaps off.

HANDLE FRESH CHILIES Handle, but don't touch! We recommend wearing thin rubber gloves to protect your skin from the burning compounds in chilies. If you don't have gloves, be sure to wash your hands thoroughly with soap when you're done. And don't touch your eyes when you've been handling chilies.

Do you know how to...

SEED A CUCUMBER When a cucumber has big seeds and a lot of pulp in the center, seed the cuke, leaving just the crisp flesh. To remove the seeds, halve the cucumber lengthwise, then use a teaspoon to scoop or scrape out the seedy portion.

TRIM FENNEL You can save the feathery portion of fennel tops for seasoning or garnish, but the woody stalks are inedible. Trim the stalks straight across, then trim the base of the bulb. Halve, quarter, or slice the bulb as the recipe requires.

GRATE VEGETABLES A box grater is easier to hold than a flat grater. Use the large holes for grating strips of hard vegetables such as carrots or potatoes.

PEEL GARLIC Try to peel a whole garlic clove and you'll probably end up with garlic under your fingernails. Instead, lay a wide knife blade on top of the clove and smack it with your fist to crush the garlic slightly. This will break the skin, making it easy to pull off.

MINCE HERBS OR VEGETABLES BY "ROCKING" A CHEF'S KNIFE This classic technique is a real work-saver, but a well-balanced chef's knife with a wedge-shaped blade is required. Roughly cut the food to be minced in smallish portions, then mound it on a cutting board. Hold down the tip of the knife with the fingertips of one hand and rock the knife up and down with the other hand, moving the blade back and forth across the food. Re-mound the food occasionally for even mincing.

SNIP HERBS Sometimes it's quicker to snip herbs (especially feathery ones like dill) with scissors than to try to mince them with a knife. Hold the herb by the stem and snip off the leaves in tiny bits.

SLIVER FRESH HERBS The French call fine slivers of fresh leafy herbs (or any greens) a *chiffonade*. The fastest way to make a chiffonade of herbs such as basil or mint is to stack a few leaves, then roll them up tightly. Slice the roll crosswise to yield strips of the desired width.

MINCE FRESH GINGER When you need a substantial amount of fresh ginger, peel a good-sized knob (use a vegetable peeler or a paring knife), then cut it into thin coins. Stack the coins and cut them crosswise into thin sticks. Finally, chop the sticks crosswise into a fine mince.

MINCE AN ONION Peel the onion, then shave a slice off one side so it stands steady. Make a series of parallel cuts to (but not through) the root end. Turn the onion 90°, shave off a piece again, and make a series of cuts perpendicular to the first. Finally, cut the onion crosswise and it will fall into very fine pieces.

SLICE AN ONION This will give you crescent-shaped slivers of onion: Halve the onion through the root end. Lay each half flat on the cutting board and slice crosswise. Keep the fingertips holding the onion tucked under so they don't get nicked!

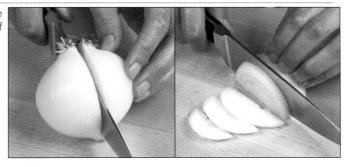

CUT VEGETABLES ON THE DIAGONAL Vegetables like carrots, zucchini, or celery look more elegant if you slice them on a long diagonal instead of straight across. And, because more surface area is exposed, the vegetable will cook more quickly.

CLEAN LEEKS Leeks almost always have a lot of dirt just where the green leaves branch off from the white stem. If the recipe calls for whole leeks, halve the leek down to this joint and rinse out the dirt. But if the leek is to be sliced or chopped, cut it up first, then rinse the pieces in a bowl of warm water.

Do you know how to...

CLEAN MUSHROOMS The less time fresh mushrooms spend in water, the better (they'll soak it up). So it's a good idea to clean the mushrooms with a damp cloth or paper towel, or a soft brush. Rub gently; if the dirt is stubborn, run the mushrooms under a light spray of cold water, then pat them dry.

PREPARE FRESH SHIITAKE MUSHROOMS Shiitake mushrooms are much denser than button mushrooms—especially the stems, which are really too tough to eat. Cut off the stems (save them for soup-making or discard them), then cut the meaty caps as directed in the recipe.

STRING SUGAR SNAP PEAS (OR SNOW PEAS) Sugar snap peas and their cousins, snow peas, should have their strings removed before cooking. Pinch the top of the pod to start the string, then peel it off. For sugar snaps, (big, mature ones especially), repeat to pull off the string on the other side of the pod.

CORE TOMATOES You can see that the tomato's stem is attached to a little white core (which does not share the tomato's terrific taste or texture). So when a recipe says to "core" tomatoes, this is the part you want to remove, by cutting out a cone-shaped portion of the top of the tomato.

PEEL TOMATOES Why peel tomatoes before cooking them? If you don't, the skin will come off as the tomatoes cook, but it will never soften and will end up as unpleasantly chewy bits in the sauce or soup. So many recipes direct you to peel tomatoes. The best way to do this is to blanch the tomatoes in boiling water to loosen their skins. Lower a few tomatoes at a time into a big pot of boiling water. Leave them in for about 20 seconds, or until the skins split, then lift them out with a slotted spoon. The skins will slip off ever so easily.

PIT OLIVES BY CRUSHING Pitting olives is a breeze if you use this simple trick: Place the olives on a cutting board and gently crush them under the blade of a chef's knife (no need to pound, just press firmly). The olives will split and the pits will be easy to remove.

SQUEEZE SPINACH DRY Frozen spinach is a real time-saver when you need cooked spinach as an ingredient. But be sure to squeeze the spinach dry, or its liquid will make the dish watery. After thawing the spinach, press it in a strainer to get out most of the liquid, then finish by squeezing it in your hand.

GRATE PARMESAN The easy way to grate Parmesan and other hard cheeses is with a rotary grater—and fresh grated is *so* much better than pre-grated cheese! Just put in a chunk of cheese, close the top, and crank the handle. Some rotary graters have interchangeable blades for fine and coarse grating.

SPLIT A CHICKEN LEG To divide a whole chicken leg into drumstick and thigh, first find the joint. You can wiggle the leg to feel where the joint is, but there is also a line of fat that runs along the joint. Work a knife through the meat and skin down into the joint and then through to the other side.

SHELL AND DEVEIN SHRIMP In-shell shrimp are much cheaper than shelled, so this is a good skill to perfect! Start by pulling off the legs, then slip your thumbs under the shell to pop it off. To devein, make a shallow cut down the back of the shrimp, then use the tip of the knife to pull out the black vein.

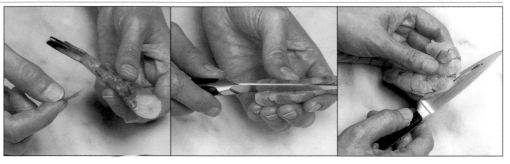

USE A SHRIMP DEVEINER Specially designed deveining tools make quick work of deveining shrimp. You slip them into the head end of the shell and push them toward the tail. As the wider part of the deveiner goes in, it splits the shell apart; the pointed end strips out the vein at the same time.

DEBEARD MUSSELS Although most mussels are pretty clean when you buy them, some have strands of hairlike fiber (called a beard) that have to be pulled out. Cook the mussels right away after debearding—they must be alive when you cook them, and they'll die shortly after debearding.

QUARTER SCALLOPS Bay scallops are expensive and not always available, but you can recreate the "bay scallop experience" by cutting up sea scallops, which are about four times as large. Cut them into equal quarters or thirds so that they cook evenly.

POUND MEAT OR POULTRY CUTLETS Veal cutlets, pork medallions, boneless chicken breasts, and turkey breast slices cook faster and look more elegant when flattened to an even thickness. Place between sheets of plastic wrap and pound gently with a meat pounder or small skillet.

Do you know how to...

CUT MEAT FOR STIR-FRYING
For quick, even cooking, cut meat for stir-fries into thin, even strips. First, trim any visible fat from the meat. If it's a wide cut, like this flank steak, halve it lengthwise. Then cut ¼-inch-thick strips crosswise. The work will go more easily if you first chill the meat in the freezer for a few minutes.

TELL WHEN FISH IS DONE
Some recipes say to cook fish "until it flakes easily," but if it falls apart at a touch, it's overdone. Fish should separate readily when you test it, but should still look moist and the slightest bit translucent. The center will continue to cook from retained heat after the fish is taken from the pan.

TELL WHEN SHRIMP ARE DONE Shrimp have a built-in doneness signal: They turn from a translucent greenish-gray to an opaque but slightly pearly white (on the inside) and seashell pink (on the outside). This happens in a matter of minutes, so watch carefully: Overcooked shrimp will be tough.

TELL WHEN MEAT IS DONE
Give the meat a gentle poke, then compare with the resilience of the spot inside your thumb joint. Is the meat as soft and jiggly as your hand at rest? Then it's rare. A bit firmer and springier, as when you make a loose fist? Medium. Firm as a clenched fist? The meat is well done.

TELL WHEN CHICKEN IS DONE
Rare steak is great, but nobody should eat under-cooked chicken. Cut about halfway into the chicken: The flesh should be opaque white and the juices clear or yellowish, not pink. ⚠ At right, we show what **under-cooked chicken** looks like.

USE A GRAVY SEPARATOR
Instead of skimming the fat off a pan of drippings, get one of these ingenious gadgets. You just pour in pan juices and let them settle for a moment. The fat rises to the top, and you can pour off the defatted juices through the spout, which, as you see, comes up from the bottom.

DEGLAZE A PAN Deglazing is a method in which the caramelized meat juices (called a glaze) that come from sautéing meat or poultry are used to make a sauce or gravy. Here's how to deglaze a pan to make a sauce: Pour off excess fat. Whisk liquid (usually broth, wine, or water) into the skillet, scraping up the browned bits (the caramelized juices) from the bottom and sides of the pan. (This is best done over low heat.) You can then serve the deglazed juices as the simplest of sauces (perhaps reduced slightly to concentrate the flavors), or you can thicken them with flour, or enrich them with cream.

MAKE BEURRE MANIÉ The classic French "kneaded butter" is the secret to smoothly thickened sauces and soups. Knead together equal amounts of softened butter and flour (roughly, 2 tablespoons of each will thicken 1 cup sauce). Whisk small bits of beurre manié into the sauce just until incorporated.

STEAM FOOD There are many ways to accomplish this healthy cooking method. A collapsible steamer basket (near right) converts any tightly covered pot into a steamer. Some pots come with their own steamer inserts (middle). An Asian bamboo steamer (far right) fits nicely inside a wok.

ROAST AND PEEL PEPPERS This doesn't have to be a labor-intensive job if you do it our way. Cut the peppers into flat panels lengthwise (the shape of the pepper will dictate how many panels you get). Roast the peppers skin side up and as close to the heat source (of a broiler or outdoor grill) as possible, until the skin is completely charred. After roasting, pile the peppers in a bowl; cover with a plate and let steam for 15 minutes. The steaming will loosen the charred skin for easy peeling. Thick, meaty peppers (they feel heavy when you heft them) are best for roasting. Thin-walled peppers can cook away to nothing.

Do you know how to...

MAKE BREAD CRUMBS Have you ever read a recipe that called for fresh bread crumbs and wondered what the heck they were? Well, they're really just finely crumbled bread. To make them with a food processor, tear fresh bread into pieces and process until the crumbs are the size you want (they can be quite fine, as shown). To make crumbs by hand, cut sliced bread into narrow strips, stack them, and chop them crosswise. This will make coarser crumbs. In either case, the crumbs will be easier to make if you use slightly stale bread.

MEASURE LIQUIDS Be sure to use a see-through liquid measuring cup (there really is a difference between liquid and dry measures). You'll get the most accurate measure if you check at eye level (by bending down to counter height), rather than looking down from above or picking up the cup.

MEASURE SOLID FATS Cleaning a greasy measuring cup is no fun, so try this "displacement method." Subtract the amount of fat you need from 1 cup, then pour that amount of water into a measuring cup—e.g., to measure ¼ cup fat, use ¾ cup water. Then add fat by spoonfuls until the water level reaches 1 cup.

MEASURE DRY INGREDIENTS Dry ingredients should be measured in dry measures, which usually come in a graduated set. (A liquid measure—see above—will actually give an inaccurate amount of a dry ingredient.) You can measure some dry ingredients, such as sugar, by scooping with the measuring cup itself. But very powdery ingredients such as flour, cornstarch, confectioners' sugar, and cocoa would be compacted by scooping and require the "spoon and level" technique: Lightly spoon the ingredient into a dry measuring cup; don't pack it in. Then level off the top with the back of a knife.

CUT BUTTER INTO FLOUR Pastry dough and crumb toppings require a special method to mix—but not thoroughly blend—the butter and flour. Toss the well-chilled chunks of butter with the flour (near right), then cut into the butter with a pastry blender (middle) or 2 table knives used scissor fashion.

ROLL OUT PIE DOUGH Quick, cool moves make for a tender, flaky pie dough. Working on a floured surface, pat a chilled ball of dough into a disk, then roll it, with short outward strokes, into a circle about 2 inches wider than the pan all around. Drape one side of the dough over the rolling pin and transfer the dough to the pie plate. Gently pat the dough into the bottom of the plate, being careful not to stretch or tear the dough. Trim the dough evenly all around. After filling the pie, roll out a second portion of dough and place it on top. Trim the top crust and fold under the edges of both crusts. Crimp the edge with a fork to seal the crusts together.

BLIND-BAKE A PIE SHELL For some pies, you need to bake the crust empty, or "blind," before filling. To keep the crust from bubbling and buckling as it bakes, line it with foil, then weight it with dried beans or rice (you can also use specially made pie weights, which are small ceramic or aluminum "pebbles"). After baking, remove the foil and weights, and prick the bottom of the crust to release steam. If you do a lot of pie baking, you should save the beans or rice to use the next time you blind-bake a pie shell—but don't plan to cook them for dinner.

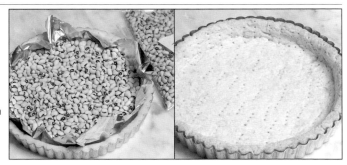

TOAST NUTS Depending on how many nuts you are toasting, you can either do this in a skillet on the stove or in a baking pan in the oven. For relatively small amounts, place the nuts in an ungreased heavy skillet and toast over medium heat. Stir or shake them often, and keep an eye on them: As soon as they are done, turn them out of the pan so that they don't scorch. Toast larger quantities of nuts on a baking sheet in a 325°F. oven. Again, keep an eye on them. The amount of time it takes to toast nuts will vary with the type of nut and whether or not they are whole, sliced, or chopped.

Do you know how to...

SKIN HAZELNUTS The papery brown skin on hazelnuts clings tightly. To remove it, toast the nuts in a 325°F oven for about 10 minutes, then wrap them in a kitchen towel and rub vigorously. Most, but not all, of the skin will come off, so don't worry if a little skin is left on.

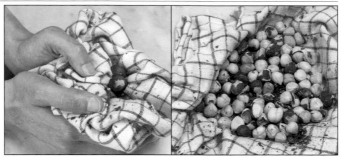

LINE A CAKE PAN Depending on the recipe, a cake pan may need to be lined, greased, floured—or some combination of the three. To line a pan, trace its outline on waxed paper and cut out the shape. Fit the waxed paper into the pan and, if the recipe requires it, grease or grease and flour the waxed paper.

TELL WHEN A CAKE IS DONE A cake tester or thin skewer inserted in the center should come out clean (**the cake at right is not quite done**—it has a few minutes to go). There are other signs, too: The cake will have pulled away from the sides of the pan, and when you touch the cake gently, it will spring back.

PROOF AND DISSOLVE YEAST Always "proof" yeast to be sure it's still active: Sprinkle the yeast and a pinch of sugar into a small bowl of warm (105° to 115°F) water. Let stand for 1 minute, then stir to dissolve the yeast. A layer of foam will form on top within about 5 minutes. If not, the yeast is not good.

PREPARE YEAST DOUGH To knead: Push the dough away from you with the heel of your hand, then fold it toward you and give the dough a quarter turn. Repeat the process until the dough is smooth and elastic. After the dough has risen, deflate it with your fist before shaping into loaves.

BEAT EGG WHITES Always separate eggs over a small bowl, and *then* transfer the whites to a dry, clean mixing bowl. This method ensures that you will not get any egg yolk into the egg whites by accident. (The fat in the yolk would keep the whites from beating properly.) To beat egg whites, start with the mixer on low speed and beat the whites until foamy (top, middle). Then increase the speed and beat until you have what the recipe calls for: soft peaks (top, right), which slowly droop over, or stiff peaks (bottom, left), which hold their angular shape after you lift out the beaters.
⚠ Watch carefully: Beat too long and the egg whites will get dry and "broken" (far right)—and you'll have to start over.

MELT CHOCOLATE Place the chocolate, cut into chunks, in a bowl set over very hot (but not actively boiling) water; let stand, stirring occasionally. To microwave, place the blocks of chocolate in a bowl and cook on High for 1 to 3 minutes. The chocolate will keep its shape (and appear unmelted) until you stir it.

WHIP CREAM Chill the cream, bowl, and beaters in the freezer, especially if your kitchen is warm. Beat the cream on medium speed until soft peaks form (near right).
⚠ Watch carefully: A few seconds of overbeating and cream will turn to butter (at far right, cream that is past the point of no return).

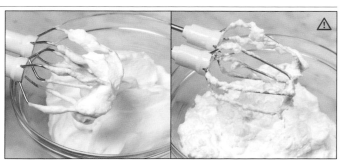

Do you know how to...

FOLD INGREDIENTS TOGETHER When you want to combine something fluffy (such as beaten egg whites or the whipped cream shown here) with something denser and heavier (such as melted chocolate), you need to fold —not stir—the two together. Using a gentle under-and-over motion with a rubber spatula, cut down to the bottom of the bowl, then bring the spatula up to the top and "fold" the cream over the chocolate. Rotate the bowl 45° and repeat. Fold *just* until blended (a few streaks are okay); the object is to combine the two ingredients without deflating the fluffy one.

TELL WHEN CUSTARD IS DONE You'll know when custard is done by checking to see if it will coat the back of a spoon. A thin custard (like crème anglaise, or custard sauce) will simply coat the spoon, but a thicker custard will leave a clear track when you run your finger down the spoon.

CHILL FOOD IN AN ICE BATH When you want to chill something quickly (custard, for example), pour the hot food into a metal or glass bowl and place that in a larger bowl of ice and water. Stirring speeds the cooling.

FILL A PASTRY BAG Not such an awkward task when you do it this way: Fit the piping tip into the bag, then fold over the top of the bag to form a deep cuff. Hold the bag under the cuff with one hand while you put in the cream, custard, or icing. Then unroll the cuff and twist it over the filling.

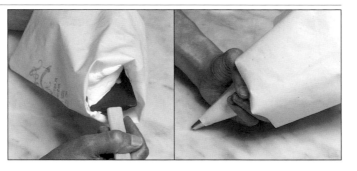

THICKEN WITH CORNSTARCH Cornstarch makes beautifully glossy sauces, but if you stir dry cornstarch into simmering sauce, you'll never get rid of the lumps. Instead, blend the cornstarch with cold liquid before stirring it into the sauce. Cook gently—don't boil the sauce or it may separate.

STRAIN FRUIT PUREE Straining seems like a chore, but a dessert sauce made from berries is a lot more elegant if it's not filled with tiny seeds. After pureeing the fruit in a food processor or blender, turn it into a sieve and press it through with a wooden spoon or rubber spatula.

appetizers & Starters

Bruschetta PLUS

Bruschetta are great appetizers to serve when you've got a mixture of kids and adults. The kids can have the crisp toasts with no topping at all. Or you can really kid-customize the bruschetta and sprinkle them with Parmesan or shredded mozzarella before you put them in the oven.

Prep time per topping: 15 minutes/Bake time: 10 minutes

These garlicky toasts topped with savory spreads are a classic Italian appetizer. Make just one batch of toasts and one topping, or toast more bread and make two, three, or all four toppings. Short cut: Serve the toppings on crackers or with tortilla chips.

Bruschetta toppings (recipes follow)

1 loaf crusty Italian bread, 24 inches long (about 11 ounces)

3 tablespoons olive oil

2 garlic cloves, peeled and halved

1. Make one of the toppings; set aside.
2. Preheat oven to 400°F.
3. Cut bread on diagonal into scant ½-inch-thick slices. Brush bread on one side with oil. Transfer slices to baking sheet and bake about 7 minutes, or until golden and crisp. With cut garlic cloves, very lightly rub crisp sides of toast; discard garlic. Divide the topping evenly among the garlic toasts. *Makes about 32 bruschetta/40 cals, 1g fat per bruschetta without topping*

Tomato, Olive & Mint Topping In small skillet, heat 1 teaspoon olive oil over low heat. Add 1 minced small garlic clove and cook 1 minute, or until tender. In

Bruschetta with (left to right) Tomato, Bell Pepper & Almond Topping; Roasted Poblano Topping; and Smoky White Bean Topping.

medium bowl, stir together sautéed garlic, 1 pound seeded and coarsely chopped tomatoes, ⅓ cup pitted and coarsely chopped Kalamata olives, ¼ cup chopped mint leaves (or basil leaves), 2 teaspoons olive oil, and ½ teaspoon salt. *Makes 2½ cups/9 cals, .7g fat per tablespoon*

Roasted Poblano Topping Preheat broiler. Place 2 halved and seeded poblano peppers, skin side up, on broiler pan. Broil 6 inches from heat until skin is charred, about 7 minutes. When cool enough to handle, peel and thinly sliver cross-wise. In 10-inch skillet, heat 2 teaspoons olive oil over medium heat. Add 1 minced small red onion and 1 minced garlic clove and cook, stirring, about 7 minutes, or until onion is tender. Stir in ¼ cup chopped parsley, 1 tablespoon fresh lemon juice, 1 teaspoon olive oil, ½ teaspoon salt, and the roasted peppers. Remove from heat. *Makes 1 generous cup/15 cals, .9g fat per tablespoon*

Smoky White Bean Topping In medium bowl, with potato masher, mash 1 can (19 ounces) white beans, rinsed and drained, with 2 tablespoons olive oil, 4 teaspoons sesame oil, 4 teaspoons water, 2 teaspoons fresh lemon juice, ¼ teaspoon natural-hickory liquid smoke, and ¼ teaspoon salt. Stir in ⅓ cup finely shredded carrots. *Makes 2 cups/35 cals, 2g fat per tablespoon*

Tomato, Bell Pepper & Almond Topping In 10-inch skillet, heat 1 tablespoon olive oil over low heat. Add 1 minced medium onion and 2 minced garlic cloves and cook, stirring frequently, about 7 minutes, or until onion is tender. Add 1 red and 1 yellow bell pepper, both diced, and cook, stirring frequently, about 5 minutes, or until crisp-tender. Add ½ cup chopped, drained canned tomatoes and ¼ teaspoon salt, and cook about 3 minutes, or until lightly thickened. Stir in 3 tablespoons raisins and 3 tablespoons coarsely chopped almonds. *Makes 2 cups/15 cals, .8g fat per tablespoon*

Absolutely Nuts

Prep time: 10 minutes/Bake time: 25 minutes

If you want your guests (or family) to have an appetite for dinner, be stingy with these spice-gilded nuts, because they *will* all get eaten.

4 teaspoons chili powder	2 cups unsalted cashews (12 ounces)
4 teaspoons sugar	
1½ teaspoons dried thyme	1¼ cups pecan halves (8 ounces)
1¼ teaspoons salt	4 tablespoons unsalted butter, melted

1. Preheat oven to 350°F.
2. In large bowl, stir together chili powder, sugar, thyme, and salt. Add cashews, pecans, and butter and toss well. Transfer to jelly-roll pan and bake, turning nuts occasionally, 25 minutes, or until fragrant and crisp. Cool to room temperature before serving. *Makes 4 cups/250 cals, 23g fat per ¼ cup*

Garnish each bruschetta with a small fresh herb leaf or sprig, such as chives, mint, parsley, cilantro, or basil. If the herb is also used in the topping, all the better.

In a pinch

Poblano peppers—deep-green chilies about 4 inches long—have a flavor somewhere between a sweet green pepper and a jalapeño. However, the Roasted Poblano Topping at left will be just fine if you make it with a plain old bell pepper. Just add heat (like a pinch of cayenne or some minced pickled jalapeño pepper) to give it some kick. Roast the bell peppers the same way you would the poblanos.

For a change, go Absolutely Nuts with other nut combinations: Try pistachios and almonds. A change of herb can also bring new dimensions to this recipe: Experiment with rosemary instead of thyme (but use only 1 teaspoon, minced).

Chunky Guacamole with Chili-Lime Chips

Prep time: 20 minutes/Cook time: 15 minutes

Guacamole seems to have replaced the sour cream-onion dip as the definitive party food. And here's a definitive recipe, which is virtually foolproof as long as the avocados are good and ripe. A ripe avocado will yield to gentle finger pressure.

Chili-Lime Chips (recipe follows)
2 ripe avocados, pitted and peeled
1 small tomato, finely chopped
⅓ cup finely diced red onion

1 jalapeño pepper, seeded and finely diced
2 tablespoons fresh lime juice
½ teaspoon salt
⅓ cup chopped cilantro

1. Make Chili-Lime Chips.
2. In large bowl, mash avocados with potato masher or back of large spoon until chunky, not smooth. Stir in tomato, onion, jalapeño, lime juice, and salt; toss until well combined. Add cilantro; toss again. Serve with chips on side. *Makes 6 servings/120 cals, 10g fat per serving without chips*

Chili-Lime Chips Preheat oven to 375°F. In small bowl, stir together 2 tablespoons fresh lime juice, 2 tablespoons olive oil, 1 teaspoon chili powder, ½ teaspoon salt, and ½ teaspoon sugar. Brush mixture on one side of each of 12 corn tortillas (6-inch diameter) and cut into 6 wedges each. Arrange wedges in single layer on baking sheets and bake 10 to 12 minutes, turning midway, or until crisp. *Makes 72 chips/13 cals, .5g fat per chip*

Roasted Tomato Salsa

Prep time: 15 minutes/Cook time: 10 minutes

Roasting tomatoes deepens and enriches their flavor (think of what happens when you roast bell peppers). Add to that a chipotle pepper and you have a truly unusual salsa. Just the thing to serve with Smoky Quesadillas (page 27) or alongside Chunky Guacamole (above) as a dip for tortilla chips.

2 pounds plum tomatoes
2 tablespoons red wine vinegar
1 tablespoon olive oil
1 tablespoon tomato paste
¼ teaspoon natural-hickory liquid smoke (optional)

1 chipotle pepper in adobo sauce, finely chopped
½ teaspoon salt
½ cup chopped cilantro
2 scallions, thinly sliced
¾ teaspoon ground cumin

1. Preheat broiler.

2. Cut each tomato in half. Place, cut side down, on broiler pan. Broil 6 inches from heat about 5 minutes, or until skin is nicely charred. Remove from pan and when cool enough to handle, coarsely chop. Transfer to large bowl and toss with vinegar, oil, tomato paste, liquid smoke, chipotle, and salt until well coated. Add cilantro and scallions and toss again.

3. In small skillet, toast cumin over low heat 1 minute, or until fragrant. Add to tomato mixture and toss again. For maximum flavor, let stand 30 minutes. At serving time, if there is excess liquid in bowl, drain off half of it. *Makes 3 cups/30 cals, 1g fat per ¼ cup*

Dynamite Black Bean Dip

Prep time: 15 minutes/Cook time: 1 hour 40 minutes

Although this scrumptious Southwestern dip takes a little time to make, consider the fact that if you bought this amount of bean dip in jars at the supermarket, it would cost about 15 bucks! If you don't have time to cook dried beans, you can use canned beans (see "In a Pinch," at right), although you will sacrifice some flavor this way.

1½ cups dried black beans (10 ounces), picked over and rinsed

2 large garlic cloves

1 picce (3 x ½ inch) lemon zest

1¼ teaspoons salt

½ fresh jalapeño pepper, with seeds

¼ cup whole cilantro sprigs, plus ½ cup chopped cilantro

¼ cup whole scallion greens, plus ¼ cup sliced scallions

1 tablespoon ground cumin

1 pickled jalapeño pepper, stem removed

2 tablespoons distilled white vinegar

4 teaspoons fresh lemon juice

1. In 4-quart saucepan, combine black beans, garlic, lemon zest, ½ teaspoon salt, fresh jalapeño, cilantro sprigs, scallion greens, and water to cover by 2 inches and bring to a boil over medium heat. Reduce to a simmer, partially cover, and cook about 1½ hours, or until beans are tender. Drain and reserve any liquid.

2. Meanwhile, in small skillet, toast cumin over low heat about 2 minutes, or until fragrant and slightly browned.

3. Transfer drained beans to food processor and add pickled jalapeño, vinegar, lemon juice, toasted cumin, and remaining ¾ teaspoon salt. Puree until smooth, adding some of reserved liquid if mixture is too thick to puree. Transfer dip to bowl and stir in chopped cilantro and sliced scallions. *Makes 3½ cups/20 cals, 0g fat per tablespoon*

THE **RIGHT** STUFF

Chipotle chilies, a hot item on restaurant menus these days, are simply jalapeños that have been dried and smoked. Their smoky-sweet flavor is a delicious addition to Mexican and Tex-Mex dishes. Chipotles come dried, pickled, or packed in a thick, piquant sauce called adobo, which is made with chilies, vinegar, and herbs.

In a pinch

You can make the bean dip with 3 to 4 cups of canned black beans, well rinsed and drained. To compensate for some of the flavor lost by not using the ingredients in the bean-cooking step, add 1 teaspoon each grated lemon zest and garlic powder (yup, you heard right) to the mixture in step 3.

Different Spins

Use the black bean dip as a a terrific low-fat alternative to the refried beans in Huevos Rancheros (page 130) or as a sandwich spread: Try it with smoked turkey and grilled onions on toasted peasant bread, or in Lahvash Pinwheels (page 29).

For an ultra-luxe first course, accompany the Smoked Salmon on Herbed Potato Pancakes with a spoonful of salmon caviar.

Smoked Salmon on Herbed Potato Pancakes

Prep time: 15 minutes/Cook time: 30 minutes

In Russia, smoked salmon (and caviar) are served on diminutive pancakes called blini, with a dollop of sour cream as the finishing touch. We've pulled a switch, substituting silver-dollar-sized potato pancakes, fragrant with tarragon, for the blini.

1 egg
1 pound baking potatoes, peeled and shredded
3 tablespoons snipped chives
½ teaspoon dried tarragon
½ teaspoon salt

¼ teaspoon freshly ground black pepper
2 tablespoons olive oil
4 ounces smoked salmon, thinly sliced
⅓ cup sour cream

1. Preheat oven to 400°F.
2. In medium bowl, lightly beat the egg. Add potatoes, 2 tablespoons chives, tarragon, salt, and pepper and stir until well combined.

3. In 10-inch nonstick skillet, heat 1 tablespoon oil over medium heat. Drop potato mixture, by tablespoonfuls, into skillet and cook until pancakes are golden brown on one side, about 3 minutes. Turn pancakes over and cook 2 minutes, or until lightly browned. Transfer to a baking sheet, arranging pancakes in one layer. Repeat with remaining 1 tablespoon oil and potato mixture for a total of 16 pancakes.

4. Transfer baking sheet to oven and bake pancakes about 15 minutes, or until crisp on the outside and creamy within. Transfer to serving platter.

5. Top each pancake with a slice of salmon, sour cream, and a sprinkling of remaining chives. *Makes 4 servings/220 cals, 13g fat per serving*

Smoky Quesadillas with Roasted Corn

Prep time: 20 minutes/Cook time: 20 minutes

A quesadilla is the irresistible Southwestern equivalent of the grilled cheese sandwich. Our version includes spiced, roasted corn and features the lush texture and tangy taste of goat cheese. Cut into wedges, the quesadillas are divine finger food, but a whole cheese-filled tortilla "sandwich" makes a great light lunch, too. If you're making these for kids, you might want to stick with a more kid-friendly cheese: Try this with all Monterey Jack cheese (about 2 cups shredded). Baked unwrapped, the tortillas get a little crisp; if you'd prefer them to stay soft, wrap the quesadillas in foil (brushed with a little oil) before baking them.

3 teaspoons olive oil
2 tablespoons fresh lime juice
¾ teaspoon ground cumin
¾ teaspoon ground coriander
2 ears corn, shucked
1 small onion, minced
8 flour tortillas (8-inch diameter)

1 cup shredded smoked Cheddar cheese (4 ounces)
1 log (4 ounces) soft goat cheese, crumbled
½ cup chopped cilantro
1 scallion, thinly sliced
½ teaspoon chili powder

1. Preheat broiler.

2. In small bowl, stir together 1 teaspoon oil, 1 tablespoon lime juice, cumin, and coriander. Rub corn all over with mixture; broil corn 6 inches from heat about 7 minutes, or until piping hot and lightly charred, turning ears as they cook. When cool enough to handle, scrape corn into medium bowl.

3. Meanwhile, in 8-inch skillet, heat remaining 2 teaspoons oil over medium heat. Sauté onion about 7 minutes, or until tender. Add to corn in bowl.

4. Preheat oven to 400°F.

5. Lay 2 tortillas on each of two cookie sheets. Sprinkle Cheddar and goat cheese over them. Add cilantro, scallion, chili powder, and remaining 1 tablespoon lime juice to corn mixture. Sprinkle mixture evenly over cheese. Top with remaining tortillas.

6. Bake quesadillas 5 to 10 minutes, turning once. Cut quesadillas into wedges. Serve hot. *Makes 8 servings/265 cals, 12g fat per serving*

KNOW HOW

Use the medium holes on a box grater to shred the potatoes for the Herbed Potato Pancakes, but do not do this too far in advance or the potatoes will turn brown.

In a pinch

For the Smoky Quesadillas: When fresh corn is out of season, substitute 1 cup (half a 10-ounce package) of frozen corn kernels, thawed, drained, and well dried with paper towels. Sauté the corn along with the onion.

THE RIGHT STUFF

For years now, goat cheese (chèvre in French) has been widely available in the United States. No longer just a gourmet item imported from Europe, goat cheese is made all across this country, from Vermont to California and points in between. The goat cheese sold in four-ounce logs is pretty mild (they're not aged very long), but they do have a touch of the distinctive tang that makes goat cheese so addictive.

We'll Never *shh*
Tell

Want to turn a roast chicken from the deli into a company meal? Just supplement the chicken with a super-quick first-course soup. Here are two canny options: One is based on canned creamed corn, the other on canned pumpkin (which is loaded with that amazingly healthful stuff, beta carotene). If you have a minute to spare, top the pumpkin soup with toasted pumpkin seeds. Partying on short notice? Bring home some chips (or ready-to-eat peeled and cut vegetables such as baby carrots, celery sticks, and broccoli florets) and whirl up one or more of our Four Easy Dips. They all start with the same basic recipe and they're made from ingredients you can keep on the shelf, ready to go in a flash. Ditto the Italian Party Mix, a mucho-munchy snack you can make in advance and store in a big jar or a jumbo zip-seal plastic bag.

Quick Corn Chowder

In 3-quart saucepan, cook 4 ounces (about 5 slices) chopped bacon over medium heat about 7 minutes, or until crisp; transfer to paper towels to drain. Stir in 1 chopped small onion and 1 diced small green bell pepper about 5 minutes, or until vegetables are tender. Stir in 2 cans (14¾ ounces each) creamed corn, 2 cups milk, ¾ teaspoon freshly ground black pepper, and ½ teaspoon salt and simmer 5 minutes, or until heated through. Serve with bacon on top. Makes 6 servings/190 cals, 6g fat per serving

Pronto Pumpkin Soup

In 3-quart saucepan, combine 16-ounce can solid-pack pumpkin, 1 cup chicken broth, ½ cup heavy or whipping cream, ½ cup water, ⅓ cup grated Parmesan cheese, ½ teaspoon dried sage, ¼ teaspoon salt, and ¼ teaspoon freshly ground black pepper. Bring to a boil, reduce to a simmer, and cover. Simmer 7 minutes, or until richly flavored. Top with toasted shelled pumpkin seeds if desired. Makes 4 servings/180 cals, 14g fat per serving

Four Easy Dips

Red Pepper Dip (this is the base recipe): In small pan of boiling water, blanch 4 garlic cloves 2 minutes; drain and place in food processor. Add 2 cups drained jarred roasted red peppers, ½ cup natural (unblanched) almonds, ¼ cup tomato paste, 2 tablespoons olive oil, and ½ teaspoon salt, and process until smooth. Makes 2 cups/50 cals, 4g fat per 2 tablespoons

Creamy Red Pepper Dip: Into 1 recipe Red Pepper Dip, stir ½ cup sour cream. Makes 2½ cups/50 cals, 4g fat per 2 tablespoons

Pesto Red Pepper Dip: Into 1 recipe Red Pepper Dip, stir ¼ cup store-bought pesto. Makes 2¼ cups/60 cals, 5g fat per 2 tablespoons

Chili Red Pepper Dip: Into 1 recipe Red Pepper Dip, stir 1 can (4½ ounces) drained chopped mild green chilies and 2 teaspoons chili powder. Makes 2¼ cups/45 cals, 4g fat per 2 tablespoons

Italian Party Mix

In large bowl, toss together well 8 cups crisp corn cereal squares, 2 cups thin pretzel sticks, 1½ cups coarsely chopped natural (unblanched) almonds, 1 cup grated Parmesan cheese, and 1 teaspoon cayenne. Add ⅓ cup olive oil and toss again. Spread mixture evenly in jelly-roll pan and bake in preheated 350°F oven 15 minutes, or until crisp and cheese is crusty. Cool and store in airtight containers. Makes 12 cups/70 cals, 4g fat per ¼ cup

Lahvash Pinwheels

Prep time: 5 minutes per spread/Cook time: 10 minutes/Chill time: 1 hour

You've probably seen these impressive hors d'oeuvres on caterers' trays at weddings and cocktail parties; surprisingly, they're no big deal to make. You start with lahvash, a soft Middle Eastern flatbread the consistency of a flaky flour tortilla. Spread the lahvash with something creamy (we give you three options), add thinly sliced meat, roll up the lahvash, and refrigerate for a while to firm. Slicing the roll yields pretty pinwheels. Our spreads and fillings are just a starting point: You can coat the lahvash with other spreadables, such as store-bought flavored cream cheese, hummus, or our Dynamite Black Bean Dip (page 25). Grilled vegetables can stand in for the meat. And a sprinkling of fresh basil or cilantro couldn't hurt. The possibilities are pretty much endless.

Lahvash, a/k/a Lavash or Mountain Shepherd Bread, is a flat (though yeasted) bread originally from the Near East. Lahvash comes in two forms: One is hard and cracker-like, and the other is soft and flexible. It's the soft type you want for these pinwheel hors d'oeuvres. If you can find a brand of lahvash that comes in a rectangular sheet, you're all set; if you can find only the big round sheets of lahvash, trim them to a rectangular shape before filling and rolling them. Save the scraps for "sampling" the fillings!

Cream cheese spreads (recipes follow)

1 tablespoon olive oil

2 large onions, halved and thinly sliced

1 teaspoon sugar

2 rectangular lahvash sheets, each 8 x 10 inches

4 ounces very thinly sliced baked ham, roast beef, prosciutto, or smoked turkey

1. Make one of the cream cheese spreads; set aside at room temperature.

2. Meanwhile, in 10-inch skillet, heat oil over medium heat. Add onions, sprinkle sugar over them, and cook, stirring frequently, about 7 minutes, or until light golden and tender but not mushy; set aside.

3. To assemble: Spread cream cheese spread evenly over each lahvash. Top with meat of choice and onions. Roll lahvash up lengthwise and wrap tightly in plastic wrap. Refrigerate 1 hour before slicing into ½-inch-wide pinwheels. *Makes 30 pinwheels/30 cals, .8g fat per pinwheel without cream cheese spread*

Basil Cream Cheese Spread With electric mixer, beat 8 ounces softened cream cheese and 1 tablespoon milk until whipped. Beat in ½ cup chopped basil, ¼ teaspoon salt, and ¼ teaspoon freshly ground black pepper until combined. *Makes 1¼ cups/40 cals, 4g fat per tablespoon*

Chutney Cream Cheese Spread With electric mixer, beat 8 ounces softened cream cheese and 2 teaspoons fresh lime juice until whipped. Beat in ¼ cup finely chopped mango chutney, ½ teaspoon curry powder, and ¼ teaspoon salt until combined. *Makes 1¼ cups/50 cals, 4g fat per tablespoon*

Cilantro Cream Cheese Spread With electric mixer, beat 8 ounces softened cream cheese and 1 tablespoon milk until whipped. Beat in ⅓ cup chopped cilantro, ½ teaspoon ground coriander, and ¼ teaspoon salt until combined. *Makes 1¼ cups/40 cals, 4g fat per tablespoon*

Although hazelnuts are delicious, it is a bit of a chore to skin them, so try this salad with almonds or pecans instead. Just be sure to toast them in the oven for maximum flavor.

KNOW HOW

It's awfully tricky to make melon balls unless you have a handy gadget called a melon baller (stop giggling), which looks like a miniature ice cream scoop. It comes in two shapes, round and oval, and makes, respectively, spheres and footballs. If you don't have one, just cut the melon into ½-inch cubes for this salad.

Warm Scallop Salad with Light Lemon-Shallot Vinaigrette

Prep time: 25 minutes/Cook time: 15 minutes

This sublime salad of freshly cooked scallops bathed in a warm vinaigrette is an elegant way to start a sitdown dinner. (P.S. It also makes a great light supper or lunch.) Since the scallops do need to be prepared just before serving, you'll want to choose a main course and dessert that require little last-minute attention. How about Perfectly Moist Roast Chicken (page 67) and store-bought chocolate ice cream with hot Butterscotch Sauce (page 153)?

¼ cup hazelnuts (1 ounce)
½ cup clam juice or chicken broth
½ cup finely chopped tomato
½ teaspoon grated lemon zest
1 pound sea scallops, halved horizontally

Light Lemon-Shallot Vinaigrette (recipe follows)
4 cups torn Bibb lettuce
2 cups honeydew melon balls
2 cups cantaloupe balls

1. Preheat oven to 375°F.
2. Toast hazelnuts on baking sheet about 7 minutes, or until skins begin to wrinkle and nuts are fragrant. With kitchen towel, rub hazelnuts until skins come off. (Some bits of skin will remain even after rubbing.) Coarsely chop nuts.
3. In 10-inch skillet, bring clam juice, tomato, lemon zest, and ¼ cup water to a simmer over low heat. Add scallops and poach about 3 minutes, or just until cooked through. With slotted spoon, transfer scallops and tomato to bowl; set aside.
4. Make Light Lemon-Shallot Vinaigrette.
5. Divide lettuce among 4 serving plates. Scatter melon balls evenly on top. Arrange scallops and tomato on salads and spoon warm vinaigrette over each. Garnish salads with hazelnuts. Serve at once. *Makes 6 servings/210 cals, 11g fat per serving*

Light Lemon-Shallot Vinaigrette In small skillet, heat 1 tablespoon olive oil over low heat. Add 1 minced medium shallot and 2 scallions (white part only), minced, and cook 2 minutes. Add ¼ cup fresh lemon juice, 2 teaspoons Dijon mustard, ½ teaspoon salt, 2 tablespoons water, and 2 tablespoons olive oil, stirring to combine. Bring to a boil and cook about 2 minutes, or until dressing has thickened and no longer appears separated. Swirl in 1 tablespoon minced parsley (optional). *Makes ½ cup/100 cals, 10g fat per 2 tablespoons*

A plate of pretty pastels, the Warm Scallop Salad is perfect for a springtime dinner. Serve it with a French baguette or some soft breadsticks. ▶

Five-Flavor Eggplant

Prep time: 15 minutes/Cook time: 35 minutes

Here's a wonderful appetizer that even non-eggplant fans will love. (Really! We've even tried it on kids.) Follow the Asian eggplant with a simple but flavorful main dish such as Grilled Flank Steak with Soy-Ginger Marinade (page 40) or Broiled Chicken Breasts with Chili Butter (page 58).

THE **RIGHT** STUFF

Japanese eggplants are small, slender, and deep purple. Their flavor is more delicate than that of regular eggplants, and they have a thinner skin and fewer seeds. If you can't get Japanese eggplants (or very small Italian eggplants) try to find the smallest regular eggplants you can and cut them into 1-inch cubes. Cut the cubes from the portion of the eggplant that has the fewest seeds.

2 pounds Japanese eggplants or small Italian eggplants

2 teaspoons peanut or other vegetable oil

2 tablespoons minced peeled fresh ginger

3 garlic cloves, minced

⅓ cup rice vinegar

2 tablespoons sugar

1 tablespoon soy sauce

1 tablespoon sesame oil

¼ teaspoon salt

3 tablespoons chopped cilantro

1 teaspoon sesame seeds

1. If using Japanese eggplants, cut into 1-inch chunks. If using Italian eggplants, halve lengthwise and slice 1 inch thick. Place half of eggplant in a vegetable steamer. Cover and steam about 15 minutes, or until tender. Transfer to medium bowl. Steam remaining eggplant in same manner and transfer to bowl.

2. In small skillet or saucepan, heat peanut oil over low heat. Add ginger and garlic and cook, stirring frequently, about 2 minutes, or until tender. Add vinegar, sugar, soy sauce, sesame oil, and salt and bring to a boil, stirring until sugar has dissolved, about 1 minute. Pour over steamed eggplant and toss to combine. Cool to room temperature, cover, and refrigerate until serving time.

3. Add cilantro; toss to combine. Serve chilled or at room temperature. Sprinkle with sesame seeds before serving. *Makes 4 cups/70 cals, 3g fat per ½ cup*

Golden Gazpacho

Prep time: 15 minutes/Chill time: 2 hours

Yellow tomatoes brighten this new take on a classic Spanish soup (but regular tomatoes would be fine); carrot juice is the "secret ingredient" that pumps up the brilliant golden color. Be sure that you don't overprocess the vegetables—the soup should have a bit of a chunky, crunchy character. And it should be served well chilled.

THE **RIGHT** STUFF

You'll find carrot juice in cans at your supermarket (usually where you find fruit juices in cans). You can also order up some freshly made carrot juice at your local juice bar.

1½ pounds yellow tomatoes, seeded and cut into large chunks

1 large cucumber, peeled, halved lengthwise, seeded, and cut into large chunks

1 yellow bell pepper, cut into large chunks

1 small red onion, quartered

½ cup canned carrot juice

¼ cup distilled white vinegar

2 tablespoons olive oil

¾ teaspoon salt

In food processor or blender, combine all ingredients and process until finely chopped but still a bit chunky. Transfer soup to large bowl, cover, and refrigerate 2 hours, or until well chilled. Stir before serving. *Makes 4 servings/130 cals, 7g fat per serving*

Red Pepper Soup with Chive Cream

Prep time: 20 minutes/Cook time: 35 minutes

They say that you "eat with your eyes" before you even taste a dish, and this soup is truly a visual feast. It's very simple—and actually, a lot of fun—to make the sunburst pattern on top of the crimson pepper puree (see photo, at right). The visual promise is matched by the taste of this richly flavored soup, spiked with a hint of fresh ginger and a splash of balsamic vinegar. An apple is added to the soup mixture for two reasons: The natural sweetness of the apple underscores that of the red peppers, and the apple, when it's pureed, adds some texture and heft to the soup.

1 tablespoon olive oil	1 cup chicken broth
2 scallions, thinly sliced	1 tablespoon balsamic vinegar
1 tablespoon chopped peeled fresh ginger	½ teaspoon salt
1 garlic clove, finely chopped	¼ teaspoon crushed red pepper flakes
1 small Granny Smith apple, peeled and thinly sliced	⅓ cup reduced-fat sour cream
4 red bell peppers (2 pounds), thinly sliced	3 tablespoons snipped chives or minced scallion greens
	2 tablespoons milk

1. In 4- to 5-quart Dutch oven or large saucepan, heat oil over low heat. Add scallions, ginger, and garlic and cook, stirring frequently, about 2 minutes, or until scallions are tender. Add apple and cook about 4 minutes, or until crisp-tender.

2. Add bell peppers, stir to combine, and cook, stirring frequently, about 7 minutes, or until peppers are tender.

3. Add broth, vinegar, salt, red pepper flakes, and 1 cup water and bring to a boil. Reduce to a simmer, cover, and cook about 20 minutes, or until peppers are very soft and the soup is richly seasoned.

4. Meanwhile, make chive cream: In mini food processor, combine the sour cream, chives, and milk and process until smooth. (If you don't have a mini food processor, just stir ingredients together. The sour cream mixture will have flecks of chive in it instead of being a solid color, but it will taste just as good.)

5. Working in batches, transfer the soup to food processor or blender and puree. Divide soup evenly among 4 bowls. Drizzle each serving with chive cream. *Makes 4 servings/145 cals, 7g fat per serving*

Show off

Here's a great restaurant trick to dress up any pureed soup. It doesn't have to be a special topping (like the chive cream shown below on the Red Pepper Soup); it can be just sour cream, thinned with a little milk to bring it to the right consistency.

Spoon a circle of the chive cream onto the bowl of soup, then "feather" it using in-and-out strokes of a skewer or toothpick. Once you've got the knack, try other patterns. For example, drizzle the chive cream in parallel lines and then draw the skewer lightly through them in perpendicular lines (think of the top of a Napoleon).

Double-Mushroom Bisque

Prep time: 20 minutes/Cook time: 45 minutes

Start a meal with this smooth, deeply flavorful cream soup made with two kinds of mushroom: fresh and dried shiitakes, plus the more familiar button mushrooms. They're combined with leeks, garlic, and potato in this velvety bisque. The soup is topped with crispy bits of sautéed prosciutto. When you serve a rich, creamy soup as a first course, you can follow it with a fairly simple (unsauced) entrée—maybe Sesame-Pepper Tuna Steaks (page 81) or Stuffed Chicken Breasts (page 71). If you're in the mood to spend a little more money, try another type of dried mushroom, such as porcini or cèpes (Italian and French versions, respectively, of the same variety), in place of the shiitakes.

½ ounce dried shiitake mushrooms

2 teaspoons olive oil

2 ounces prosciutto, finely chopped (¼ cup)

2 leeks, halved lengthwise and cut into ½-inch pieces

3 garlic cloves, finely chopped

½ pound fresh shiitake mushrooms, stemmed and caps thinly sliced

1 package (10 ounces) button mushrooms, thinly sliced

1 all-purpose potato (about 6 ounces), peeled and cut into ½-inch cubes

½ teaspoon dried sage

¼ teaspoon freshly ground black pepper

¼ teaspoon salt

⅛ teaspoon ground nutmeg

1 can (14½ ounces) chicken broth

⅓ cup heavy or whipping cream

1. In small bowl, combine dried mushrooms with 1 cup hot water. Let stand 20 minutes, or until softened. With slotted spoon, remove mushrooms from bowl, reserving soaking liquid. Strain liquid through sieve lined with a paper towel or cheesecloth; set aside. Rinse mushrooms well and finely chop; set aside.

2. In 4- to 5-quart Dutch oven or large saucepan, heat oil over medium-low heat. Add prosciutto and cook about 3 minutes, or until lightly crisped. Remove with slotted spoon and set aside. Add leeks and garlic to pan and cook, stirring frequently, about 7 minutes, or until leeks are tender. Add fresh shiitakes, button mushrooms, potato, and reserved chopped mushrooms and cook, stirring frequently, about 10 minutes, or until fresh mushrooms are tender and juicy.

3. Sprinkle sage, pepper, salt, and nutmeg over mushroom mixture and stir to coat. Add broth, 1 cup water, and reserved mushroom soaking liquid and bring to a boil. Reduce to a simmer, cover, and cook about 20 minutes, or until potato cubes are very tender and soup is richly flavored.

4. Stir in cream and remove pan from heat. Divide soup among soup bowls, sprinkle each serving with some of the prosciutto, and serve. *Makes 6 servings/160 cals, 9g fat per serving*

THE RIGHT STUFF

Shiitake mushrooms, which originated in Asia, are now grown in the United States as well. Sometimes called "Golden Oak Mushrooms" because they're grown on oak logs, shiitakes have a rich, meaty flavor. The caps of the fresh mushrooms (at left) are 3 to 6 inches across; the stems are so tough that they're usually not eaten. (Save them, though, for making flavorful mushroom broth.) Dried shiitakes (at left) are widely available and need to be soaked before using. As with the fresh mushrooms, the stems are not used.

Lighten Up!

There's less than a tablespoon of cream in each serving of the Double-Mushroom Bisque, but to go even lighter, substitute light cream (half-and-half) or whole milk for the heavy cream.

beef *Veal* pork & *lamb*

Burgers PLUS

Prep time: 10 minutes/Cook time: 6 minutes for medium-rare

Anyone can cook a burger—right? Well, if you've ever eaten a dry, tough, tasteless beef patty, you know that they're not quite foolproof. For guaranteed moist, flavorful results, our basic burger recipe adds Dijon mustard and Worcestershire sauce to the ground sirloin; the variations below use other mix-ins. This recipe makes real Fred Flintstone-size portions. For more modest appetites, shape the meat into 6 patties instead.

2 pounds ground sirloin	2 teaspoons Worcestershire sauce
4 teaspoons Dijon mustard	¾ teaspoon salt

1. Preheat broiler or prepare grill.

2. In medium bowl, stir together beef, mustard, Worcestershire, and salt. Shape into 4 burgers, each 1 inch thick.

3. Broil burgers on broiler pan 6 inches from heat until cooked to desired degree of doneness, about 3 minutes per side for medium-rare. Or grill burgers over medium heat 3 to 4 minutes per side for medium-rare. *Makes 4 servings/405 cals, 24g fat per serving*

Mustard & Caper Burgers Prepare basic burger recipe through step 2, but add 1 (additional) tablespoon Dijon mustard and 2 tablespoons rinsed and drained capers (or minced dill pickles) to burger mixture. Proceed as for basic recipe. *Makes 4 servings/410 cals, 24g fat per serving*

Cheese-Stuffed Burgers In small bowl, mash 4 ounces feta, blue, or goat cheese with 1 ounce (2 tablespoons) cream cheese until well combined. Stir in 1 tablespoon snipped chives or scallion greens. Prepare basic burger recipe through step 2. With your thumb, make an indentation in the center of each burger. Push cheese mixture into indentation and shape meat around it to enclose. Proceed as for basic recipe. *Makes 4 servings/505 cals, 32g fat per serving*

Chili & Scallion Burgers Prepare basic burger recipe through step 2, but add 1 can (4½ ounces) drained, chopped mild green chilies, ¼ cup chopped cilantro, 2 thinly sliced scallions, and 2 teaspoons green jalapeño pepper sauce to basic burger mixture. Proceed as for basic recipe. *Makes 4 servings/415 cals, 24g fat per serving*

Water Chestnut-Ginger Burgers Prepare basic burger recipe through step 2, but add ⅓ cup coarsely chopped water chestnuts, 2 tablespoons soy sauce, 1 teaspoon ground ginger, 1 teaspoon sesame oil, and ½ teaspoon light brown sugar to basic burger mixture. Proceed as for basic recipe. *Makes 4 servings/430 cals, 25g fat per serving*

Not Your Mother's Meat Loaf

Prep time: 25 minutes/Cook time: 1 hour 15 minutes

Even if your mother was a meat loaf *meister*, chances are she flavored the thing with nothing more exotic than ketchup or chili sauce. We *have* used a touch of ketchup here, but this mixture of ground beef and veal is also seasoned with ginger, nutmeg, cloves, and pepper—a variation on a French seasoning mixture called *quatre épices* (four spices) that is often used for pâté. The meat loaf is baked in a loaf pan lined with bacon, as it would be for a French *terrine*. The bacon adds flavor to the meat loaf, but also ensures that it will not dry out as it bakes.

10 slices thin-cut bacon (6 ounces)

1 tablespoon olive oil

1 onion, minced

2 garlic cloves, minced

1½ pounds ground sirloin

1 pound ground veal

2 eggs

2 tablespoons Dijon mustard

2 tablespoons ketchup

2 slices (2 ounces) firm white
   sandwich bread, finely crumbled
   (1 cup)

⅓ cup milk

1½ teaspoons salt

1 teaspoon ground ginger

1 teaspoon dried thyme

½ teaspoon freshly ground black
   pepper

¼ teaspoon ground nutmeg

⅛ teaspoon ground cloves

1. Preheat oven to 350°F. Use 8 of the bacon slices to line 9 x 5 x 3-inch glass loaf pan (see photo at right); set pan aside.

2. In 10-inch skillet, heat oil over low heat. Add onion and garlic and cook, stirring frequently, about 7 minutes, until onion is tender. Transfer to large bowl and cool to room temperature.

3. Add sirloin, veal, eggs, mustard, ketchup, bread crumbs, milk, salt, ginger, thyme, pepper, nutmeg, and cloves to sautéed onion mixture. With your hands (messy, but the best way), mix meat loaf ingredients until well combined. Transfer mixture to prepared pan and pack down by banging it on work surface. Smooth top, then arrange bacon overhangs to cover top. Use 2 remaining bacon slices to cover loaf completely. Cover pan with double layer of aluminum foil.

4. Bake about 1 hour, or until juices run clear when loaf is tested with a knife. Uncover and bake 15 minutes more, or until bacon is lightly crisped. Let cool 10 minutes before inverting loaf onto serving platter with lip; discard juices. Or, cool to room temperature and refrigerate. To unmold chilled loaf, run a thin knife around edge of pan and invert loaf onto platter. *Makes 8 servings/350 cals, 21g fat per serving*

Serve this sophisticated meat loaf hot, or chill it and serve it like a French country pâté— with sliced French bread, Dijon mustard, and the little French gherkin pickles called *cornichons*.

To line the loaf pan with bacon, lay 5 slices crosswise to cover the bottom and come up the sides. The ends will hang over (and will be used to cover the meat loaf later). Cut 3 more bacon slices in half and use the half slices to cover the two ends of the pan; again, leave overhangs.

Big-Batch Chili

In a pinch

The chili is best when the beans are cooked from scratch, but canned beans will work, too—use 2 to 2½ cups (from about two 15-ounce cans). Rinse and drain the beans thoroughly, discarding the liquid from the can. Replace the 1½ cups bean cooking liquid called for in the chili recipe with chicken broth or water.

Prep time: 15 minutes plus bean soaking/ Cook time: 2 hours 40 minutes

Steaming, spicy chili. Icy beer. Warm tortillas. Something for dessert (well, maybe). Feeding a bunch of friends can be so easy, especially if you've made the chili days ahead and just have to reheat it at serving time. This big batch is big on flavor: The spices are toasted in the pan to bring out their full bouquet and, as in a Mexican *mole* sauce, there's a touch of chocolate for richness.

Savory Beans (page 97)

2 tablespoons olive oil

2 large onions, finely chopped

5 garlic cloves, minced

2 carrots, quartered lengthwise and thinly sliced

2 tablespoons ground cumin

2 tablespoons ground coriander

3 tablespoons chili powder

3 pounds ground sirloin

1 can (28 ounces) plum tomatoes in puree, coarsely chopped

¾ cup chopped cilantro

1 square (1 ounce) semisweet chocolate, chopped

2½ teaspoons salt

¾ teaspoon cayenne pepper

Present the Black & White Steak au Poivre atop egg noodles or fettuccine, accompanied with crisp-tender asparagus.

1. Make the Savory Beans. Drain, reserving 1½ cups cooking liquid.
2. In 5-quart Dutch oven or large flameproof casserole, heat oil over medium heat. Add onions and garlic and cook, stirring frequently, about 7 minutes, or until onions are tender. Add carrots and cook about 5 minutes, or until tender.
3. Meanwhile, in small ungreased skillet, heat cumin and coriander over low heat, stirring, about 3 minutes, or until fragrant and lightly browned. Stir toasted spices and chili powder into vegetable mixture in Dutch oven. Add sirloin and cook, stirring frequently, about 5 minutes, or until meat is no longer pink. Stir in tomatoes and their puree, ½ cup cilantro, chocolate, salt, cayenne, Savory Beans, and reserved cooking liquid. Bring to a boil, reduce heat to a simmer, and cover. Cook, stirring occasionally, 30 minutes, or until richly flavored. Stir in remaining ¼ cup cilantro and serve. *Makes 8 servings/590 cals, 31g fat per serving*

Black & White Steak au Poivre

Prep time: 10 minutes/Cook time: 25 minutes

This two-tone take on peppered steak is lavished with a creamy flamed-brandy sauce. Reach for this recipe when the guest list or the occasion—or both—calls for something drop-dead impressive.

3 bell peppers, preferably a mix of red, yellow, and green	4 teaspoons vegetable oil
1 tablespoon black peppercorns	¼ cup brandy
1 tablespoon white peppercorns	½ cup chicken broth
1 teaspoon coriander seeds	½ cup heavy or whipping cream
4 boneless sirloin steaks (8 ounces each), well trimmed	4 teaspoons Dijon mustard

1. Preheat broiler. Cut peppers lengthwise into flat panels (for how-to photos, see page 15). Place pepper pieces, skin side up, on broiler pan. Broil 6 inches from heat until skin is charred, about 10 minutes. When cool enough to handle, peel and cut crosswise into ½-inch-wide slices; set aside.
2. With mortar and pestle (or in a zip-seal plastic bag, see photo at right), lightly crush peppercorns and coriander seeds just until cracked; place in wide shallow dish. Dip steaks into peppercorn mixture, pressing it onto both sides.
3. In 10-inch skillet, heat oil over medium-high heat. Add steaks and cook about 3 minutes per side, or until browned. Reduce heat to medium and cook to desired degree of doneness, 2 to 3 minutes for medium-rare. Transfer steaks to dinner plates; cover loosely with foil to keep warm.
4. Remove pan from heat, add brandy, and, averting face, carefully ignite brandy with a match. Return pan to heat and cook mixture until flame dies out, about 45 seconds. Add broth and cook over medium-high heat about 4 minutes, or until reduced by half. Whisk in cream and cook 2 minutes, or until lightly thickened. Whisk in mustard and stir in roasted pepper strips. Spoon sauce over steaks and serve. *Makes 4 servings/490 cals, 26g fat per serving*

Show off

Surround the chili pot with a choice of toppings and stir-ins: Sour cream, grated cheese, chopped scallions, minced cilantro, sliced pickled jalapeños, and tortilla chips.

KNOW HOW

If you don't have a mortar and pestle, as most people don't, you can crush hard spices like peppercorns and coriander by smacking them with the bottom of a small skillet (and having them fly all over the kitchen), or with this much neater method. Place the peppercorns in a zip-seal plastic bag and make a few passes over the bag with a rolling pin (or a straight-sided wine bottle).

Pan-Seared Beef with Wasabi Sauce

Prep time: 15 minutes/Cook time: 10 minutes for medium-rare

Creamy horseradish sauce over rare beef is a British institution. Here's the same idea with an Eastern twist: The sour-cream sauce is spiked with Japanese wasabi.

1½ teaspoons wasabi powder
⅔ cup sour cream
1 tablespoon snipped chives or scallion greens
1 tablespoon chopped parsley

2 teaspoons tarragon vinegar
½ teaspoon salt
1 tablespoon vegetable oil
4 beef filet steaks (8 ounces each)

1. In medium bowl, combine wasabi powder with 1 tablespoon cold water and stir until smooth. Add sour cream, chives, parsley, vinegar, and ¼ teaspoon salt and stir to combine. Cover and refrigerate until ready to serve.

2. In 10-inch skillet, heat oil over medium-high heat. Sprinkle beef with remaining ¼ teaspoon salt and sear about 3 minutes per side for rare. Reduce heat to medium and cook, turning occasionally, to desired degree of doneness, about 5 minutes per side for medium-rare. Serve beef with wasabi sauce. *Makes 4 servings/755 cals, 64g fat per serving*

One of the nicer features of flank steak is that it's a lean cut of meat. The downside of this is that it can be tough unless you know how to slice it. Carve the steak across the grain and on a diagonal to the cutting board. This makes slices with shorter meat fibers and less resistance to the tooth— that is to say, tender.

Grilled Flank Steak PLUS

Prep time: 5 minutes/Marinating time: 1 to 8 hours/Cook time: 10 minutes

Flank is a great cut because although lean, it's very tasty. The secret to success is twofold: Do not cook it beyond the medium-rare stage, or it will start to toughen up, and carve it properly (see photo at left). Treating the steak to one of our three tangy marinades tenderizes it (a little) and flavors it (a lot).

Marinades (recipes follow)
One 1½-pound flank steak

1. In a large shallow dish (or zip-seal plastic bag, see "Know How," opposite page), make one of the marinades. Add flank steak and turn to coat. Refrigerate, turning occasionally, for at least 1 hour or up to 8 hours.

2. Preheat broiler or prepare grill.

3. Lift meat from marinade (discard marinade) and broil 6 inches from heat 5 minutes per side for medium-rare. Or grill over medium-high heat for a total of 7 minutes. Let stand 10 minutes before slicing across the grain and on the diagonal. *Makes 4 servings/280 cals, 16g fat per serving without marinade*

Balsamic Vinegar-Ketchup Marinade Combine ¼ cup balsamic vinegar, 2 tablespoons ketchup, 1 tablespoon olive or vegetable oil, 2 teaspoons dark brown sugar, 1 teaspoon red hot pepper sauce, ½ teaspoon dried oregano, and ½ teaspoon salt. *Makes ½ cup/25 cals, 2g fat per tablespoon*

Soy-Ginger Marinade Combine 3 tablespoons soy sauce, 2 tablespoons sesame oil, 1 tablespoon dark brown sugar, 2 crushed and peeled garlic cloves, 1 tablespoon finely chopped peeled ginger, and 2 strips orange zest (3 x ½ inch each). *Makes ½ cup/45 cals, 3g fat per tablespoon*

Red Wine Marinade Combine ¼ cup dry red wine, 2 tablespoons olive oil, 1 tablespoon Dijon mustard, 2 crushed and peeled garlic cloves, 1 teaspoon dried rosemary, crumbled, ½ teaspoon salt, and ½ teaspoon freshly ground black pepper. *Makes ½ cup/40 cals, 3g fat per tablespoon*

Carbonnade of Beef

Prep time: 25 minutes/Cook time: 2½ hours

Just like love, you can't hurry stew. It has to, well, stew—simmer and bubble and mingle and merge, preferably for hours, until the onions and garlic melt away and the meat is fork-tender. This Belgian stew, like many stews, benefits from sitting for a day or two, during which time the flavors settle still further into a harmonious whole. So think about cooking the stew on the weekend for a weekday dinner.

- 4 tablespoons olive oil
- 2½ pounds beef chuck, cut into 1-inch chunks
- ¼ cup flour
- 2¼ pounds Spanish onions, cut into ½-inch dice
- 3 carrots, halved lengthwise and thinly sliced
- 3 garlic cloves, minced
- 1 bottle (12 ounces) dark Belgian beer
- ¾ cup chicken broth
- 2 tablespoons tomato paste
- 1 teaspoon salt
- ¾ teaspoon dried thyme
- ¼ teaspoon freshly ground black pepper
- ⅛ teaspoon ground allspice

1. In 5-quart nonstick Dutch oven or large flameproof casserole, heat 1 tablespoon oil over medium-high heat. Dredge beef in flour, shaking off excess. Sauté one-third of meat about 3 minutes per side, or until browned all over. With slotted spoon, transfer to large bowl. Repeat two more times with remaining beef, using 1 tablespoon oil per batch.
2. Preheat oven to 350°F.
3. Reduce heat under Dutch oven to medium-low. Add remaining 1 tablespoon oil, onions, carrots, and garlic and cook, stirring occasionally, about 25 minutes, or until onions are golden brown and very tender. Return beef (and any juices that have collected in the bowl) to pan, add beer, broth, tomato paste, salt, thyme, pepper, and allspice, and bring to a boil.
4. Cover the Dutch oven, place in the oven, and bake 1 hour and 45 minutes, or until meat is very tender. *Makes 6 servings/695 cals, 48g fat per serving*

Osso Buco with Lemon-Orange Gremolata

Prep time: 25 minutes/Cook time: 2 hours

Here's one for a cold winter night. Hearty osso buco, one of the signature dishes of northern Italian cooking, is made with short cross-sections of veal shank—marrow-filled bones (*osso buco* means "hollow bone") with generous portions of meat attached. The dish is a perfect example of braising that yields meltingly tender meat and a rich, thick sauce. Osso buco is traditionally finished with a sprinkling of *gremolata* (a mixture of minced citrus zest, garlic, and parsley) to counter the richness. The classic *gremolata* is made with just lemon zest, but we've added orange zest for a deeper flavor. This orange note is boosted by the orange juice used in the sauce.

- 6 meaty veal shanks, each 2 inches thick (about 4 pounds total), tied
- 3 tablespoons flour
- 2 tablespoons olive oil
- 1 medium onion, minced
- 2 garlic cloves, minced
- ¾ cup dry white wine
- 1 can (14½ ounces) whole tomatoes, chopped, with their juice
- ¾ cup chicken broth
- 2 strips (2 x ½ inch each) orange zest
- ¼ cup fresh orange juice
- 1¼ teaspoons salt
- ½ teaspoon dried sage
- ½ teaspoon dried rosemary, crumbled

1. Preheat oven to 350°F.
2. Dredge veal in flour, shaking off excess. In 5-quart Dutch oven or large flameproof casserole, heat oil over medium heat. Sauté veal about 7 minutes per side, or until golden brown. With slotted spoon, transfer veal to plate.
3. Add onion and garlic to Dutch oven, reduce heat to low, and cook about 7 minutes, or until onion is tender. Add wine, increase heat to medium, and cook 2 minutes, or until slightly reduced, scraping bottom of pan to dislodge any browned bits. Add tomatoes and their juice, broth, orange zest strips, orange juice, salt, sage, and rosemary and bring to a boil.
4. Add veal, cover, and transfer pan to oven. Bake 1½ hours, or until veal is tender.
5. While veal is cooking, make Lemon-Orange Gremolata.
6. Serve veal sprinkled with gremolata. *Makes 6 servings/325 cals, 11g fat per serving*

Lemon-Orange Gremolata In small pan of boiling water, blanch 2 peeled garlic cloves for 2 minutes; drain and finely chop. In small bowl, stir together garlic, ¼ cup chopped parsley, 1 teaspoon grated orange zest, and 1 teaspoon grated lemon zest. *Makes about 6 tablespoons (calories are insignificant)*

Serve Osso Buco with orzo (rice-shaped pasta) and peas—or with plain rice. ▶

Glazed Pork Tenderloin

Prep time: 15 minutes/Marinating time: 1 to 8 hours/Cook time: 15 minutes

The secret to the deep deliciousness of this five-ingredient recipe lies in two Chinese components: hoisin sauce and oyster sauce. Hoisin sauce is soybean-based, sweet and spicy; oyster sauce, made with oysters and soy sauce, has a pungent, savory taste. Both products are sold in many supermarkets, but you'll find better quality sauces (with more soybean and more oyster) at Asian markets.

Different Spins

For an incredible sandwich, put slices of Glazed Pork Tenderloin on a toasted roll spread with mayonnaise (stir a little hoisin into the mayo); top with tomato and thinly sliced avocado.

3 tablespoons hoisin sauce
3 tablespoons oyster sauce
1 tablespoon honey

2 teaspoons fresh lemon juice
1 pound well-trimmed pork tenderloin

1. In small bowl, whisk together hoisin, oyster sauce, honey, and lemon juice. Transfer to large zip-seal plastic bag, add pork, and turn to coat. Seal and refrigerate for at least 1 hour or up to 8 hours.
2. Preheat broiler. Line broiler pan with foil; place pork on pan and brush with marinade. Reserve remaining marinade.
3. Broil pork 8 inches from heat 15 minutes, turning every 5 minutes and basting with marinade, until cooked through. (If your broiler does not allow you to broil 8 inches from heat source, roast tenderloin in preheated 450°F oven 15 to 20 minutes, basting every 5 minutes.) Let stand for 10 minutes before slicing. *Makes 4 servings/225 cals, 5g fat per serving*

THE **RIGHT** STUFF

Pork loin comes from the pig's back and includes both the center loin and sirloin. Both of these are cut and sold as chops as well as bone-in and boneless roasts. Pork *tenderloin*, on the other hand, is a particularly choice cut—it's a uniquely tender, boneless strip from the bottom of the sirloin.

Roast Pork Loin with Dried Fruit Compote

Prep time: 25 minutes/Cook time: 1 hour 25 minutes

Pork with applesauce: old-fashioned, homey, and basically boring. Pork with an autumnal compote of dried apples, pears, and cherries, scented with vanilla and sweet spices: absolutely delicious and even a little dressy. You can make the compote ahead of time—several days ahead, if it suits your schedule. The fruit will soak up even more of the red wine it's cooked in, and the compote tastes best chilled.

1 boneless center-cut pork loin roast (3 pounds)
2 garlic cloves, thinly sliced lengthwise
2 tablespoons Dijon mustard

1 tablespoon light brown sugar
1 teaspoon salt
¾ teaspoon dried sage
Dried Fruit Compote (page 146)

To suffuse the Roast Pork Loin (right) with garlic flavor, cut shallow slits in the meat with the tip of a knife and insert slices of garlic—a technique traditionally used with lamb (see page 52).

1. Preheat oven to 425°F.
2. Cut slits into the fat side of the pork loin and insert the garlic slices (see photo at left). In small bowl, stir together mustard, brown sugar, salt, and sage. Rub mixture all over pork.

3. Place pork on a rack in a roasting pan and roast 20 minutes, or until lightly browned. Reduce oven to 350°F, cover pork with foil, and roast 1 hour to 1 hour 5 minutes or until just done (155°F on meat thermometer). Let stand 10 minutes (the internal temperature will rise to 160°F) before carving. Serve with chilled compote. *Makes 8 servings/305 cals, 17g fat per serving without compote*

Kansas City BBQ'd Ribs

Prep time: 15 minutes/Marinating time: 1 to 8 hours
Cook time: 2 hours 15 minutes

Kansas City is widely considered the barbecue capital of the United States. That's barbecue as in spice-rubbed, sauce-slathered, slow-smoked pork, not backyard burgers. Serve these sauce-soaked spareribs K.C. style, with heaping helpings of coleslaw and stacks of fries. At some of Kansas City's premier barbecue joints, the french fries are cooked in lard . . . you might prefer our chilied-up Crispy Steak Fries (page 95).

4 teaspoons sugar	1 rack (3¼ pounds) pork spareribs
1½ teaspoons salt	1 cup canned tomato puree
1½ teaspoons paprika	3 tablespoons light molasses
1½ teaspoons chili powder	2 tablespoons cider vinegar
¾ teaspoon freshly ground black pepper	1 teaspoon red hot pepper sauce
¾ teaspoon dried sage	¾ teaspoon natural-hickory liquid smoke (optional)
½ teaspoon dried thyme	¼ teaspoon ground cinnamon
¼ teaspoon cayenne pepper	

1. In small bowl, stir together sugar, salt, paprika, chili powder, black pepper, sage, thyme, and cayenne. Rub mixture onto spareribs. Cover and refrigerate at least 1 hour or up to 8 hours.

2. Meanwhile, in medium bowl, stir together tomato puree, molasses, vinegar, hot sauce, liquid smoke, and cinnamon; set sauce aside.

3. Preheat oven to 350°F. Place a flat rack in a large roasting pan and pour 1 to 2 inches of water into roasting pan (it's easier and safer to do this with the roasting pan already sitting on oven shelf so you don't have to carry the sloshing roasting pan across the kitchen). Place ribs on rack over the water (the water should not touch the meat) and cover pan loosely with aluminum foil.

4. Bake ribs 1 hour 15 minutes. Remove and discard foil. Set aside rack with ribs, then pour water out of roasting pan. Return ribs (still on rack) to pan. Brush ribs with one-fourth of sauce. Bake ribs, uncovered, brushing with remaining sauce, 1 hour, or until meat is very tender.

5. Cut into individual ribs and serve. *Makes 4 servings/665 cals, 44g fat per serving*

KNOW HOW

If you're grilling the ribs outdoors, use indirect heat to keep the fat and sauce from dripping onto the coals and causing flare-ups: Heat the coals 'til they're covered with white ash, then push them to the sides of the grill. Place a disposable foil pan in the center of the coals to catch the dripping fat. Position the ribs in the center of the grilling rack so that they sit above the pan, not the coals—there will be plenty of indirect heat to cook the meat.

THE **RIGHT** STUFF

Pork spareribs, which come from the belly of the pig, are mostly bone (plus lots of fat), but the meat on those bones is some of the tastiest you'll ever eat. Baking the ribs on a rack lets much of the fat drip off (the water in the drip pan keeps the fat from smoking, and also helps keep the ribs moist). Another option for Kansas City BBQ'd Ribs is baby back ribs, which come from the top of the loin. They're leaner and meatier, but also pricier.

As with any Chinese stir-fry, rice is the accompaniment of choice for Szechuan Pork.

Szechuan Pork

Prep time: 25 minutes/Cook time: 10 minutes

It's worth a trip to an Asian market to hunt up some Asian chili paste with garlic, the unique cooking sauce that gives this stir-fry real Szechuan flavor.

1½ pounds boneless pork butt, well trimmed

2 tablespoons soy sauce

2 tablespoons dry sherry

1 teaspoon cornstarch

4 teaspoons vegetable oil

2 red bell peppers, cut into ½ x 2-inch strips

2 ribs celery, cut into 2-inch-long matchsticks

6 scallions, cut into 2-inch lengths

2 tablespoons minced peeled fresh ginger

½ cup chicken broth

1½ teaspoons Asian chili paste with garlic

1. Thinly slice pork, then cut into ½-inch-wide strips. In medium bowl, stir together soy sauce, sherry, and cornstarch. Add pork and toss to coat.

2. In 12-inch skillet, heat oil over medium-high heat. With slotted spoon, lift pork from marinade, reserving marinade. Add pork and stir-fry 2 minutes, or until cooked through. With slotted spoon, transfer to large plate.

3. Add peppers and celery to pan, reduce heat to medium, and stir-fry 3 minutes, or until peppers are crisp-tender. Add scallions and ginger and stir-fry 3 minutes, or until scallions are tender.

4. In small bowl, whisk together broth, chili paste, and reserved marinade. Pour into pan and bring to a boil. Reduce heat to low, return pork to pan, and cook 1 minute, or until sauce is lightly thickened and pork is heated through. *Makes 4 servings/350 cals, 19g fat per serving*

Pork Satay with Spicy Peanut Sauce

Prep time: 25 minutes/Cook time: 6 minutes

Satay (or saté) are enjoyed in many Southeast Asian countries as an appetizer or street snack. A marinated cucumber salad with just a hint of chili is the traditional side dish. This recipe makes a main course for four, but could also serve six to twelve as an appetizer. Try this easy grill with chicken or turkey strips instead of pork.

Asian Cucumber Salad (recipe follows)

2 tablespoons fresh lime juice

¼ cup canned unsweetened coconut milk

3 tablespoons creamy or chunky peanut butter

2 tablespoons fresh mint leaves

2 tablespoons fresh basil leaves

1½ teaspoons red hot pepper sauce

1 teaspoon soy sauce

1 pound pork tenderloin

1½ teaspoons ground coriander

¾ teaspoon salt

½ teaspoon sugar

1. Make Asian Cucumber Salad and set aside.

2. In food processor or blender, process lime juice, coconut milk, peanut butter, mint, basil, hot sauce, soy sauce, and 1 tablespoon water until smooth; set sauce aside.

3. Preheat broiler.

4. Cut tenderloin crosswise into thirds (pieces about 4 inches long). Cut each piece lengthwise into ½-inch-thick slices. In medium bowl, combine coriander, salt, and sugar. Add pork and toss to coat. Thread 2 pork slices each onto 10-inch skewers (see "Know How," at right).

5. Arrange skewers in one layer on broiler pan and broil 6 inches from heat for 3 minutes per side, or until pork is cooked through. Serve skewers with peanut sauce and cucumber salad. *Makes 4 servings/260 cals, 16g fat per serving without salad*

Asian Cucumber Salad In 1-quart saucepan, combine ¼ cup lime juice, 1 tablespoon sugar, and ¼ teaspoon crushed red pepper flakes and bring to a boil. Boil 1 minute; cool to room temperature. Add 1 diced European (hothouse) cucumber and 1 chopped red bell pepper, and toss to combine. Cover and chill salad until ready to serve. *Makes 4 servings/30 cals, 1g fat per serving*

KNOW HOW

Thread the strips of pork onto the skewers ribbon-wise. This stretches them flat so that they cook quickly and evenly. If you use bamboo skewers, as shown, be sure that you soak them in water for at least 30 minutes before broiling or grilling to keep them from charring.

THE **RIGHT** STUFF

Coconut milk is made by pureeing coconut meat with water and then straining off the "milk"; it is unsweetened and sold in cans in some supermarkets and in Asian and Hispanic markets. Coconut milk is not to be confused with cream of coconut, which is a thicker, sweetened coconut milk with added stabilizers. (It's what people use to make piña coladas and can usually be found where cocktail mixers are sold.)

Herbed Pork Chops with Tangy Cider Sauce

Prep time: 10 minutes/Cook time: 20 minutes

A big, meaty pork chop sharing a plate with, say, Crushed Potatoes (page 94) is a meal to gladden the heart. If it's still grilling weather, cook the chops outdoors. The cider sauce would also be good over sautéed chicken breasts or turkey cutlets.

1 bay leaf, crumbled	¼ teaspoon dried sage
½ teaspoon dried thyme	4 end-cut loin pork chops, each
½ teaspoon dried oregano	1 inch thick (2½ pounds total
½ teaspoon salt	weight), trimmed of fat
¼ teaspoon freshly ground black pepper	Tangy Cider Sauce (recipe follows)

1. Preheat broiler.

2. In small bowl, stir together bay leaf, thyme, oregano, salt, pepper, and sage. Rub mixture onto pork chops.

3. Broil chops on broiler pan 6 inches from heat 5 to 6 minutes per side, or until cooked through but still juicy. Transfer to platter; cover loosely to keep warm.

4. Meanwhile, make Tangy Cider Sauce. Spoon sauce over pork chops. *Makes 4 servings/310 cals, 15g fat per serving without sauce*

Tangy Cider Sauce In 1-quart saucepan, combine 1 cup thawed frozen apple juice concentrate, 2 tablespoons cider vinegar, 1½ teaspoons Dijon mustard, ¼ teaspoon salt, and ¼ teaspoon freshly ground black pepper. Bring to a boil. Remove pan from heat, stir in 2 tablespoons chopped parsley (optional) and 1 tablespoon unsalted butter, cut up. *Makes about 1 cup/145 cals, 3g fat per ¼ cup*

Pork Piccata

Prep time: 15 minutes/Cook time: 10 minutes

Pork piccata is a speedy, surefire choice for a weeknight dinner. Usually made with veal scaloppini, this Italian restaurant classic is more affordable but just as scrumptious when made with pork cutlets.

1¼ pounds boneless pork loin, cut into 12 slices	2 tablespoons olive oil
½ teaspoon salt	2 garlic cloves, minced
¼ teaspoon freshly ground black pepper	½ cup chicken broth
½ teaspoon grated lemon zest	¼ cup fresh lemon juice
¼ cup flour	1 tablespoon unsalted butter, cut up

1. Place pork slices between 2 layers of wax paper or aluminum foil and with flat side of meat mallet or small skillet, lightly pound ¼ inch thick. In small bowl, combine ¼ teaspoon salt, the pepper, and lemon zest. Rub onto both sides of pork. Dredge pork in flour, shaking off excess.

2. In 12-inch skillet, heat 1 tablespoon oil over medium heat. Add half the pork and sauté 2 minutes per side, or until golden brown and cooked through. Transfer to platter and cover loosely with foil to keep warm. Sauté remaining pork in remaining 1 tablespoon oil in same manner, transferring to platter when done.

3. Reduce heat to low, add garlic to skillet, and cook 2 minutes, or until tender. Add broth, lemon juice, and remaining ¼ teaspoon salt; raise heat to high, and cook 1 minute. Remove skillet from heat, add butter, and swirl until butter melts and sauce is lightly thickened. Spoon sauce over pork. *Makes 4 servings/405 cals, 28g fat per serving*

A Bowl of Green

Prep time: 25 minutes/Cook time: 1 hour 55 minutes

If the typical tomato-based Texas-style chili is called "a bowl o' red," it stands to reason that its New Mexican cousin, a pork-and-hominy stew made with green chilies, would be called "a bowl of green." Serve the chili with cornbread or warm tortillas.

2 pounds well-trimmed pork butt or shoulder, cut into 1-inch chunks	1 cup chicken broth
¼ cup flour	½ cup chopped cilantro
2 tablespoons olive or vegetable oil	¾ teaspoon salt
1 large onion, cut into ½-inch cubes	½ teaspoon freshly ground black pepper
3 garlic cloves, minced	1 can (15 ounces) hominy, rinsed and drained
2 green bell peppers, cut into 1-inch squares	1 tablespoon fresh lime juice
2 pickled jalapeño peppers, minced	

1. Preheat oven to 350°F. Dredge pork in flour, shaking off excess.

2. In 5-quart nonstick Dutch oven or large flameproof casserole, heat 1 tablespoon oil over medium-high heat. Add half the pork and cook, turning occasionally, for 5 minutes, or until golden brown all over. With slotted spoon, transfer pork to large plate. Brown remaining pork in remaining 1 tablespoon oil in same manner; transfer to plate.

3. Add onion and garlic to pan, reduce heat to medium, and cook, stirring frequently, for about 7 minutes, or until onion is tender. Add bell peppers and jalapeños and cook, stirring frequently, about 5 minutes, or until bell peppers are crisp-tender. Add broth, cilantro, salt, pepper, and ⅓ cup water and bring to a boil.

4. Return pork (and any juices that have collected on plate) to pan, cover, and transfer casserole to oven. Bake chili 1 hour. Stir in hominy and bake 30 minutes, or until pork is tender. Remove and stir in lime juice. *Makes 4 servings/560 cals, 27g fat per serving*

Show off

For a stylish presentation, arrange each portion of pork piccata on a bed of crisp, fresh salad greens. Or, as is done in some Italian restaurants, serve the salad on *top* of the pork. Choose flavorful, assertive greens such as arugula, escarole, or watercress.

THE **RIGHT** STUFF

Hominy is hulled, degermed dried corn (the germ is the nucleus of the corn kernel). Reconstituted whole-kernel dried hominy, sold in cans, is ready to use in chilis and stews. You probably know ground dried hominy by its more familiar name: That's grits, ma'am.

Crumb-Crusted Honey-Mustard Ham

Prep time: 15 minutes/Cook time: 1 hour 5 minutes

Take your basic ham sandwich and turn it inside out, and you have the concept behind this boneless baked ham spread with honey-mustard and then covered with herbed rye-bread crumbs. The coating bakes into a crispy crust. You don't have to save this for a special occasion: Make it for the family on the weekend, and then use the leftovers during the week. For example, try some chopped ham in the Freestyle Frittata (page 132) or use slices to make Cuban Sandwiches (page 53).

1 boneless baked ham (8½ pounds)
¼ cup Dijon mustard
2 tablespoons honey
7 ounces rye bread with caraway seeds (6 to 7 slices)

½ cup chopped parsley
2 tablespoons snipped chives
2 tablespoons olive oil
Honey-Mustard Sauce (recipe follows)

1. Preheat oven to 400°F. Place ham on rack in roasting pan.
2. In small bowl, blend mustard and honey. Brush over ham.

Help yourself to some "ham in rye": That temptingly crunchy coating consists of rye-bread crumbs mixed with chives and parsley.

3. In food processor, process bread to measure 4 cups coarse crumbs. Transfer to large bowl, add parsley and chives, and toss well. Add oil and toss again. Pat crumb mixture over ham, covering completely. Tent ham with aluminum foil.

4. Bake ham 45 minutes, or until heated through. Remove foil and bake 20 minutes longer, or until crusty.

5. Meanwhile, make Honey-Mustard Sauce.

6. Slice ham and serve with sauce. *Makes 24 servings/325 cals, 16g fat per serving without sauce*

Honey-Mustard Sauce In small bowl, stir together ¾ cup Dijon mustard, 2 tablespoons honey, and 1 tablespoon fresh lemon juice until well blended. Fold in 1½ cups finely diced gherkin pickles and ⅓ cup minced red onion. *Makes 2¾ cups/35 cals, .5g fat per 2 tablespoons*

For true mustard fans: Instead of making the Honey-Mustard Sauce for the ham, stock up on the great mustards of the world—French, German, Polish, Cajun . . . and offer them, straight from the jar.

Spicy Lamb Curry

Prep time: 30 minutes/Cook time: 1 hour 55 minutes

Some people would never think of preparing Indian food at home, especially if there's an Indian restaurant in the neighborhood. But curry is a terrific choice for an informal weekend dinner: It's really nothing more than solid comfort food, spiced up a little. This lamb curry is especially simple because it's braised in the oven, which leaves you an hour and a half free before dinner for any other preparations you need to make. Or, if it's been a killer week, just put your feet up and do *nothing*.

2 pounds boneless lamb shoulder, cut into 1-inch chunks	1 teaspoon ground ginger
¼ cup flour	½ teaspoon salt
3 tablespoons olive oil	¼ teaspoon cayenne pepper
1 medium onion, minced	1 can (14½ ounces) whole tomatoes, chopped, with their juice
2 garlic cloves, minced	
2 teaspoons curry powder	½ cup chicken broth
1 teaspoon ground cumin	¼ cup plain low-fat yogurt

1. Preheat oven to 350°F.

2. Dredge lamb in flour, shaking off excess. In 5-quart nonstick Dutch oven or large flameproof casserole, heat 1 tablespoon oil over medium-high heat. Add half the lamb and sauté 3 minutes per side, or until lightly browned. With slotted spoon, transfer lamb to bowl. Sauté remaining lamb in 1 tablespoon oil in same manner; transfer to bowl.

3. Reduce heat under pan to low. Add remaining 1 tablespoon oil, onion, and garlic and cook 7 minutes, or until onion is tender. Add curry powder, cumin, ginger, salt, and cayenne and cook 1 minute. Stir in tomatoes and broth and bring to a boil.

4. Return lamb to pan (along with any juices collected in the bowl), cover, and bake for 1½ hours, or until lamb is tender. Remove from oven and stir in yogurt. *Makes 6 servings/520 cals, 40g fat per serving*

Don't send the Spicy Lamb Curry to the table all alone—surround it with traditional curry accompaniments. First and foremost, a steaming bowl of rice. Then add colorful little bowls filled with garnishes like mango chutney (or our Apricot-Tomato Chutney, page 54), chopped cilantro, sliced scallions, flaked coconut, chopped nuts, and dried fruits. An Indian bread, such as naan, adds an authentic touch. Many supermarkets sell naan in packages, all ready to warm and serve.

Fennel-Grilled Leg of Lamb

A butterflied leg of lamb is a leg of lamb that has been boned and then slit open horizontally so that it opens out to make a larger, thinner piece for grilling or broiling. This is *definitely* a job for the butcher. Even with a professional in charge, the meat will be slightly uneven in thickness. For the best results, have the lamb at room temperature before you cook it. Check the temperature with a meat thermometer (medium-rare lamb will read 135°). The thinner (end) sections will cook first, so remove them as soon they are done and continue cooking until the thicker portions are done.

THE **RIGHT** STUFF

Pernod is a licorice-flavored apéritif from France. There are other similar liquors you could use for the lamb, including Ricard and pastis (from France), ouzo (from Greece), arak (from various parts of the Middle East), or raki (from Turkey). In a pinch, you could also use one of the sweeter licorice-flavored liqueurs, such as Sambuca (from Italy) or anisette (from France).

Prep time: 20 minutes/Marinating time: 3 hours or overnight
Grill or broil time: 30 minutes

This mouth-watering grilled lamb recipe was inspired by the Provençal method of grilling fish over a fire topped with fennel stalks. If you're cooking the lamb outdoors, you can toss some fresh or dried fennel stalks, fronds, or even seeds onto the coals; the aroma will permeate the lamb, underscoring the flavor of the fennel seeds and Pernod in the marinade.

1 tablespoon plus 1 teaspoon salt
2 teaspoons fennel seeds, lightly crushed
1½ teaspoons grated lemon zest
½ teaspoon cumin seeds, lightly crushed
1 boneless leg of lamb, butterflied (4½ pounds)

2 garlic cloves, thinly slivered lengthwise
¼ cup Pernod
½ cup plain low-fat yogurt
Spiced Yogurt Sauce (recipe follows)

1. In small bowl, stir together salt, fennel seeds, lemon zest, and cumin seeds. Rub mixture onto both sides of lamb. With tip of sharp paring knife, make slits in lamb and insert garlic slivers into slits. Transfer lamb to wide shallow pan and sprinkle with Pernod. Spread yogurt over lamb. Cover with plastic wrap and refrigerate at least 3 hours or overnight.

2. Preheat broiler or prepare grill. Make Spiced Yogurt Sauce and refrigerate until serving time.

3. Place lamb on broiler rack. Broil 8 inches from heat 15 minutes per side, or until medium-rare. Or grill over medium heat 10 to 15 minutes for thinner portions and an additional 15 for the thicker portions.

4. Slice lamb and serve with Spiced Yogurt Sauce.   *Makes 8 servings/505 cals, 31g fat per serving without sauce*

Spiced Yogurt Sauce In small skillet, toast 1 teaspoon lightly crushed fennel seeds and ½ teaspoon lightly crushed cumin seeds over medium-low heat for 3 minutes, or until fragrant and lightly colored. Transfer to medium bowl, stir in ¼ teaspoon freshly ground black pepper, ½ teaspoon grated lemon zest, ¼ teaspoon salt, and 1 cup plain low-fat yogurt. Add 3 tablespoons chopped parsley and combine. *Makes about 1 cup/20 cals, .5g fat per 2 tablespoons*

We'll Never shh Tell

Not every meaty meal has to involve a man-sized roast. You can turn out simple, quick lunches and dinners using cooked ham or roast beef from the deli (leftovers work, too), or with quick-from-scratch ingredients like bacon and sausage. The grilled Cuban sandwich is a classic from a little-known cuisine; in Cuban snack shops they're made with a special sandwich press (which works like a waffle iron), but we use a small skillet to flatten the sandwiches as they cook. The black bean soup offers another taste of Latin America; combine soup and sandwich for a hearty meal. Our In-the-Bag BLT Salad turns another favorite sandwich virtually inside out: It's a big bowl of lettuce, tomatoes, and bacon, with the role of the bread played by crisp croutons. The Thai Beef Salad Roll-Ups are exotic without requiring any out-of-the-way ingredients.

Cuban Sandwiches

Halve 4 sandwich-sized English muffins; spread 1 teaspoon softened unsalted butter on each split side. Divide 8 ounces thinly sliced Muenster or Monterey Jack cheese and 4 ounces thinly sliced smoked ham among 4 buttered halves. Top ham on each sandwich with 2 pickled hot pepper rings; arrange remaining muffin halves on top. In 12-inch skillet, heat 2 tablespoons vegetable oil over low heat. Add sandwiches and put small heavy skillet directly on top as weight. Cook sandwiches 3 minutes, remove small skillet, turn sandwiches, and replace skillet. Cook sandwiches 3 minutes more, or until cheese has melted. Serve hot. Makes 4 servings/530 cals, 31g fat per serving

Un-Canny Black Bean Soup

In 3-quart saucepan, heat 1 tablespoon olive oil over medium heat. Add 3 thinly sliced scallions and 2 minced garlic cloves and cook 1 minute, or until tender. Add 1 can (19 ounces) black beans, rinsed and drained, 1 cup chicken broth, ½ cup water, and 2 tablespoons tomato paste and bring to a boil. Reduce heat to a simmer, cover, and cook 10 minutes, or until richly flavored. With potato masher or wooden spoon, mash about one-third of beans directly in pan. Add ½ pound thinly sliced garlic sausage and ½ cup chopped cilantro and cook gently until sausage is heated through. Serve with wedges of lemon. Makes 4 servings/360 cals, 27g fat per serving

In-the-Bag BLT Salad

In 10-inch skillet, cook 8 bacon slices over medium heat until crisp. Drain on paper towels, then crumble. In large bowl, combine one 10-ounce package prewashed and torn romaine lettuce, 2 cups packaged croutons, 2 medium diced tomatoes, ⅓ cup bottled Italian dressing, and crumbled bacon. Toss together well. Makes 4 servings/250 cals, 17g fat per serving

Thai Beef Salad Roll-Ups

In small bowl, stir together 1 cup bottled lemon or lime vinaigrette, 2 tablespoons soy sauce, and ½ teaspoon crushed red pepper flakes. Lay 12 large Boston lettuce leaves, open side up, on work surface. Top with ½ pound slivered deli roast beef, 1 cup packaged shredded carrots, and 1 cup alfalfa sprouts. Drizzle about 1 teaspoon dressing on top and roll each leaf up. Use remaining dressing as a dipping sauce for the roll-ups. Makes 4 servings/230 cals, 16g fat per serving

Different Spins

The Apricot-Tomato Chutney has a life beyond lamb chops. Serve leftover chutney (or make up a second batch) with any kind of cold meat. And take a cue from the English: Try chutney in a grilled Cheddar sandwich. Absolutely fabulous!

KNOW HOW

The spice mixture for these lamb chops is called a dry rub. You can use it on other meat (or poultry) as well. Try rubbing it on Grilled Flank Steak (page 40), letting the steak "marinate" for at least 1 hour. Because flank is lean, rub the steak with 1 or 2 tablespoons of olive oil before grilling or broiling.

Moroccan Lamb Chops with Apricot-Tomato Chutney

Prep time: 15 minutes/Marinating time: at least 1 hour
Cook time: 30 minutes

Some Moroccan meals require long, tedious, complicated preparations—but not this one! It's simply grilled lamb chops rubbed with pungent spices, partnered with a chutney that you can make well ahead of time. Two highly appropriate side dishes are equally easy to make: Golden Couscous (page 124) and Moroccan Carrot Salad (page 101). Serve the meal with strong mint tea, hot or iced.

¾ teaspoon sugar

¼ teaspoon paprika

¼ teaspoon turmeric

¼ teaspoon ground cumin

¼ teaspoon ground coriander

¼ teaspoon ground ginger

¼ teaspoon salt

Generous pinch of freshly ground black pepper

8 loin lamb chops, each 1 inch thick (3 pounds total), well trimmed

Apricot-Tomato Chutney (recipe follows)

1. In small bowl, combine sugar, paprika, turmeric, cumin, coriander, ginger, salt, and pepper. Rub mixture onto lamb chops. Cover with plastic wrap and refrigerate at least 1 hour or up to 4 hours.
2. Make Apricot-Tomato Chutney.
3. Preheat broiler.
4. Broil chops on broiler pan 6 inches from heat 4 minutes per side for medium-rare. Serve with chutney. *Makes 4 servings/525 cals, 24g fat per serving without chutney*

Apricot-Tomato Chutney In small bowl, stir together ¾ teaspoon paprika, ¾ teaspoon cumin, ¾ teaspoon coriander, ½ teaspoon ginger, ½ teaspoon salt, and a generous pinch of black pepper. In 3-quart nonaluminum saucepan, stir together spice mixture, ⅔ cup distilled white vinegar, and ⅓ cup packed dark brown sugar and bring to a boil. Stir in 1 diced red bell pepper, 1 diced small onion, 1 cup diced dried apricots, and 1 seeded and chopped medium tomato. Bring to a boil, reduce heat to a simmer, cover, and cook 20 minutes, or until pepper and onion are tender and chutney is slightly thickened. *Makes 1 cup/176 cals, .5g fat per ¼ cup*

chicken
turkey
& game hens

Toasty tortilla strips do a turn as "noodles" in this hearty homestyle chicken soup, made with tomato, corn, and lots of chicken.

Mexican Grandma's Chicken Soup

Prep time: 25 minutes/Cook time: 20 minutes

Even if your grandmother wasn't Mexican, she probably served you something like this heart-warming chicken and vegetable soup—it's basically a big bowl of unconditional love. It's the least you could do for a friend (or yourself) after a grueling workweek, isn't it?

In a pinch

Just about any soup you can think of is better when prepared with homemade stock, but if you don't have Rich Chicken Stock (opposite page) on hand, you can make this chicken soup with 2 cups of canned chicken broth plus 2 cups of water. We dilute the canned broth to more closely approximate the taste of homemade stock, but if you'd prefer, you can use 4 cups of full-strength canned broth (regular or reduced-sodium).

3 tablespoons olive oil

1 pound skinless, boneless chicken thighs, cut into 2 x ½-inch-wide strips

6 scallions, thinly sliced

3 garlic cloves, minced

1 pickled jalapeño pepper, stemmed and minced

4 cups Rich Chicken Stock (opposite page)

1 can (4½ ounces) chopped mild green chilies, drained

1 large tomato, coarsely chopped

½ cup chopped cilantro

½ teaspoon dried oregano

½ teaspoon salt

1 cup frozen corn kernels

8 corn tortillas (6 inches in diameter)

2 tablespoons fresh lime juice

1. In 5-quart Dutch oven or large flameproof casserole, heat 1 tablespoon oil over medium heat. Add chicken and cook, stirring frequently, about 2 minutes, or until no longer pink. Add scallions, garlic, and jalapeño and cook 1 minute. Add stock, chilies, tomato, ¼ cup cilantro, oregano, and salt and bring to a boil. Reduce heat to a simmer, cover, and cook 10 minutes, or until richly flavored. Stir in corn and cook about 2 minutes, or just until heated through.

2. Meanwhile, cut tortillas into ½-inch-wide strips. In 10-inch skillet, heat remaining 2 tablespoons oil over medium heat. Add tortilla strips and cook about 4 minutes, or just until lightly crisped. Set aside a couple of strips for garnish.

3. Drop remaining strips into soup and stir in lime juice and remaining ¼ cup cilantro. Ladle into bowls and garnish with tortilla strips. *Makes 4 servings/440 cals, 18g fat per serving*

Rich Chicken Stock

Prep time: 15 minutes/Cook time: 4 hours

This stock is exceptionally rich in flavor and color because the chicken is browned in the oven first (but you *could* skip this step). To make the stock, you'll need a really big pot—but not a heavy or expensive one. An inexpensive stockpot (or spaghetti pot) from a discount store is fine. Second, be sure to skim off the gray foam that rises to the surface: This makes for a clear stock. And the stock should cook at a simmer—just barely bubbling—rather than a rolling boil.

5 pounds chicken drumsticks and thighs	3 medium carrots, cut up
6 garlic cloves, unpeeled	2 ribs celery, cut up
2 large onions, unpeeled and quartered	½ cup canned tomatoes with their juice
	½ cup parsley sprigs

1. Preheat oven to 450°F.

2. Place chicken on baking sheet and roast about 20 minutes, or until lightly browned. Transfer to 8-quart stockpot.

3. Add cold water to cover chicken by 2 inches (about 4 quarts). Bring to a boil, skimming any foam that rises to surface. Reduce heat to a simmer and add garlic, onions with their skins, carrots, celery, tomatoes, and parsley. Partially cover and simmer 3 hours, or until stock is richly flavored. Strain, discarding solids (yes, including the chicken; all of its flavor should now be in the stock).

4. Cool to room temperature. You can skim the fat from the stock by using a gravy separator (see page 14); or you can chill the stock in the refrigerator to harden the layer of fat, which you can then easily remove. Store the stock in the refrigerator or freezer (see "Know How," at right). Refrigerated stock will keep for a week or two, but if not used within 3 days, bring the stock to a rolling boil and boil for at least 3 minutes before using. *Makes 2½ quarts /35 cals, 1g fat per cup*

KNOW HOW

The freezer's the place for your trove of Rich Chicken Stock. Cool the stock to tepid (you can speed up the process by placing the uncovered pot in a sinkful of cold water). Ladle the cooled stock into 1-cup containers (plastic yogurt containers are fine for this purpose). Or, if you use small amounts of stock in recipes, pour the stock into ice-cube trays. When they're frozen, pop them out and store in the freezer in a large zip-seal plastic bag. You can keep the frozen stock for up to 3 months.

Different Spins

Leave that can in the cupboard and stir up some homemade chicken-noodle soup. Toss a handful of really thin egg noodles (or broken spaghetti, linguine, or fettuccine) into a pot of Rich Chicken Stock; simmer until the noodles are tender. Season to taste with salt and black pepper. Add diced leftover cooked vegetables, chicken, or turkey. A handful of minced fresh basil, dill, or parsley is a great addition, too.

Broiled Chicken Breasts PLUS

Prep time: 20 minutes plus chilling time for butter/Cook time: 20 minutes

Here, a really simple cooking method—broiling—is matched with the simplest of "sauces": compound butter. Make one or all of these seasoned butters to keep in the freezer. You can use them on chicken, as here, on steamed vegetables, fish (see Fish en Papillote, page 79), or even steak. This broiled chicken recipe uses only one-third of the compound butter, so you can double or triple the broiled chicken and not have to increase the butter recipe.

For the compound butter: After beating in the flavorings, scrape the butter onto a sheet of wax paper and pat it into a rough oblong 6 inches long. Then start wrapping the paper around the butter, gradually rolling it into a smoothly shaped log as you would for ice-box cookies. If you're freezing the butter, wrap again, in foil (be sure to label it).

Compound butters (recipes follow)

1 teaspoon dried rosemary, crumbled, or tarragon

¾ teaspoon salt

½ teaspoon freshly ground black pepper

2 tablespoons olive oil

4 bone-in chicken breast halves (about 2½ pounds)

1. Make compound butter of choice; wrap and chill for at least 2 hours to firm.
2. Preheat broiler.
3. In small bowl, stir together rosemary, salt, and pepper. Add oil and mix well. Carefully run fingers under chicken skin without tearing or removing it. Rub some mixture under skin; then rub remaining mixture all over the outside of chicken.
4. Place chicken, skin side down, on broiler pan and broil 8 inches from heat 10 minutes. Turn and broil 6 to 8 minutes more, or until just done. Transfer chicken to dinner plates and place ½-inch-thick slice compound butter on top of each breast half. If you or your guests would prefer to eat the chicken without skin, bring the compound butter slices to the table so each diner can remove the skin and then top the chicken with the butter. *Makes 4 servings/235 cals, 6g fat per serving without skin or butter*

Chili Butter With electric mixer on medium speed, beat 1 stick (8 tablespoons) softened unsalted butter, 2 teaspoons chili powder, ½ teaspoon ground cumin, ½ teaspoon ground coriander, ½ teaspoon grated lime zest, ¼ teaspoon salt, and ¼ teaspoon freshly ground black pepper until well combined. On sheet of wax paper, shape into 6-inch log. Wrap and chill or freeze. *Makes 12 servings/70 cals, 8g fat per serving*

Herb Butter With electric mixer on medium speed, beat 1 stick (8 tablespoons) softened unsalted butter until creamy. Add 2 tablespoons chopped parsley, ½ teaspoon dried thyme, ½ teaspoon dried crumbled rosemary, ¼ teaspoon salt, and ¼ teaspoon freshly ground black pepper and beat until well combined. On sheet of wax paper, shape into 6-inch log. Wrap and chill or freeze. *Makes 12 servings/70 cals, 8g fat per serving*

Red Wine-Scallion Butter In small skillet, heat 2 teaspoons olive oil over low heat. Add ¼ cup minced scallions (white part only) and cook, stirring frequently, about 7 minutes, or until tender. Add ⅔ cup full-bodied red wine (such as Pinot Noir), raise heat to high, and cook about 5 minutes, or until scallions have absorbed

THE **RIGHT** STUFF

A word of caution in case it ever remotely occurred to you to use a so-called cooking wine in the Red Wine compound butter: Don't! Cooking wine is poor-quality stuff and usually has salt added to it. Buy a decent wine and—obviously —serve the rest of the bottle with the meal.

almost all wine. Cool to room temperature. With electric mixer on medium speed, beat 1 stick (8 tablespoons) softened unsalted butter and ¼ teaspoon salt until soft. Beat in scallions until well combined. On sheet of wax paper, shape into 6-inch log. Wrap and chill or freeze. *Makes 12 servings/85 cals, 8g fat per serving*

Toasted Hazelnut Butter In 350°F oven, in a baking pan, bake ⅓ cup hazelnuts until skins loosen and nuts are fragrant, about 10 minutes. Rub nuts in kitchen towel until skins come off (some bits will remain). Transfer to food processor, add 1 stick (8 tablespoons) softened unsalted butter, ¼ teaspoon salt, ¼ teaspoon grated nutmeg, and ⅛ teaspoon cayenne pepper, and process until well combined. On sheet of wax paper, shape into 6-inch log. Wrap and chill or freeze. *Makes 12 servings/90 cals, 10g fat per serving*

Teriyaki Chicken Stir-Fry

Prep time: 20 minutes/Marinating time: 30 minutes/Cook time: 15 minutes

Okay, this recipe is not strictly authentic. Technically teriyaki refers to broiled, not stir-fried, foods. But the marinade, made with soy sauce, honey, sake, and ginger, has real teriyaki taste. And you get to toss a bunch of healthful veggies into the pan, too.

1¼ pounds skinless, boneless chicken breast halves	3 scallions, thinly sliced
2 tablespoons soy sauce	1 tablespoon minced peeled fresh ginger
2 tablespoons sake, dry sherry, or white wine	½ pound shiitake or button mushrooms, trimmed and sliced
1 tablespoon honey	½ pound bok choy, cut crosswise into ½-inch-wide strips
2 teaspoons cornstarch	½ teaspoon salt
1 teaspoon sesame oil	½ cup chicken broth
6 teaspoons vegetable oil	

1. Cut each chicken breast crosswise into ½-inch-wide strips.

2. In medium bowl, whisk together soy sauce, sake, honey, cornstarch, and sesame oil. Add chicken strips, tossing to coat. Cover and refrigerate 30 minutes.

3. In 12-inch nonstick skillet, heat 4 teaspoons vegetable oil over medium-high heat. Lift chicken from marinade, reserving marinade, and stir-fry chicken 4 minutes, or until golden brown and just cooked through. With slotted spoon, transfer to plate.

4. Add remaining 2 teaspoons oil to pan. Add scallions and ginger, reduce heat to medium, and stir-fry 1 minute, or until tender. Add mushrooms and cook, tossing frequently, 3 minutes, or until crisp-tender. Add bok choy and salt and stir-fry 4 minutes, or until bok choy is crisp-tender. Add broth and bring to a boil.

5. Return chicken with reserved marinade to pan, bring to a boil, and cook 1 minute, or until chicken is nicely coated and cooked through. *Makes 4 servings/290 cals, 10g fat per serving*

Chicken Sauté PLUS

Prep time: 15 minutes/Cook time: 25 minutes

The sautéed chicken breasts look just fine served with a scrumptious sauce, but for dress-up, cut each chicken breast crosswise on a slight diagonal into six or seven slices, fan them on a bed of rice or creamy mashed potatoes, and then top with the sauce.

KNOW HOW

Here's your entrée into the world of flambé: To flame the Rich Bourbon Sauce, pour the bourbon into the skillet off the heat. Return the pan to low heat to heat up the bourbon enough to ignite. Avert your face as you hold a match *above* the pan—you're igniting the fumes, not the liquid. A long match is a smart idea and a big help here.

If you can master the knack of making a pan sauce, you'll have a lot more options for a quick dinner. The basic idea is simple: When you sauté poultry (or meat), it creates delicious, caramelized meat juices in the pan. By stirring a liquid into the pan drippings, you have the beginnings of a pan sauce. Once you've tried these three versions, you'll undoubtedly come up with a few of your own.

4 skinless, boneless chicken breast halves (1½ pounds)

½ teaspoon salt

¼ teaspoon freshly ground black pepper

1 tablespoon olive oil

Pan sauces (recipes follow)

1. Sprinkle chicken with salt and pepper.
2. In 10-inch skillet, heat oil over medium heat. Add chicken and sauté about 7 minutes, or until golden brown. Turn and cook 6 to 7 minutes more, or until just cooked through. Transfer chicken breasts to a plate (cover loosely to keep warm).
3. Make pan sauce of choice. Return chicken to pan and heat, spooning sauce over chicken, until heated through. *Makes 4 servings/215 cals, 5g fat per serving without sauce*

Balsamic Sauce Sauté chicken as above. Pour off all but a light skim of fat from pan. Add 2 tablespoons balsamic vinegar and 2 teaspoons tomato paste, stirring to incorporate any pan drippings, and cook 3 minutes. Add ½ cup chicken broth and cook 3 minutes. In small bowl, with fingers, knead together 1 tablespoon unsalted butter and 2 teaspoons flour. Whisk into pan and cook 2 minutes, or until sauce is lightly thickened. *Makes 4 servings/35 cals, 3g fat per serving*

Rich Bourbon Sauce Sauté chicken as above. Pour off all but a light skim of fat from pan. Off heat, add ¼ cup bourbon. Return pan to heat, carefully ignite bourbon (see "Know How" at left), and cook until flame subsides. Add ¾ cup chicken broth, ¼ teaspoon freshly ground black pepper, and ¼ teaspoon salt. Bring to a boil and cook 4 minutes. In small bowl, with fingers, knead together 1 tablespoon unsalted butter and 2 teaspoons flour. Whisk into pan and cook 2 minutes, or until sauce is lightly thickened. *Makes 4 servings/55 cals, 3g fat per serving*

Light Tomato Sauce with Thyme Sauté chicken as above. Pour off all but a light skim of fat from pan. Add 2 minced garlic cloves and cook 1 minute. Add 2 chopped tomatoes and 1 teaspoon minced fresh thyme (or ½ teaspoon dried) and cook 3 minutes. Add ½ cup chicken broth and ¼ teaspoon salt and simmer until sauce is lightly thickened. *Makes 4 servings/20 cals, .4g fat per serving*

The thyme-scented tomato sauce is almost a side dish in itself. Green beans color up the meal. ▶

Lighten Up!

There's very little oil in the barbecue sauce, so if you use skinless
(bone-in) chicken breasts in place
of chicken legs with the skin on,
you'll have a very low-fat dish.
Check for doneness a little sooner
—white meat cooks faster
than dark.

Secret-Ingredient Barbecued Chicken

Prep time: 15 minutes/Cook time: 35 minutes

And the Secret Ingredient is: Coffee! But you'd never guess, because there's a lot more going on here and the coffee does its deep, dark thing in a subtle way.

Secret-Ingredient Barbecue Sauce
  (recipe follows)
4 chicken legs, split into drumsticks
  and thighs (2½ pounds)

1 tablespoon paprika
½ teaspoon salt
½ teaspoon freshly ground black
  pepper

1. Make Secret-Ingredient Barbecue Sauce; set aside.
2. Preheat broiler or preheat grill. If using broiler, line baking pan with foil.
3. Sprinkle chicken with paprika, salt, and pepper. Place chicken on broiler rack and brush one-fourth of barbecue sauce over it. Broil 8 inches from heat 4 minutes. Brush with one-third of remaining sauce and broil 4 minutes. Turn, brush with half of remaining sauce, and broil 4 minutes. Brush with remaining sauce and broil 5 to 8 minutes, or until cooked through. Or grill chicken over medium heat for 20 minutes.
Makes 4 servings/485 cals, 22g fat per serving (with sauce)

Team up the chicken with your own favorite barbecue go-withs. We've opted for tomato salad, slaw, and sweet bicolor corn on the cob.

Secret-Ingredient Barbecue Sauce In 10-inch skillet, heat 2 teaspoons olive oil over medium heat. Add 1 minced small onion and 2 minced garlic cloves and cook, stirring frequently, about 7 minutes, or until tender. Add ⅔ cup ketchup, ¼ cup firmly packed brown sugar, ⅓ cup brewed coffee, 2 tablespoons molasses, 1 tablespoon red wine vinegar, 1 teaspoon ground ginger, and ¼ teaspoon salt. Bring to a boil. Reduce to a simmer, cover, and cook 5 minutes, or until thick. Store covered in refrigerator. *Makes 1½ cups/105 cals, 2g fat per ¼ cup*

Chicken Birds

Prep time: 25 minutes/Cook time: 30 minutes

There are just so many dinner parties you can give where you serve roast chicken. Here's an impressive (but relatively easy) way to get you out of that rut. Based on "veal birds"—cutlets stuffed and rolled into packets to resemble plump little squabs—the wrapper here is boneless chicken thighs. Luckily, the supermarket has done a lot of the work for you by selling chicken thighs already boned and skinned.

¼ cup dried Chinese black mushrooms	½ teaspoon salt
4 ounces ground pork	2 tablespoons flour
3 scallions, thinly sliced	1 tablespoon vegetable oil
3 tablespoons hoisin sauce	½ cup chicken broth
¼ teaspoon ground ginger	1½ teaspoons cornstarch blended with 1 tablespoon cold water
8 skinless, boneless chicken thighs (about 2 pounds)	

1. In small heatproof bowl, combine mushrooms and ¾ cup boiling water. Let stand 20 minutes, or until softened. Lift mushrooms from soaking liquid, rinse, and finely chop. Strain liquid through a coffee filter or strainer lined with paper towels; reserve.
2. In medium bowl, stir together pork, scallions, 2 tablespoons hoisin sauce, ginger, and reserved mushrooms.
3. Place chicken between sheets of wax paper. With flat side of meat mallet or bottom of skillet, pound thighs ¼ inch thick. Place thighs, smooth side down, on work surface. Sprinkle with ¼ teaspoon salt. Spread pork mixture over thighs. Starting at one short end, roll each thigh up jelly-roll fashion and secure with toothpick. Dredge rolls in flour, shaking off excess.
4. In 10-inch skillet, heat oil over medium-high heat. Sauté rolls, turning them, about 4 minutes, or until browned all over. Reduce heat to medium. Add reserved mushroom soaking liquid and cook 5 minutes, or until reduced by half. Add broth, remaining 1 tablespoon hoisin, and remaining ¼ teaspoon salt and bring to a boil. Reduce heat to a simmer and cover. Cook about 20 minutes, or until chicken is tender and sauce is lightly thickened.
5. Remove toothpicks and divide chicken among 4 dinner plates. Stir cornstarch mixture, add to pan, and boil 1 minute. Spoon sauce over chicken and serve. *Makes 4 servings/440 cals, 19g fat per serving*

KNOW HOW

Yes, you can make the barbecue sauce ahead of time; store it in the refrigerator in a tightly covered container for up to 1 month. You can also make a much bigger batch of it. Just double or triple all the ingredients. WARNING: Do not, however, save any *leftover* barbecue sauce if you dipped the brush into it after touching the raw chicken. This could contaminate the sauce with salmonella.

Get out a colorful serving platter and fill it with brown-rice pilaf (or the Barley Pilaf with Caramelized Onions on page 128). Perch the Chicken Birds on top of those amber waves of grain.

In a pinch

For the Chicken Bird stuffing, you can use 3 tablespoons plum or apricot jam blended with 2 teaspoons soy sauce in place of the hoisin sauce.

Coq au Vin Nouveau

Prep time: 25 minutes/Cook time: 1 hour 5 minutes

Ah, oui, le Beaujolais Nouveau. Such a blushing ruby color, such a flirtatiously fruity flavor—and such a lovely wine for cooking. This youngest of reds is just the thing to lighten up good old *coq au vin*, which is usually made with a heavier wine. We've lightened up the dish in another way, too: We've spared you peeling a bushel of tiny little boiling onions (a traditional component of this dish) by simply substituting chopped onion instead. Nobody'll notice. Especially if you pour more of that wonderful Beaujolais with the meal.

4 strips bacon, cut into 1-inch pieces

One 3½-pound chicken, cut into 8 pieces, skin removed

¼ cup flour

1 tablespoon olive oil

12 garlic cloves, peeled

1 medium onion, finely chopped

3 carrots, halved lengthwise and cut into 1-inch lengths

⅔ cup red wine, preferably Beaujolais Nouveau

1 cup chicken broth

½ cup canned tomatoes, chopped, with their juice

½ teaspoon dried thyme

½ teaspoon salt

Chopped parsley, for garnish

1. In 5-quart Dutch oven or large flameproof casserole, cook the bacon over medium heat for about 5 minutes, or until crisp. With slotted spoon, transfer bacon to paper towels to drain.

2. Dredge chicken in flour, shaking off excess. Add oil and heat over medium heat. Add chicken and sauté about 4 minutes per side, or until golden brown. With slotted spoon, transfer chicken to plate.

3. Add garlic and onion to pan and cook about 5 minutes, or until onion is lightly golden. Add carrots and cook about 5 minutes, or until lightly colored. Add wine and cook 5 minutes, or until reduced by half.

4. Add broth, tomatoes with their juice, thyme, and salt, and bring to a boil. Return chicken and bacon to pan and return to a boil.

5. Reduce heat to low, cover, and simmer chicken about 20 minutes, turning pieces midway, or until breast meat is tender. Remove breasts; set aside. Continue cooking dark meat about 15 minutes more, or until tender. Return breasts to pan and cook about 2 minutes, or just until heated through. Transfer to a serving tureen if desired and garnish with chopped parsley. *Makes 4 servings/490 cals, 24g fat per serving*

A brimming tureen of Coq au Vin Nouveau, accompanied with braised leeks. ▶

Thai Chicken & Noodles

In a pinch

A true Thai dish would use fish sauce, but we've found that anchovy paste provides a similar richness and saltiness and is a good substitute. On the other hand, if you're not inclined to run out and buy anchovy paste for this dish (it's also great for Caesar salad, by the way), you could get away with using a small amount of grated Parmesan instead.

Prep time: 20 minutes/Marinating time: 1 hour/Cook time: 20 minutes

This toss of noodles, vegetables, and chicken pretty much defines Thai cuisine in its variety of flavors and textures.

1 cup chicken broth

3 slices (each ¼ inch thick) unpeeled fresh ginger

1 pound skinless, boneless chicken breasts

4 ounces dried Thai rice noodles, preferably thin

⅓ cup fresh lime juice

3 tablespoons soy sauce

3 tablespoons vegetable oil

1 tablespoon plus 2 teaspoons brown sugar

1½ teaspoons anchovy paste

1 red bell pepper, cut into ¼ x 2-inch strips

2 cups fresh mung bean sprouts

½ cup chopped cilantro

⅓ cup coarsely chopped peanuts

1. In 10-inch skillet, bring broth and ginger to a boil over medium heat. Add chicken, reduce heat to low, and cover. Poach 10 minutes, or until cooked through, turning chicken midway. Remove from heat and cool to room temperature. With slotted spoon, transfer chicken to plate; discard broth mixture.

Thai Chicken & Noodles delights with its rainbow of flavors. The savor of soy against the tang of lime and the bite of fresh ginger—wow!

2. Break rice noodles in half. In large pan of boiling water, cook noodles according to package directions; drain.

3. In large bowl, whisk together lime juice, soy sauce, oil, brown sugar, and anchovy paste. Add bell pepper, bean sprouts, and cilantro.

4. Slice chicken crosswise on diagonal into 1-inch-wide strips; add to bowl. Divide mixture evenly among 4 dinner plates and sprinkle with chopped peanuts. *Makes 4 servings/450 cals, 18g fat per serving*

Perfectly Moist Roast Chicken

Prep time: 15 minutes/Cook time: 1 hour 15 minutes

You stuff the chicken before roasting it, but there's no stuffing. How's that? What you put into the bird is a whole lemon, an entire head of garlic, and some fresh rosemary, so flavor and moisture come from right inside the chicken as it roasts. Another plumpness preserver: Start roasting the chicken breast side down, and turn it over when the roasting is half done. This keeps the breast meat from drying out—a common disappointment among novice chicken-roasters.

1 teaspoon salt	1 head garlic, unpeeled
One 4-pound chicken, giblets removed, rinsed and patted dry	2 tablespoons olive oil
	2 tablespoons flour
3 sprigs fresh rosemary	1½ cups chicken broth
1 lemon, pricked all over with a fork	

1. Preheat oven to 425°F.

2. Rub ¼ teaspoon salt into chicken cavity, then insert rosemary, lemon, and garlic. With cotton string, tie together chicken legs. Lift wings toward neck, then fold them under back of chicken to pin them in place. Rub under skin with some oil; brush remaining oil over outer skin and sprinkle with ½ teaspoon salt.

3. Roast, breast side down, on rack in roasting pan 30 minutes. Turn breast side up and roast 30 minutes more, or until cooked through (see "Know How," at right). Transfer to platter and let stand 10 minutes before carving. Discard rosemary, lemon, and garlic from interior of chicken.

4. Pour off all but 2 tablespoons fat from pan. Place pan over 2 burners, on medium heat. Whisk in flour until well combined. Whisk in broth and remaining ¼ teaspoon salt and simmer, whisking occasionally, 5 minutes, or until gravy is lightly thickened. Carve chicken and serve with gravy. *Makes 4 servings/590 cals, 35g fat per serving*

In a pinch

Those Thai rice noodles may be a little tough to track down. If you can't find any, you can substitute about 8 ounces of linguine or spaghettini, cooked according to package directions.

KNOW HOW

You can't fool around when you're cooking poultry: Because of the risk of salmonella, the bird must be absolutely, unequivocally done before you serve it. "Done" means that a meat thermometer inserted in the thigh will register 175°, and that the juices run clear (not pink) when you cut into the thickest part of the meat with the tip of a knife.

Different Spins

If you're a garlic fan, you can use some of the garlic that has cooked inside the roast chicken to add more body and flavor to the gravy. Take a couple of the cloves, squeeze them out of their skins, mash them with a fork, and stir into the gravy.

Oven-Fried Chicken PLUS

Different Spins

Customize your batch of oven-fried chicken: Instead of cooking a cut-up whole chicken, buy a total of 4 pounds of your preferred chicken parts—breasts, legs, and/or thighs.

Lighten Up!

You can make the Oven-Fried Chicken with skinless chicken. But to make it easy on yourself— don't try cutting up and skinning a whole chicken—just buy the parts already skinned. And, if you are really counting fat grams, use only white meat, which is lower in fat than dark.

In a pinch

If you can't find chipotle chilies for the Chipotle-Ketchup Sauce, just stir some chili powder (to taste) into the ketchup.

Prep time: 10 minutes /Marinating time: 1 hour or up to 8 hours
Cook time: 40 minutes

Get out a big basket and call your friends: This chicken wants to go on a picnic. Bathed in an old-fashioned buttermilk marinade, then coated in Parmesan bread crumbs, the chicken is baked to crunchy perfection. We give you three dipping sauces to choose from; they can travel to the picnic in jars, along with some cool salad "sides." How about our One Potato, Two Potato salad (page 107)?

2 cups buttermilk
2 tablespoons honey
½ teaspoon dried oregano
¼ teaspoon cayenne pepper
One 4-pound chicken, cut into
    8 pieces
Dipping sauces (recipes follow)

1 cup dried bread crumbs
⅓ cup chopped parsley
2 tablespoons grated Parmesan
    cheese
¼ teaspoon salt
3 tablespoons olive or vegetable oil

1. In large bowl, stir together buttermilk, honey, oregano, and cayenne. Add chicken, cover, and refrigerate at least 1 hour or up to 8 hours.

2. While chicken soaks, make dipping sauce of choice; set aside.

3. Preheat oven to 350°F.

4. In shallow bowl, stir together bread crumbs, parsley, Parmesan, and salt. Dredge chicken in crumb mixture, shaking off excess. Transfer to jelly-roll pan and drizzle oil over top.

5. Bake chicken, without turning, for 30 minutes. Check breasts for doneness and remove if cooked through. Continue baking dark meat pieces about 10 minutes longer, or until cooked through and golden brown. Serve with dipping sauce. *Makes 6 servings/610 cals, 40g fat per serving without dipping sauce*

Apricot-Lemon Sauce In medium bowl, stir together ½ cup apricot jam, ¼ cup fresh lemon juice, 2 tablespoons honey, ¾ teaspoon ground ginger, and ¼ teaspoon salt. *Makes scant 1 cup/65 cals, .1g fat per 2 tablespoons*

Chipotle-Ketchup Sauce In small food processor, process 1 cup ketchup, 2 canned chipotle chilies in adobo sauce, and 4 teaspoons fresh lime juice until smooth. *Makes generous 1 cup/30 cals, .2g fat per 2 tablespoons*

Creamy Blue Cheese Sauce In medium bowl, with fork mash ¾ cup crumbled blue cheese (3 ounces). Stir in ¾ cup buttermilk, ¾ teaspoon Worcestershire sauce, and ½ teaspoon red hot pepper sauce. *Makes generous 1 cup/45 cals, 3g fat per 2 tablespoons*

We'll Never shh Tell

It seems to us that every time we go to the supermarket, someone has come up with yet another way to package chicken. With skin, but no bones. With bones, but no skin. With both. With neither. And that doesn't even touch on the myriad ready-to-cook and ready-to-eat forms, such as chicken pre-cut for stir-fry, or this era's boon to mankind: the fully cooked roast chicken from the deli. Our recipes take advantage of several types of ready-to-go poultry with some surprising pantry-shelf ingredients for four great main dishes. And it's easy to turn them into meals. The Chicken Pesto Presto is a natural served with fettuccine; the Enchiladas Suizas ("Swiss" because they're made with a cream sauce) just need a salad on the side. The Smoked Turkey Salad begs for a big, crusty loaf of bread, and Devilishly Easy Chicken can go to the table with a store-bought potato or pasta salad.

Chicken Pesto Presto

Spread 1 tablespoon store-bought pesto under skin of each of 4 bone-in chicken breast halves (10 ounces each). Broil bone side up on broiler pan 8 inches from heat 8 minutes, or until browned. Meanwhile, in small bowl, stir together ¼ cup store-bought pesto and 2 tablespoons sour cream. Spread pesto cream over skin on chicken. Broil, skin side up, 7 to 10 minutes, or until cooked through. Makes 4 servings/490 cals, 26g fat per serving

Enchiladas Suizas

In medium bowl, whisk 1 cup milk into 2 tablespoons flour. Stir in ½ cup bottled salsa verde. Dip eight 6-inch corn tortillas, one at a time, into salsa-milk mixture. Sprinkle ½ pound shredded Monterey Jack cheese and 6 ounces shredded deli chicken (or roast turkey) over tortillas. Spread 1 tablespoon plain salsa verde over each tortilla and roll up. Arrange tortillas, seam side down, in one layer in buttered 11 x 7-inch glass baking dish. Pour remaining salsa-milk mixture over tortillas. Bake in preheated 350°F oven 30 minutes, or until piping hot. (The rolls may unravel slightly during baking; not to worry--they still taste *muy bueno*.) Makes 4 servings/450 cals, 23g fat per serving

Smoked Turkey Salad

In large bowl, whisk together ⅓ cup store-bought vinaigrette (if lemon is available, use it; otherwise use another flavored vinaigrette), 1 tablespoon apricot jam, 2 tablespoons fresh lemon juice, 1 tablespoon Dijon mustard, and ¼ teaspoon freshly ground black pepper. Add 1 package (10 ounces) prewashed and torn salad greens, ½ pound cubed (½ inch) smoked turkey, 1 pint cherry tomatoes, halved, and ½ cup chopped honey-roasted cashews and toss to combine. Makes 4 servings/225 cals, 11g fat per serving

Devilishly Easy Chicken

Place 4 skinless, boneless chicken breast halves (6 ounces each) between sheets of wax paper. With meat mallet or bottom of small skillet, pound chicken ¼ inch thick. Sprinkle ½ teaspoon each of salt and freshly ground black pepper over chicken. In small bowl, stir together ⅓ cup regular or light mayonnaise, ¼ cup grated Parmesan cheese, 1 tablespoon drained white horseradish, and ¼ teaspoon crushed red pepper flakes. Spread mixture over top of chicken breasts. Broil chicken on broiler pan 6 inches from heat, without turning, 7 minutes, or until golden brown and cooked through. Makes 4 servings/410 cals, 25g fat per serving

Jamaican Jerk Chicken

In a pinch

In a way, marinating the chicken overnight is a timesaver: All you have to do at serving time is stick it under the broiler. But if you need to make the dish on really short notice, just rub on the spice paste and put the chicken right in the oven—marinating is not mandatory!

**Prep time: 30 minutes/Marinating time: 3 hours or overnight
Cook time: 25 minutes**

Hey, mon, here's a taste of the tropics, broiled chicken division. A hot-sweet spice paste rubbed on the chicken gives it true Island flavor. The pineapple-mango salsa, though an optional accompaniment, does a nice job of balancing the pungency. The chicken is meant to be broiled, but if you can't broil 8 inches from the heat in your oven, bake the chicken at 450°F for 30 to 35 minutes.

Tropical Fruit Salsa (recipe follows)

4 teaspoons ground allspice

6 scallions, thinly sliced

3 garlic cloves, minced

1 tablespoon minced peeled fresh ginger

3 pickled jalapeños, stemmed and minced

3 tablespoons fresh lime juice

1 tablespoon brown sugar

¾ teaspoon salt

½ teaspoon freshly ground black pepper

3 tablespoons olive oil

4 chicken legs, split into drumsticks and thighs (2½ pounds)

Serve Jamaican Jerk Chicken and its accompanying tropical salsa with rice and grilled baby vegetables.

1. Make Tropical Fruit Salsa, cover, and refrigerate until serving time.

2. In large bowl, stir together allspice, scallions, garlic, ginger, jalapeños, lime juice, brown sugar, salt, and black pepper. Add oil and stir to make a paste. Rub jerk paste all over chicken. Cover and refrigerate at least 3 hours or up to overnight.

3. Preheat broiler or prepare grill.

4. Broil chicken pieces on broiler rack 8 inches from heat 25 minutes, turning several times, or until cooked through. Transfer chicken to heated platter and serve with salsa. Or grill chicken over medium heat 20 to 25 minutes. *Makes 4 servings/450 cals, 29g fat per serving without salsa*

Tropical Fruit Salsa In medium bowl, combine 3 cups of ½-inch pieces fresh pineapple, 1 mango, peeled and cut into ½-inch pieces, 1 red bell pepper, cut into ¼-inch dice, 2 tablespoons honey, and 2 tablespoons fresh lime juice. *Makes 4 cups/130 cals, .7g fat per cup*

Stuffed Chicken Breasts

Prep time: 25 minutes/Cook time: 50 minutes

Putting flavorings under chicken skin is a neat trick. It can be as simple as a slice of lemon or a fresh herb sprig. Or it can be something richer and heftier, like this filling made with cheese, sun-dried tomatoes, and olives. Once you get the idea, you can make up all sorts of stuff to tuck under chicken skin. Serve this with one of the Vegetable Purees on page 101.

To stuff the chicken breasts, use your fingers to carefully separate the skin from the flesh. Take care to leave the skin attached at the sides so the stuffing won't fall out. Then gently pack in the stuffing, spreading it evenly; pat the skin back in place.

¼ cup sun-dried tomatoes, not oil-packed	¼ cup chopped fresh basil or parsley
4 ounces soft goat cheese or feta cheese, crumbled	¼ teaspoon freshly ground black pepper
1 egg, lightly beaten	4 bone-in chicken breast halves (2½ pounds)
¼ cup brine-cured olives, such as Kalamata, finely chopped	1 tablespoon olive oil
¼ cup golden or dark raisins	¼ teaspoon salt

1. Preheat oven to 350°F. Lightly grease 13 x 9-inch glass baking dish.

2. In small pan of boiling water, blanch sun-dried tomatoes 5 minutes, or until softened. Drain, cool, and finely chop. In medium bowl, combine sun-dried tomatoes, goat cheese, egg, olives, raisins, basil, and pepper.

3. Lift skin on each chicken breast and stuff olive mixture carefully under skin, spreading it evenly (see photo at right); pat skin back down over stuffing. Brush skin with oil and sprinkle with salt.

4. Bake chicken, stuffed side up, in baking dish 45 minutes, or until cooked through. *Makes 4 servings/505 cals, 26g fat per serving*

Go ahead and gild the lily: Serve the Stuffed Chicken Breasts with one of the compound butters on pages 58 and 59.

The Holiday Bird

Prep time: 55 minutes/Cook time: 4 hours 10 minutes

Trussing makes for a handsome, tidily tucked-in bird. But skewers and laces are unnecessarily fussy, if you ask us. First put a slice of bread over the stuffing to keep it from drying out, and then use one of the Quick Trusses below to keep the drumsticks together.

Quick Truss #1: Slip the ends of the drumsticks either through the band of skin at the bottom of the cavity opening or through the skin beneath "the part that goes over the fence last."

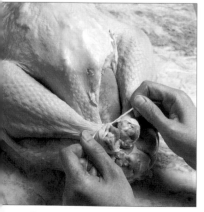

Quick Truss #2: Lasso the drumsticks and tie them tightly together with cotton string.

So you've finally volunteered to make the Big Meal on the Big Day, and everybody is coming. Not to worry! Read this recipe. Take a deep breath. Read the recipe again and make your shopping list. And on the day, don't forget to delegate. Aunts and cousins and friends are going to crowd into the kitchen anyway before the meal, so you might as well have nice little tasks all ready for them. Salad tossing, gravy stirring, napkin folding—you don't have to do it all yourself. This recipe is for a 12-pound turkey. If you are roasting a larger bird, consult the Poultry Roasting Chart on page 174.

Classic Bread Stuffing with Sausage (recipe follows)

4 tablespoons unsalted butter, softened

½ cup minced scallions, white part only

1 tablespoon minced fresh rosemary or 1½ teaspoons dried

1 tablespoon minced fresh thyme or 1½ teaspoons dried

¾ teaspoon salt

One 10- to 12-pound turkey, giblets removed and reserved; liver discarded

1 slice bread, preferably the heel

1 cup chicken broth

3 tablespoons flour

1. Make Classic Bread Stuffing with Sausage; set aside.

2. Preheat oven to 425°F.

3. In small bowl, with wooden spoon, combine butter, scallions, rosemary, thyme, and ½ teaspoon salt.

4. Rinse turkey inside and out and pat dry. Rub cavity with remaining ¼ teaspoon salt. Carefully lift skin of turkey with fingers and spread herb butter over breast. Spoon 6 cups stuffing into turkey cavity and seal cavity with slice of bread. Quick-truss turkey (see photos at left). Lift wings toward neck, then fold them under back of chicken to pin them in place. Spread remaining stuffing evenly in 13 x 9-inch glass baking dish and toss with broth; set aside.

5. Place turkey, breast side down, on rack in roasting pan. Roast turkey 45 minutes, or until nicely browned.

6. Meanwhile, in 3-quart saucepan, combine turkey giblets and 3 cups water. Bring to a boil, reduce heat to low, and partially cover. Simmer for 1 hour. Strain, discarding giblets.

7. Lower oven temperature to 350°F. Turn turkey breast side up and roast 2½ hours longer, basting frequently with pan drippings, until meat thermometer inserted in breast registers 160°F. (If turkey is overbrowning, tent with foil.) Bake reserved stuffing for last 30 minutes of cooking time. Transfer turkey to carving board and keep baked stuffing warm, loosely covered.

8. Pour off all but 3 tablespoons of pan drippings. Place roasting pan over 2 burners both set on low heat. Whisk in flour and cook, whisking constantly, 3 minutes, or until lightly browned. Whisk in giblet stock. Cook, stirring, until gravy is slightly thickened. Remove trussing string from turkey. Carve and serve with stuffing and gravy. *Makes 8 servings/830 cals, 42g fat per serving with stuffing and gravy*

Classic Bread Stuffing with Sausage In 12-inch skillet, crumble in 1 pound sweet Italian sausages, casings removed, and cook, stirring frequently, for 5 minutes, or until lightly browned and cooked through. With slotted spoon, transfer to bowl. Add 4 minced large onions and 6 minced garlic cloves to skillet and cook, stirring frequently, 12 minutes, or until onions are golden brown and tender. Add 4 ribs celery cut into ½-inch dice and cook 5 minutes, or until crisp-tender. Let cool. Preheat oven to 350°F. Toast 10 cups sourdough bread (or French bread) cubes (¾-inch) on baking sheet 7 minutes, or until crisp. Transfer to large bowl and add 1 cup chicken broth, ⅓ cup chopped parsley, 1½ teaspoons dried sage, ¾ teaspoon salt, ¼ teaspoon freshly ground black pepper, cooked sausage, and onion mixture. Toss well, add 4 tablespoons melted unsalted butter, and toss again. *Makes 12 cups/245 cals, 13g fat per cup*

Grilled Cornish Hens with Southwestern Rub

Prep time: 15 minutes/Cook time: 20 minutes

Cornish hens are real cuties, and when halved they're as easy to cook as chicken breasts. Come to think of it, you could do this recipe with chicken, if you'd rather. If you're making this for young kids, you might want to either leave out the cayenne pepper from the rub, or just sprinkle their birds with the salt and sugar.

Avocado Corn Relish (recipe follows)

1 teaspoon dried oregano

1 teaspoon ground cumin

1 teaspoon ground coriander

¾ teaspoon salt

½ teaspoon sugar

¼ teaspoon cayenne pepper

2 Cornish game hens (each about 1½ pounds), halved lengthwise

1. Make Avocado Corn Relish, cover, and refrigerate.

2. Preheat broiler or prepare grill.

3. In small bowl, stir together oregano, cumin, coriander, salt, sugar, and cayenne. With fingertips, carefully lift skin on each hen without tearing or removing it. Rub spice mixture under and over skin and onto bone side of hen halves.

4. Broil hens, skin side down, on broiler pan 8 inches from heat about 10 minutes, or until browned. Turn hens and broil 8 to 10 minutes more, or until cooked through. Or grill hens over medium heat for 5 to 7 minutes per side. Serve hens with Avocado Corn Relish spooned over top. *Makes 4 servings/375 cals, 26g fat per serving without relish*

Avocado Corn Relish In medium bowl, toss together gently 1 avocado (8 ounces), pitted, peeled, and cut into ¼-inch chunks, 1 cup thawed frozen corn, 1 small diced tomato, ¼ cup minced red onion, 1 tablespoon red wine vinegar, 1 teaspoon chili powder, and ¼ teaspoon salt. *Makes 2 cups/60 cals, 3g fat per ¼ cup*

KNOW HOW

If you want to roast an unstuffed turkey, the roasting time for a 12-pound bird will go down—check for doneness about 40 minutes sooner than for a stuffed turkey. For roasting larger birds, stuffed or unstuffed, consult the Poultry Roasting Chart on page 174.

Show off

Thanksgiving's the time to go for broke on garnishing. Put the turkey on a platter and surround it with miniature fruits—lady apples, seckel pears, kumquats, and those tiny Champagne grapes, interspersed with lavish herb sprigs or with lemon leaves.

KNOW HOW

Poultry shears are sometimes called kitchen shears and they're good for lots of jobs. But they're unbeatable for cutting up poultry. To halve a game hen, first snip right along the backbone, then turn the hen over and cut along the length of the breastbone.

Turkey Cutlets Normandy

Prep time: 30 minutes/Cook time: 30 minutes

THE RIGHT STUFF

You have several options for the splash of apple in the Turkey Cutlets Normandy. Applejack is an American apple brandy that's been around since Colonial times. Calvados is its French counterpart. Regular grape brandy adds flavor, but you sacrifice the apple kick. For a nonalcoholic option, you can use apple cider. (Note that most of the alcohol burns off anyway when the brandy is cooked.)

Turkey cutlets or scallops are one "convenience food" that's worth its weight in gold: The leanest of all meats, boneless turkey breast cutlets couldn't be quicker to prepare. One wonderful way to go is with sautéed apples, apple brandy, and cream. What's not to like? To streamline the recipe for a weeknight, skip the applejack step and increase the chicken broth to ½ cup.

12 slices turkey breast, each ½ inch thick (about 1½ pounds)

3 tablespoons flour

½ teaspoon salt

¼ teaspoon freshly ground black pepper

2 tablespoons olive oil

1 small onion, minced

2 Granny Smith apples, unpeeled, and cut into ¼-inch-thick slices

1 tablespoon sugar

¼ cup applejack, Calvados, or brandy

⅓ cup chicken broth

½ cup heavy or whipping cream

2 tablespoons chopped parsley

1. Place turkey slices between 2 sheets of wax paper or foil. With meat mallet or bottom of skillet, pound slices ¼ inch thick. On plate, stir together flour, ¼ teaspoon salt, and pepper. Dredge slices in seasoned flour, shaking off excess.

With the Turkey Cutlets Normandy, serve a mix of white and wild rice, molded in custard cups, and lightly sautéed zucchini.

2. In 10-inch nonstick skillet, heat 1 tablespoon oil over medium-high heat. Add 3 turkey slices and sauté about 2 minutes per side, or until golden brown and cooked through. Transfer to platter and cover loosely with foil to keep warm. Add 3 more slices to pan and sauté in same manner; transfer to platter. Add remaining 1 tablespoon oil to pan and cook remaining turkey in 2 batches as above.

3. Add onion to pan, reduce heat to medium, and cook 5 minutes, or until lightly browned. Add apples and sugar and sauté 4 minutes, or until lightly caramelized. Remove pan from heat and pour applejack into pan. Return pan to heat, carefully ignite applejack (see "Know How," page 60), and cook until flame subsides.

4. Add broth and remaining ¼ teaspoon salt and bring to a boil. Cook 3 minutes, or until apples are tender and broth has evaporated. Add cream and cook 1 minute, or until sauce is lightly thickened. Add parsley and stir to combine. Serve turkey topped with sauce. *Makes 4 servings/460 cals, 19g fat per serving*

Thai Green Curry

Prep time: 30 minutes/Cook time: 30 minutes

This Thai curry is powerfully flavored with cilantro, jalapeños, and lime zest—quite different from the more familiar Indian curries.

Green Curry Paste (recipe follows)	1½ pounds turkey breast or skinless, boneless chicken thighs, cut into 1-inch chunks
1 pound all-purpose potatoes, peeled and cut into ½-inch chunks	
1 tablespoon vegetable oil	½ pound green beans, cut into 2-inch lengths
1 cup canned unsweetened coconut milk	1 teaspoon sugar

1. Make Green Curry Paste and set aside.

2. In large pan of boiling water, cook potatoes 5 minutes. Drain.

3. In 5-quart Dutch oven or large casserole, heat oil over medium heat. Add curry paste and cook 1 minute. Add ½ cup coconut milk and cook about 4 minutes, or until almost dry.

4. Add turkey and ¼ cup coconut milk and cook, stirring frequently, until turkey is no longer pink. Add potatoes, beans, sugar, and remaining ¼ cup coconut milk and bring to a boil. Reduce to a simmer, cover, and cook about 15 minutes, or until turkey is cooked through and potatoes and beans are tender. *Makes 4 servings/435 cals, 22g fat per serving*

Green Curry Paste In food processor or blender, combine 3 garlic cloves, 1 tablespoon coarsely chopped fresh ginger, 3 fresh jalapeño peppers (or 4 pickled jalapeños), ¾ cup cleaned cilantro sprigs (preferably with roots), 2 strips (3 x ½ inch each) lime zest, 2 strips (3 x ½ inch) lemon zest, 1 shallot, ¾ teaspoon salt, and 2 tablespoons water and process until smooth. *Makes 1 cup/12 cals, .1g fat per ¼ cup*

THE **RIGHT** STUFF

Basic to Mexican, Indian, and many other of the world's cuisines, cilantro was little known by most Americans until recently. But once you have developed a taste for it, cilantro can be nearly addictive. It's sometimes called Chinese parsley, and it does look a lot like flat-leaf parsley. The distinctive fragrance is the giveaway (pinch a leaf to be sure). If you can, buy cilantro with its roots intact. Store it like a little bouquet, in a jar of water. Wash the roots and chop them right in with the leaves and stems—the roots hold the richest flavor. Cilantro also travels under the name "coriander" because its seeds are the source of that pungent, citrus-y spice.

In a pinch

You can use whole milk (or half-and-half) instead of coconut milk. Use ¾ cup total; add ¼ cup with the curry paste and the rest with the turkey in step 4. To get some of the special sweetness that coconut adds, you could use a couple of drops of coconut extract (watch out; it overpowers other flavors easily).

Turkey Burgers PLUS

Prep time: 20 minutes/Cook time: 20 minutes

With all the hype about turkey burgers, you would think that they had negotiated world peace or something. Not quite, but in their own modest way they've permanently altered the burger scene. Turkey's milder flavor and drier texture (compared to beef) do call for some extra help: We've added sautéed onions and garlic, sour cream, and fresh bread crumbs. Use this recipe as is, or as the jumping-off point for one of the variations below.

2 teaspoons olive oil	1½ pounds ground turkey
1 small onion, minced	¾ teaspoon salt
2 garlic cloves, minced	½ teaspoon dried sage (optional)
¼ cup reduced-fat sour cream	½ teaspoon freshly ground black pepper
1 slice firm white sandwich bread, crumbled	

1. In small skillet, heat oil over low heat. Add onion and garlic and cook, stirring frequently, about 7 minutes, or until tender. Transfer to medium bowl and stir in sour cream and bread crumbs. Add turkey, salt, sage, and pepper. Shape mixture into 4 patties.

2. Preheat broiler.

3. Broil patties on broiler pan 6 inches from heat 5 minutes per side, or until golden brown and cooked through. *Makes 4 servings/360 cals, 22g fat per serving*

Chutney-Mustard Turkey Burgers Prepare basic burger recipe through step 1, but add ¼ cup minced mango chutney and 1 tablespoon Dijon mustard to burger mixture. Proceed as for basic recipe. *Makes 4 servings/425 cals, 22g fat per serving*

Cheddar-Chili Turkey Burgers Prepare basic burger recipe through step 1, but add ¼ cup finely shredded Cheddar cheese and 2 finely minced pickled jalapeños to burger mixture. Proceed as for basic recipe. *Makes 4 servings/395 cals, 24g fat per serving*

Apple & Almond Turkey Burgers Prepare basic burger recipe through step 1, but add ¼ cup shredded Granny Smith apple and 2 tablespoons minced toasted almonds to burger mixture. Proceed as for basic recipe. *Makes 4 servings/390 cals, 24g fat per serving*

Spicy Carrot Turkey Burgers Prepare basic burger recipe through step 1, but add ¼ cup finely shredded carrot and ½ teaspoon red hot pepper sauce to burger mixture. Proceed as for basic recipe. *Makes 4 servings/365 cals, 22g fat per serving*

Show off

As long as you have the broiler up and running, broil thick slices of red onion (brush with some olive oil first) to serve with the burger.

Lighten Up!

When you buy a product labeled "ground turkey," you're getting a mix of light meat, dark meat, and skin—which is not particularly low in fat. For a leaner burger, look for ground skinless turkey breast, which, being all white meat, is very low in fat. If you can't find this in your market, make your own ground turkey (see below).

KNOW HOW

It's really simple to make ground turkey at home. Just buy a piece of skinless turkey breast, cut it into chunks, and drop them into the food processor as you pulse the machine on and off. Check frequently so you don't over-chop the turkey; it should have some texture—and not be a paste.

fish & Shellfish

Poached Salmon PLUS

Prep time: 15 minutes/Cook time: 10 minutes

KNOW HOW

Poaching fish is a quick, basic cooking technique you should know. All you do is place the fish in a shallow pan of liquid that's kept at a gentle simmer; most cooks use a seasoned poaching liquid that the French call a *court bouillon.* Put in the fish skin side up so that the flesh is completely immersed, and remove the skin after cooking. You can do this when the fish is still hot— or, if serving the fish chilled, after cooling.

We've all heard those stories about someone poaching a whole salmon in the dishwasher. Maybe it works, maybe it doesn't, but it's way easier to poach fillets in a skillet on the stove. Take your pick of the sauces: They're all no-cook affairs that you just stir up in a bowl. If you're serving the salmon cold, refrigerate the sauce, too.

Sauces (recipes follow)
4 salmon fillets, with skin (4 to 6 ounces each)
1 cup dry white wine
1 small onion, halved and thinly sliced
1 carrot, thinly sliced
4 sprigs parsley
¼ teaspoon salt

1. Make sauce of choice; cover and set aside.

2. With your fingertips, check each fillet at thickest point for small bones; remove with fingertips or tweezers and discard.

3. In 10-inch nonreactive (i.e., not unlined aluminum or cast iron) skillet, combine wine, onion, carrot, parsley, salt, and 1 cup water. Bring to a boil over medium heat, reduce to a simmer, and add fillets, skin side up. Simmer 8 to 10 minutes, or until fish is cooked to desired doneness. With slotted spatula, transfer fillets to work surface; remove and discard skin. Discard poaching liquid.

4. Serve fillets hot or cold with sauce as accompaniment. *Makes 4 servings/260 cals, 15g fat per serving without sauce*

Parsley-Dill Sauce In medium bowl, whisk together 3 tablespoons olive oil, 2 tablespoons fresh lemon juice, 1 teaspoon Dijon mustard, and ¼ teaspoon salt. Add ¼ cup each of chopped parsley and snipped dill. Stir in ½ cup diced peeled cucumber. *Makes ¾ cup/65 cals, 7g fat per 2 tablespoons*

Different Spins

Here are some other possibilities for sauces to serve with the poached salmon (or any poached fish): Beurre Blanc (page 90), Pesto (page 118), and Light Lemon-Shallot Vinaigrette (page 30).

Creamy Lemon-Caper Sauce In medium bowl, whisk together ½ cup sour cream, 1 tablespoon mayonnaise, 1 teaspoon grated lemon zest, 1 tablespoon fresh lemon juice, and 1 teaspoon red hot pepper sauce. Stir in 4 teaspoons rinsed and drained capers. *Makes ¾ cup/70 cals, 7g fat per 2 tablespoons*

Sesame-Spinach Sauce In medium bowl, whisk together ¾ cup plain low-fat yogurt, 1 tablespoon sesame oil, and 1 teaspoon soy sauce. Stir in ¼ cup finely chopped thawed frozen spinach (be sure to squeeze the spinach dry first). Before serving, sprinkle sauce with 4 teaspoons toasted sesame seeds. *Makes 1 cup/40 cals, 3g fat per 2 tablespoons*

Carrot Vinaigrette In medium bowl, whisk together 3 tablespoons olive oil, 2 tablespoons red wine vinegar, ¼ teaspoon salt, and ⅛ teaspoon freshly ground black pepper. Stir in ¼ cup each of finely diced red bell pepper, red onion, and carrot. *Makes ¾ cup/80 cals, 8g fat per 2 tablespoons*

It's a Wrap: Fish en Papillote

Prep time: 25 minutes plus chilling time for butter/Cook time: 30 minutes

The *papillote* we're talking about is the French term for a parchment-paper packet used for sealing in moisture in baked dishes. The ingredients are assembled on a heart-shaped piece of parchment and sealed with a series of pleats (see photos at right). Fish cooked *en papillote* is an impressive achievement, and not a difficult one. However, if paper folding is not your *forte*, you can easily make the packets from foil as directed below. Open the packets carefully—the steam can burn!

Compound butters (page 58)

1⅓ cups couscous

¾ teaspoon salt

¼ cup dried currants or raisins

3 tablespoons pine nuts, toasted

1 tablespoon olive oil

1 leek, cut into ¼ x 2-inch strips, well washed

2 carrots, cut into ¼ x 2-inch matchsticks

1 red bell pepper, cut into ¼ x 2-inch strips

4 sole or flounder fillets (6 to 8 ounces each)

Fold a piece of parchment in half and cut into a heart shape (remember making valentines in third grade?). Place the ingredients on one half of the heart.

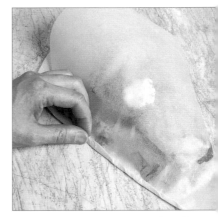

Fold the parchment over and seal the edges by making a series of small pleats. It doesn't have to be neat, but crease the pleats well to hold the edges together.

1. Make compound butter of choice; wrap and chill for at least 2 hours to firm.

2. In medium bowl, combine couscous, ½ teaspoon salt, and 2¼ cups boiling water, and toss with fork. Cover and let stand 5 minutes, or until water has been absorbed and couscous is tender. Add currants and pine nuts and toss.

3. In 10-inch skillet, heat oil over medium heat. Add leek and cook, stirring frequently, 3 minutes, or until crisp-tender. Add carrots and bell pepper and cook, stirring frequently, 4 minutes, or until carrots are tender.

4. Preheat oven to 400°F. Cut off 4 lengths of parchment paper (14 x 12 inches), fold each piece in half, and cut into a heart shape (see top photo). Alternatively, lightly oil four 12-inch squares of aluminum foil.

5. Spoon one-fourth of couscous mixture across one half of each piece of parchment or foil. Top with 1 sole fillet and sprinkle remaining ¼ teaspoon salt over all. Top fillets with julienned vegetables, dividing them evenly, and 1 slice compound butter. Pleat parchment to seal (middle photo), or fold foil in half over couscous and fish and, leaving a little headspace, fold edges up to seal.

6. Bake packets on baking sheet 15 minutes, or until the parchment packets are puffed (the foil packets won't puff). Place 1 packet on each serving plate, cut an X in the top of the packet, carefully peel back the cut edges, and serve at once. *Makes 4 servings/540 cals, 10g fat per serving without butter*

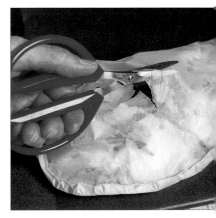

To serve, cut an "X" in the top of the parchment and peel the paper back. Watch out for steam.

Grilled Swordfish with Vegetables Basquaise

Different Spins

If you can't get swordfish (sometimes it's in short supply), substitute halibut. As a matter of fact, the Vegetables Basquaise are also great with grilled chicken that's been seasoned with the same spice rub.

Prep time: 25 minutes/Marinating time: 30 minutes/Cook time: 35 minutes

In this country, we don't hear a lot about the foods of Spain—and hardly anything about its many regional cuisines. But Spaniards consider the Basque country (on the slopes of the Pyrenees and along the Bay of Biscay) a great gastronomical center. Seafood dishes form the basis of that reputation, and fish cooked with sweet peppers and green olives is one of the defining recipes of the cuisine.

2 teaspoons paprika

¾ teaspoon ground ginger

½ teaspoon sugar

½ teaspoon freshly ground black pepper

¼ teaspoon salt

4 swordfish steaks (6 to 8 ounces each)

Vegetables Basquaise (recipe follows)

1 tablespoon olive oil

1. In small bowl, stir together paprika, ginger, sugar, pepper, and salt. Rub mixture onto both sides of fish steaks, cover, and refrigerate 30 minutes.

2. Meanwhile, make Vegetables Basquaise and keep warm.

The chunky vegetable accompaniment for grilled swordfish is a basil-scented "ragout" of sweet peppers, tomatoes, and olives.

3. Preheat broiler or prepare grill.

4. Rub oil over both sides of fish steaks. Broil on broiler pan 6 inches from heat 3 minutes per side, or until just cooked through when tested with fork. Or grill fish over medium heat for 3 minutes per side. Serve with vegetables spooned over top of each steak. *Makes 4 servings/250 cals, 11g fat per serving without vegetables*

Vegetables Basquaise In 10-inch skillet, heat 1 tablespoon olive oil over low heat. Add 1 minced small onion and 3 minced garlic cloves and cook, stirring frequently, about 7 minutes, or until onion is tender. Stir in 2 bell peppers (1 red and 1 green, cut into ½-inch squares) and cook, stirring frequently, 8 to 10 minutes, or until soft. Add 2 cups chopped tomatoes with their juice, ⅓ cup pitted and coarsely chopped green olives, ⅓ cup chopped fresh basil, and ½ teaspoon salt and bring to a boil. Reduce to a simmer and cook about 10 minutes, or until slightly thickened. *Makes 3 cups/90 cals, 5g fat per ¾ cup*

Sesame-Pepper Tuna Steaks

Prep time: 10 minutes plus marinating time for salad
Cook time: 10 minutes

Like steak au poivre, these tuna steaks are coated with pepper. But for a change of pace, the coarsely cracked black peppercorns are mixed with sesame seeds for more crunch and a wonderful nutlike flavor. Most people like tuna cooked rare—pink at the center, almost like rare beef—so we mean it when we say just 2 minutes per side.

Radish-Carrot Salad (recipe follows)

2 teaspoons whole black peppercorns

2 tablespoons sesame seeds

½ teaspoon salt

4 tuna steaks, ¾ inch thick (6 to 8 ounces each)

2 tablespoons olive oil

1. Make Radish-Carrot Salad. Cover and refrigerate at least 1 hour.

2. With mortar and pestle (or in a zip-seal plastic bag; see photo, page 39), lightly crush peppercorns. Transfer to shallow plate, add sesame seeds and salt, and stir to combine. Lay tuna steaks, one at a time, in peppercorn mixture, pressing it into flesh to coat.

3. In 10-inch skillet, heat oil over medium heat. Add tuna steaks and cook 2 minutes per side for medium-rare. Transfer tuna steaks to serving plates and top with Radish-Carrot Salad. *Makes 4 servings/345 cals, 18g fat per serving without salad*

Radish-Carrot Salad In small saucepan, bring ¼ cup distilled white vinegar, 2 tablespoons sugar, and ¼ teaspoon salt to a boil over medium heat and boil 5 minutes, or until slightly reduced. Transfer to medium bowl and cool to room temperature. Shave 2 carrots into thin, wide ribbons with a vegetable peeler and add to dressing. Thinly slice 6 to 8 medium radishes and cut each slice into ¼-inch-wide strips. Add radishes to carrots and toss to combine. *Makes 2 cups/45 cals, 1g fat per ½ cup*

Different Spins

For the outdoor-grill deprived, consider purchasing a stovetop grill pan. The raised ridges in the pan give you that great grilled look without the need to light a fire. Grease the pan lightly with oil or cooking spray and cook the fish for 3 minutes per side. (Grill pans comes in a wide variety of shapes and sizes—and colors—and are great for chicken and meat, too.)

THE **RIGHT** STUFF

Sesame seeds are cheaper if you buy them by the bag in an ethnic food store (such as an Indian market) rather than in a teeny-tiny jar from the spice aisle. Store the seeds in an airtight container in the refrigerator or freezer: They're high in fat, and with time can become rancid if kept at room temperature.

Bouillabaisse

Prep time: 40 minutes/Cook time: 50 minutes

Monkfish fillets are covered with a tough membrane that you have to remove before cooking. Slip a paring knife under the skin to loosen it, then peel the membrane off with your fingers.

Purists claim that you can't make bouillabaisse without using Mediterranean fish. But to buy into that would be to deny yourself a great culinary pleasure. Monkfish (or striped bass), clams, and shrimp make a superb bouillabaisse when flavored with the traditional orange zest, Pernod, and fennel seeds.

Rouille (recipe follows)

1 loaf French bread (12 ounces), thinly sliced

3 tablespoons olive oil

¼ cup minced onion

4 garlic cloves, minced

1 small bulb fennel (1 pound), trimmed and cut crosswise into ¼-inch-wide strips

1½ cups dry white wine

2 dozen littleneck clams, scrubbed

2 tablespoons Pernod or other anise-flavored liquor

2 cups canned tomatoes, chopped, with their juice

4 strips orange zest (½ x 3 inches each)

¾ teaspoon fennel seeds, crushed

½ teaspoon salt

1 pound skinless, boneless monkfish, cut into 1-inch chunks

1½ pounds medium shrimp, shelled and deveined

1. Make Rouille and transfer to bowl; set aside.

2. Preheat oven to 400°F.

3. Brush bread on one side with 2 tablespoons oil, transfer to baking sheet, and toast about 7 minutes, or until golden brown. Set toasts aside.

4. Meanwhile, in Dutch oven, heat remaining 1 tablespoon oil over medium heat. Add onion and garlic and cook, stirring frequently, about 5 minutes, or until the onion is tender. Add fresh fennel and sauté, stirring frequently, about 7 minutes, or until crisp-tender. Add wine and 2½ cups water and bring to a boil over high heat. Add clams and cover. Cook, checking for doneness occasionally, about 5 minutes, or until clams just open. The clams will open at different times; remove them as they open, and discard any that do not open. Set clams aside; cover loosely to keep warm.

5. Add Pernod and bring to a boil. Add tomatoes, orange zest, fennel seeds, and salt and bring to a boil. Add monkfish. Reduce to a simmer, cover, and cook 10 minutes.

6. Add shrimp and cover. Cook 3 minutes, or until shrimp are just cooked through. Return clams to pan and cook just until heated through. Remove orange zest strips if desired (they're perfectly edible).

7. Spread Rouille over toasts. Divide fish and shellfish among 8 wide shallow soup or pasta bowls and ladle broth over top. Float 2 toasts in each bowl and serve. *Makes 8 servings/340 cals, 9g fat per serving*

Rouille In small pan of boiling water, blanch 3 peeled whole garlic cloves for 2 minutes; drain. Transfer to food processor and add ¾ cup light mayonnaise, 1 roasted red pepper (preferably homemade, see how-to on page 15), 1 tablespoon tomato paste, 1 teaspoon red hot pepper sauce, and ¼ teaspoon salt, and process until smooth. *Makes 1 generous cup/80 cals, 8g fat per 2 tablespoons*

We'll Never Tell Shh

Just in case you're one of those people who still thinks that fish is hard to cook, let us clue you in: The only trick to cooking fish is not to cook it very long. And isn't that what we're all after—food that's ready *fast?* Here's are some ways with fast fish (in one case, canned fish) plus secret ingredients that make it something special. The first is a Tex-Mex take on cocktail sauce for shrimp; the second, an easy fish stew *alla marinara* (which means "sailor-style," appropriately enough). Next, a simple method for steaming snapper in the microwave (one of the few good uses for this appliance, in our humble opinion), with an Asian sesame-ginger sauce as the final flourish. Our final entry is the ultimate tuna melt, topped with Manchego, a mellow Spanish sheep's-milk cheese—though you could use Muenster, Cheddar, or smoked mozzarella in its place.

Fiery Cocktail Sauce

In medium bowl, whisk together 1 cup bottled chili sauce, 2 tablespoons fresh lime juice, 2 teaspoons ground cumin, 1 teaspoon ground coriander, ½ teaspoon dried oregano, ¼ teaspoon cayenne, and 2 minced pickled jalapeño peppers. Serve with boiled or steamed shrimp. Makes about 1¼ cups/30 cals, .2g fat per 2 tablespoons

Fish Stew alla Marinara

In small pan of boiling water, cook ¾ pound diced peeled potatoes 10 minutes, or until tender; drain and set aside. Meanwhile, in 12-inch skillet, stir together 1 jar (16 ounces) marinara sauce, ½ cup chicken broth, and ¼ cup dry white wine and bring to a boil over medium heat. Add ½ cup pimiento-stuffed olives, coarsely chopped, and cook 3 minutes to blend flavors. Add 1½ pounds skinless cod fillets, cut into 1-inch chunks, 1 teaspoon green jalapeño sauce, and potatoes. Bring to a boil, reduce to a simmer, and cover. Simmer 7 to 10 minutes, or until fish is cooked through. Add ½ cup frozen peas and cook 1 minute, or until heated through. Makes 4 servings/330 cals, 8g fat per serving

Zapped Snapper

With your fingertips, check 4 skinless red snapper fillets, each 6 ounces and ½ inch thick, for small bones; remove with your fingertips or tweezers and discard. Place fillets on microwave-safe plate and season with ¼ teaspoon each of salt and freshly ground black pepper. Tent plate loosely with plastic wrap. Microwave on High 3 minutes; turn plate and cook 3 minutes more, or until fish is cooked through and can be easily pierced with fork. Divide fillets among serving plates. Sprinkle 2 tablespoons minced scallion and 2 teaspoons finely minced peeled ginger evenly over fillets. Drizzle 2 tablespoons soy sauce and 1 teaspoon sesame oil evenly over top. In small skillet, heat 2 tablespoons vegetable oil until hot but not smoking; pour hot oil evenly over fillets and serve at once. Makes 4 servings/185 cals, 3g fat per serving

Tony Tuna Melt

In medium bowl, stir together 2 cans (6 ounces each) water-packed tuna, drained. Add 3 tablespoons mayonnaise, 2 thinly sliced scallions, and 2 teaspoons fresh lemon juice and combine well. Spread mixture on 4 slices 7-grain bread. Top each with 2 thin rings of pickled jalapeño pepper. Sprinkle with ¼ pound Manchego cheese, shredded. Broil on broiler pan 6 inches from heat 3 to 4 minutes, or until cheese is melted. Makes 4 servings/360 cals, 19g fat per serving

Nouvelle Scampi

Prep time: 20 minutes/Cook time: 10 minutes

This take on Shrimp Scampi is "nouvelle" because of the eye-opening tang of lime juice and the heady aroma of basil, miles away from the dish's restaurant origins.

1 tablespoon olive oil	¼ teaspoon cayenne pepper
1½ pounds large or jumbo shrimp, shelled and deveined	¼ teaspoon salt
3 large garlic cloves, minced	4 teaspoons unsalted butter, in pieces
⅓ cup fresh lime juice	2 tablespoons chopped basil
⅓ cup chicken broth	

1. In 10-inch nonstick skillet, heat oil over medium heat. Add shrimp and cook, tossing frequently, 3 minutes, or until just cooked through. With slotted spoon, transfer shrimp to a bowl.

2. Reduce heat to low, add garlic to pan, and cook, stirring frequently, 1 minute, or until tender. Add lime juice and cook 1 minute. Add broth, cayenne, and salt; increase heat to high and cook 2 minutes, or until slightly reduced.

3. Remove pan from heat and return shrimp to pan. Add butter and basil and swirl until butter has just melted and shrimp are coated. *Makes 4 servings/225 cals, 10g fat per serving*

THE **RIGHT** STUFF

Scampi is the Italian name for giant prawns found in European waters. Sometime in America's past a transplanted Italian chef, perhaps longing for the *scampi* of his homeland, came up with a dish called Shrimp Scampi—large shrimp cooked with butter, garlic, and white wine. Though the name nonsensically translates as "Shrimp Big Shrimp," it has become an Italian restaurant standard. To approximate what a dish made with real scampi might be, try to find shrimp that come 16 to 20 to the pound. If they're terribly expensive, you can, of course, use smaller specimens.

Sole in Tarragon Cream Sauce

Prep time: 20 minutes/Cook time: 25 minutes

We wouldn't have believed this, but it turned out to be true: Cooking fish in dry vermouth eliminates the cooking odors. Maybe it's the 40-some herbs and spices used to make vermouth—flavorings that also subtly season the lush cream sauce. By the way, when you've cooked down the vermouth, added the cream, and cooked down the sauce some more, you've made what's called a reduction sauce.

4 sole or flounder fillets (6 to 8 ounces each)	2 tablespoons unsalted butter
¾ teaspoon salt	¾ cup minced scallion whites
¼ cup minced parsley	1 cup dry white vermouth
3 tablespoons minced fresh tarragon	½ cup heavy or whipping cream

1. Lay sole fillets, skinned side up, on work surface and sprinkle with ½ teaspoon salt, 2 tablespoons parsley, and tarragon.

2. In 10-inch skillet, melt butter over low heat. Add scallions and cook, stirring frequently, 2 minutes, or until tender. Sprinkle scallions over fish; fold fillets in half crosswise.

You want just the leaves of the tarragon, not the tough stems. Hold the tarragon sprig with the leaves pointing down. Strip off the leaves by pulling the sprig between your closed thumb and forefinger. This method also works for other herbs whose leaves branch off a sturdy stem.

3. Add folded-over fillets to pan and pour vermouth over them. Place piece of wax paper directly on surface of fillets to cover. Bring liquid to a simmer over low heat and cook about 5 minutes, or until fish can easily be pierced when tested with fork. With slotted spatula, transfer fillets to 4 dinner plates and cover loosely to keep warm.

4. Increase heat to medium-high and bring liquid in pan to a boil. Cook 5 to 7 minutes, or until reduced by two-thirds. Add cream and remaining ¼ teaspoon salt and boil 4 minutes, or until sauce is thick enough to coat fish. Stir in remaining 2 tablespoons parsley. Spoon sauce over fillets and serve at once. *Makes 4 servings/375 cals, 19g fat per serving*

Snapper Escabeche

Prep time: 20 minutes/Cook time: 30 minutes/Marinating time: 2 hours

You know all about marinating food *before* you cook it; *escabeche* is one of the few dishes in which you marinate *after* cooking. In this Mexican recipe, sautéed fish fillets, along with onions, are left to chill in a sweet-and-sour sauce made with vinegar, orange juice, and raisins. It's a terrific summer dish, especially good served with a cool rice or orzo salad and some dead-ripe tomatoes sliced over pungent arugula.

4 skinless red snapper fillets, ¼ inch thick (6 to 8 ounces each)	2 teaspoons sugar
¼ cup flour	⅓ cup cider vinegar
1 tablespoon chili powder	⅓ cup fresh orange juice
¾ teaspoon salt	½ cup chicken broth
3 tablespoons olive oil	⅓ cup golden raisins (optional)
1 large onion, halved and thinly sliced	½ teaspoon dried oregano
2 garlic cloves, slivered	¼ teaspoon freshly ground black pepper

1. With your fingertips, check each snapper fillet at thickest point for small bones; remove with your fingertips or tweezers and discard.

2. On sheet of wax paper, stir together flour, chili powder, and ¼ teaspoon salt. Dredge fillets in flour mixture, shaking off excess.

3. In 10-inch nonreactive (i.e., not unlined aluminum or cast iron) skillet, heat oil over medium heat. Sauté 2 fillets for about 3 minutes per side, or until cooked through. With slotted spatula, transfer to shallow nonmetal baking dish large enough to hold all 4 fillets in one layer. Sauté remaining fillets in same manner and transfer to baking dish.

4. Add onion and garlic to pan and cook, stirring frequently, about 10 minutes, or until golden brown and tender. Sprinkle sugar over vegetables, add vinegar, and increase heat to high. Cook 1 minute. Stir in orange juice and cook 2 minutes. Add broth, raisins, oregano, remaining ½ teaspoon salt, and pepper. Bring to a boil and boil about 4 minutes, or until slightly thickened. Pour sauce over fillets, cover, and refrigerate, occasionally spooning sauce over fish, at least 2 hours or up to overnight.

5. Serve snapper fillets with onion and sauce mixture spooned over top. *Makes 4 servings/370 cals, 13g fat per serving*

Different Spins

Although tarragon works especially nicely with delicate fish like sole, you could also make the cream sauce with finely slivered fresh basil. For an unusual look, see if you can find purple-leaved opal basil.

THE RIGHT STUFF

Red snapper, one of the most prized of all fish, is usually sold with the skin on to assure you that you're getting the real thing (not some other kind of snapper). Even fillets come with the skin on. For the escabeche, you'll need to remove the skin (then rinse the fillets to wash away any loose scales).

KNOW HOW

Don't "go off the deep end" when you're frying fish, by which we mean: The oil can splatter when you add the fish to the skillet, so tilt the pan away from you (the oil will pool at the far side) and drop the fish in at the "shallow end."

Different Spins

Scallops make an equally delicious seviche. Prepare them the same way you would the shrimp—the steaming and marinating times are the same.

KNOW HOW

You practically need a toolbox to shell a whole crab, so buy fresh lump crabmeat (not the canned stuff!)—it's definitely the way to go. Even though the lump crabmeat you buy is likely to be pretty clean, it still may have tiny bits of cartilage in it. Spread the crabmeat on a baking sheet and pick through it gently with your fingers, removing any bits of cartilage or shell.

Shrimp Seviche

Prep time: 20 minutes/Cook time: 2 minutes
Marinating time: 2 hours or up to 8 hours

Not to be confused with *escabeche* (that's on page 85), South America's *seviche* is a refreshing specialty of raw seafood "cooked" in citrus juice. (The acid in the juice turns the fish firm and opaque after several hours' soaking.) To be on the safe side, we've poached the shrimp first, but the flavor is no less fresh and inviting.

- 1 pound medium shrimp, shelled and deveined
- 1¼ cups fresh orange juice
- ½ cup fresh lime juice
- 2 red bell peppers, cut into ¼-inch dice
- 1 large tomato, seeded and cut into ¼-inch dice
- 1 avocado, cubed

- 1 medium red onion, cut into ¼-inch dice
- ⅔ cup chopped cilantro
- ⅓ cup chopped fresh basil or mint (optional)
- 1 teaspoon salt
- ½ teaspoon crushed red pepper flakes

1. In medium saucepan with steamer basket set over simmering water, steam shrimp (covered) for 2 minutes, or until cooked through. Transfer shrimp to shallow bowl large enough to hold them in single layer and pour in orange and lime juices. Cover and refrigerate at least 2 hours or up to 8 hours.

2. In large bowl, stir together bell peppers, tomato, avocado, onion, cilantro, basil, salt, and red pepper flakes. Add shrimp and citrus juices and toss gently to combine. Serve chilled. *Makes 4 servings/265 cals, 10g fat per serving*

Crab Cakes with Mango Salsa

Prep time: 40 minutes/Cook time: 20 minutes

The quality of crab cakes is determined by their ratio of crabmeat to "other stuff." These score high: One pound of crab to just 3 ounces of bread crumbs, an egg white, and judicious amounts of seasoning. You can prepare the crab cakes (through step 3) several hours ahead of time; place them on a baking sheet, cover with plastic wrap or foil, and refrigerate until you're ready to sauté them.

- Mango Salsa (recipe follows)
- 3 slices firm white sandwich bread (3 ounces)
- 1 pound lump crabmeat, picked over to remove cartilage and shell
- ¼ cup mango chutney, minced
- 1 tablespoon Dijon mustard

- 2 teaspoons green jalapeño pepper sauce
- ½ teaspoon salt
- ¼ teaspoon freshly ground black pepper
- 1 large egg white
- 3 tablespoons olive oil

Spoon each portion of cool, tangy Shrimp Seviche onto a bed of lettuce and garnish with a sprig of cilantro.

1. Make Mango Salsa, cover, and refrigerate.
2. Preheat oven to 400°F.
3. In food processor, process bread to fine crumbs (or finely chop by hand). Transfer crumbs to sheet of wax paper; set aside.
4. In large bowl, stir together crabmeat, chutney, mustard, pepper sauce, salt, and black pepper. In small bowl, beat egg white to stiff peaks. Fold beaten white into crab mixture until incorporated. Shape mixture into 8 cakes. Coat each crab cake on both sides with reserved bread crumbs, patting them on to adhere.
5. In 10-inch nonstick skillet, heat 1½ tablespoons oil over medium heat. Add 4 crab cakes and sauté 2 minutes per side, or until golden brown. Transfer to baking sheet. Sauté remaining crab cakes in remaining 1½ tablespoons oil in same manner and transfer to baking sheet. Bake 7 to 8 minutes, or until heated through.
6. Divide crab cakes among 4 dinner plates and spoon mango salsa alongside.
Makes 4 servings/330 cals, 13g fat per serving without salsa

Mango Salsa In medium bowl, stir together gently 1 mango, cut into ½-inch cubes (see technique, page 9), 1 large red bell pepper, cut into ½-inch pieces, 2 thinly sliced scallions, 2 tablespoons honey, and 1 tablespoon fresh lemon juice. *Makes about 2 cups/75 cals, .2g fat per ½ cup*

Different Spins

There are lots of toppings that go well with crab cakes: Stay with the tropical theme and serve Tropical Fruit Salsa (page 71) or head for Mexico and serve with either Spicy Fresh Tomato Sauce (page 130) or Chipotle-Ketchup Sauce (page 68).

Golden Sea Scallops on Vegetable "Pappardelle"

Prep time: 15 minutes/Cook time: 20 minutes

Pappardelle are broad Italian egg noodles, so we've borrowed the name for our wide ribbons of summer squash, which are fun to make with a vegetable peeler. The secret behind the delicately crunchy, golden crust on the sautéed sea scallops is a light dusting of cornstarch.

Different Spins

If you don't feel like playing along with our "vegetable pasta" game, serve the sauced scallops over real pasta, such as fettuccine. If you're up for the veggies but not for the fancy slicing, just cut the zucchini and yellow squash into half-moons and sauté them.

4 medium zucchini (6 ounces each)

4 medium yellow summer squash (6 ounces each)

2 tablespoons unsalted butter

2 scallions, minced

2 garlic cloves, minced

1 teaspoon salt

3 tablespoons cornstarch

1 pound sea scallops, halved horizontally

2 tablespoons olive oil

1 lemon, cut into 8 wedges

1. Cut ends off zucchini and yellow summer squash. With vegetable peeler, cut thin strips down length of squash to make "ribbons" (see photo, opposite page).

2. In 12-inch nonstick skillet, heat 1 tablespoon butter over low heat. Add half the scallions and half the garlic and cook, stirring frequently, 1 minute, or until tender. Increase heat to medium, add half the squash ribbons and sprinkle with ¼ teaspoon

Ribbons of yellow summer squash and zucchini, wilted in garlicky butter, serve as a foil for crisp-coated sautéed scallops.

salt. Sauté, tossing frequently, 5 minutes, or until vegetables are tender but not mushy. Divide evenly among 4 dinner plates. Repeat with remaining 1 tablespoon butter, remaining scallion and garlic, remaining squash ribbons and ¼ teaspoon salt. Add to squash already on plates. Wipe out the skillet.

3. In small bowl, combine cornstarch and remaining ½ teaspoon salt. Spoon mixture into small strainer and sprinkle over both sides of scallops.

4. In skillet, heat 1 tablespoon oil over medium-high heat. Arrange half the scallops in pan in one layer and cook about 2 minutes, or until golden brown and crisp. With slotted spatula, transfer scallops to the dinner plates. Repeat with remaining 1 tablespoon oil and scallops. Garnish with lemon wedges. *Makes 4 servings/300 cals, 14g fat per serving*

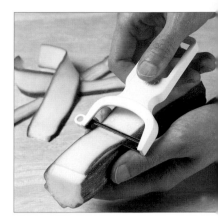

To make the vegetable "pappardelle," first trim both ends from the squash. Then run a vegetable peeler along the side of the squash to form long strips. Take it slow so the "ribbons" don't break. If the squash are especially seedy, start making ribbons and when you hit the seeds, flip the squash over and continue on the second side. Discard the seedy section (or eat it on the spot).

Moules Provençale

Prep time: 40 minutes/Cook time: 30 minutes

A bowl of mussels is a real treat, and one that your family will be pleasantly surprised to find on the dinner table. Be sure to provide a big basket of crusty peasant bread for mopping up the delicious broth (it's almost the best part of the dish). As a bonus, mussels are one of the cheapest types of seafood you can buy: When we last looked they were still under $2 per pound.

1 tablespoon olive oil	2 cups canned tomatoes, chopped, with their juice
2 leeks or 4 large scallions, white and tender green parts, diced and well rinsed	½ teaspoon ground ginger
3 garlic cloves, minced	½ teaspoon salt
1½ cups dry white wine	5 pounds mussels, debearded and scrubbed

1. In a large nonaluminum saucepan with lid, heat oil over low heat. Add leeks and garlic and cook, stirring frequently, 5 minutes, or until leeks are tender. Add wine, increase heat to high, and cook 3 minutes, or until slightly reduced.

2. Add tomatoes with their juice, ginger, salt, and 1½ cups water and bring to a boil. Add mussels, cover, and cook, shaking the pan occasionally, 12 minutes, or until shells have opened. Divide mussels among 4 shallow bowls; discard any that have not opened.

3. Spoon cooking liquid over mussels to serve. *Makes 4 servings/295 cals, 8g fat per serving*

KNOW HOW

Mussels grow in undersea colonies, attached to rocks or other surfaces by a tuft of thread-like fibers called a "beard." You need to remove the beard before cooking the mussels. The beard originates inside the mussel shell. Grab it near the shell opening and pull it out with a quick tug. Then scrub the shells with a stiff brush and rinse under cold water.

Lobster PLUS

Prep time: 10 minutes/Cook time: 20 minutes

If you can't stand the thought of cooking a live lobster, try to get over it. Or get a friend to help—a lobster feed is by definition a group activity. Take a deep breath, place the beasts in the boiling water claws-down, and cover the pot quickly. They'll be done in only minutes—in fact be sure not to overcook them, since it makes them tough. Then, arm yourself with claw-crackers (or a small hammer) and picks. And although we personally wouldn't be caught dead in a lobster bib, we would certainly appreciate something like a wet washcloth for dealing with messy fingers and hands at the end of the meal.

There's more than one way to get at the prized meat in a cooked lobster tail. Here's an easy trick: First, twist off the tail.

2 tablespoons coarse (kosher) salt or sea salt

4 live lobsters (1½ pounds each)

Dipping sauces (recipes follow)

1. Bring lobster pot (or large spaghetti pot) of water to a boil. Add salt and return to a boil. Slip lobsters carefully into boiling water and immediately cover pot. Cook lobsters 10 to 12 minutes, or until shells are red-orange. With tongs, remove lobsters and transfer to large colander to drain.

2. Meanwhile, make one (or all!) of the dipping sauces (though the Beurre Blanc would not do well with *chilled* lobsters—the cold would congeal the butter).

3. The lobsters may be served hot, at room temperature, or chilled, with sauce as accompaniment. *Makes 4 servings/145 cals, 1g fat per serving without sauce*

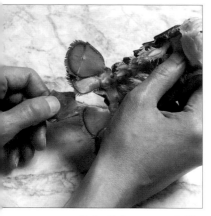

Pull off the center finlike piece from the tail. Removing it "unlocks" the meat.

Thai Dipping Sauce In small saucepan, bring ½ cup fresh lime juice, 2 tablespoons soy sauce, 2 tablespoons plus 2 teaspoons sugar, and 1½ teaspoons anchovy paste to a boil over medium heat. Cook, stirring, until sugar is dissolved. Remove pan from heat and let sauce cool. *Makes ⅔ cup/20 cals, .2g fat per tablespoon*

Beurre Blanc In small nonaluminum saucepan, combine ¼ cup minced shallots and 1 cup dry white wine and bring to a boil over medium heat. Boil 5 minutes, or until wine has almost evaporated. Whisk in 1 stick (8 tablespoons) cut-up cold unsalted butter, 1 piece at a time, until sauce is creamy. Whisk in ¼ teaspoon salt. Serve warm or make several hours in advance and refrigerate. To reheat, set over a pan of simmering water, whisking until re-emulsified. *Makes ¾ cup/70 cals, 8g fat per tablespoon*

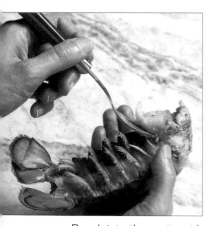

Reach into the cavity with a fork and pull out the meat. It should come out in one succulent piece.

Spicy Green Sauce In mini food processor, process 1 seeded jalapeño pepper, ¼ cup parsley leaves, 2 cut-up scallions, 3 tablespoons fresh lime juice, 2 tablespoons water, and ½ teaspoon salt until smooth. *Makes ¾ cup/3 cals, 0g fat per tablespoon*

vegetables & salads

Braised Artichoke Hearts with Pancetta

Prep time: 30 minutes/Cook time: 40 minutes

Preparing artichokes this way takes a little time, but it's worth it. The hearts—which are revealed after you remove the leaves and fuzzy "chokes"—are pure pleasure, the filet mignon of the vegetable kingdom. Since artichokes will discolor after they're cut, they're dropped into what's called *acidulated* water (water plus a few drops of lemon juice or vinegar) to keep them from darkening. The braised artichokes are flavored with pancetta, a flavorful unsmoked Italian bacon.

To prepare artichoke hearts, pull off the outer leaves, then cut across, close to the base, to remove remaining leaves.

Use a teaspoon to scoop and scrape out the fuzzy fibers that form the "choke." Discard the choke.

1 tablespoon lemon juice or white vinegar

6 medium artichokes

2 teaspoons olive oil

4 slices pancetta or smoked ham, minced (1½ ounces)

1 small onion, minced

½ pound all-purpose potatoes, peeled and cut into ¼-inch dice

½ teaspoon dried thyme

¼ teaspoon salt

1 cup chicken broth

1 cup canned white kidney beans, rinsed and drained

¼ cup chopped parsley

1 tablespoon unsalted butter, in pieces

1. Fill large bowl with cold water and add lemon juice.
2. With paring knife, cut each artichoke down to the heart, scoop out choke, and peel stem (see photos at left). Cut each artichoke heart lengthwise into ¼-inch-thick slices and immediately put slices in water with lemon juice to prevent discoloration.
3. In 10-inch skillet, heat oil over medium-low heat. Add pancetta and cook, stirring, 3 minutes, or until lightly crisped. Add onion and cook, stirring frequently, about 7 minutes, or until tender.
4. With slotted spoon, transfer artichokes from bowl to skillet. Add potatoes, thyme, and salt and stir to coat. Cover and cook 5 minutes, or until potatoes are well coated.
5. Add broth and ½ cup water to skillet and bring to a boil. Reduce to a simmer and cover. Cook about 20 minutes, or until artichokes can easily be pierced with tip of knife and potatoes are cooked through. Add beans and stir to heat through.
6. Remove from heat and stir in parsley and butter, swirling until butter melts. Serve.
Makes 4 servings/275 cals, 10g fat per serving

Braised Artichoke Hearts & Limas A traditional Italian component of the above artichoke dish would be lima beans, so for those who like lima beans and want to go for the authentic dish: Omit the white beans and add 1 cup of frozen baby lima beans in step 4, when you add the potatoes. *Makes 4 servings/280 cals, 10g fat per serving*

Trim off the remaining bases of the leaves, then peel the artichoke stem.

Portobello "Pizzas"

Prep time: 15 minutes/Cook time: 20 minutes

Until quite recently, what we now call portobello mushrooms were considered overgrown—and were usually thrown away. Luckily someone realized that older mushrooms have a lot more flavor than button-like babies (and thus a craze was born). Sturdy portobellos are used here as the "crust" for mini-pizzas.

4 portobello mushrooms (5 ounces each), stems removed	2 tomatoes, chopped (1½ cups)
2 teaspoons olive oil	½ teaspoon grated orange zest
2 garlic cloves, minced	½ teaspoon salt
⅛ teaspoon crushed red pepper flakes	¼ teaspoon dried sage
	4 ounces part-skim mozzarella cheese, shredded

1. Preheat oven to 400°F. Brush a jelly-roll pan lightly with oil.
2. Arrange mushrooms, stemmed side down, in one layer in pan and bake 15 minutes, or until tender when pierced with tip of knife.
3. Meanwhile, in 10-inch nonstick skillet, heat oil over low heat. Add garlic and red pepper flakes and cook 1 minute. Add tomatoes, orange zest, salt, and sage and simmer 5 to 7 minutes, or until slightly thickened.
4. Turn mushrooms stemmed side up. Spoon mozzarella into mushroom caps, dividing it evenly, and top with tomato mixture. Bake 5 minutes, or until cheese has melted. Serve hot. *Makes 4 servings/135 cals, 8g fat per serving*

Baked Fennel with Parmesan Shavings

Prep time: 10 minutes/Cook time: 30 minutes

Fennel grows as a tightly layered bulb, like the base of a bunch of celery, and has a faintly licorice-like flavor (its other name is anise). Raw fennel makes great crudités and salads, but it turns soft and mellow when baked, as in this popular Italian recipe.

2 bulbs fennel (about 1 pound each)	1 tablespoon fresh lemon juice
2 tablespoons olive oil	⅓ cup grated Parmesan cheese plus ¼ cup shavings
½ teaspoon grated lemon zest	

1. Preheat oven to 375°F.
2. Cut off and discard fennel stalks and fronds. Slice bulbs lengthwise ¼ inch thick.
3. In large bowl, toss fennel with oil until coated. Add lemon zest and juice and toss again. Spread fennel in 9 x 13-inch glass baking dish and sprinkle with the grated Parmesan. Bake about 30 minutes, or until tender. Arrange the Parmesan shavings over top and serve. *Makes 4 servings/165 cals, 12g fat per serving*

Crushed Potatoes

Prep time: 10 minutes/Cook time: 20 minutes

Mashed potatoes can range from way too lumpy to way too creamy (in which case they're probably instant). But some comfort-foodie chef came up with a new take: crushed or smashed potatoes, which fit somewhere in between and really hit the spot. If you're feeding folks who haven't had a home-cooked meal lately, you'll want to make a double batch. If they're garlic lovers, you can add more of that, too.

2 pounds all-purpose potatoes
1 cup chicken broth
3 garlic cloves, peeled
¾ teaspoon salt

2 tablespoons unsalted butter, softened
¼ cup whole or low-fat milk

1. Peel potatoes, halve lengthwise, and cut into thick slices.
2. In 3-quart saucepan, combine potatoes, broth, garlic, ¼ teaspoon salt, and 2 cups water and bring to a boil over medium heat. Reduce to a simmer, cover, and cook about 20 minutes, or until potatoes are tender. Drain, reserving garlic.
3. Combine potatoes and garlic in large bowl and add butter and remaining ½ teaspoon salt. With potato masher, coarsely mash, adding milk gradually until potatoes are just crushed. Serve hot. *Makes 4 servings/205 cals, 7 g fat per serving*

Gratin Dauphinoise

Prep time: 20 minutes/Cook time: 70 minutes

Time for a pop quiz on your "food French." Did you know that *gratin* doesn't mean "smothered with cheese," but rather "topped with a yummy crust"? The term, in fact, is often used to describe foods that are immersed in cream, which turns a gorgeous golden-brown in the oven. It sure works for these potatoes.

1½ cups half-and-half or light cream
1 garlic clove, peeled and halved
½ teaspoon salt

⅛ teaspoon ground nutmeg
2 pounds baking potatoes, peeled and sliced ⅛ inch thick

1. Preheat oven to 350°F.
2. In 1-quart saucepan, bring cream, garlic, salt, and nutmeg to a boil over low heat. Remove from heat.
3. Layer potato slices, overlapping them, in shallow 1½-quart casserole or 7 x 11-inch glass baking dish. Pour cream mixture over potatoes and remove and discard garlic. Cover dish with aluminum foil.
4. Bake 45 minutes. Remove foil and bake 20 minutes more, or until potatoes are fork-tender and cream is golden brown and bubbly. Let gratin stand 5 to 10 minutes to cool slightly before serving. *Makes 6 servings/170 cals, 7g fat per serving*

Crispy Steak Fries

Prep time: 10 minutes/Cook time: 1 hour 15 minutes

Flimsy fast-food fries pale (literally) before these mighty steak fries, sturdy planks o' potato with a crisp chili crust. Use a *mild* chili powder for these fries—though most chili powders are not labeled for heat level, you should be safe in assuming that a supermarket-available chili powder will be mild.

¼ cup flour

1 tablespoon chili powder

¾ teaspoon salt

½ teaspoon ground cumin

¼ teaspoon black pepper

4 large baking potatoes, 6 to 8 inches long (8 to 10 ounces each)

3 tablespoons olive or vegetable oil

1. Preheat oven to 375°F. Brush a jelly-roll pan lightly with oil.

2. In small bowl, combine flour, chili powder, salt, cumin, and pepper.

3. Cut each potato lengthwise into 8 wedges and put in large shallow bowl. Sift flour mixture over potatoes, tossing to coat.

4. Arrange potatoes in single layer in jelly-roll pan. Sift any flour mixture remaining in bowl over potatoes. Drizzle oil over all. Bake potatoes, turning occasionally, 1 hour 15 minutes, or until crisp and golden brown. *Makes 4 servings/270 cals, 11g fat per serving*

A dusting of well-seasoned flour is the secret to these steak fries. Steak is optional.

Lighten Up!

You can get away with far less oil on these steak fries if you spray them instead of drizzling them. We suggest trying one of the oil sprayers available these days. They are pump-action, non-aerosol sprayers and you fill them with your own oil. Nice to the environment and the pocketbook at the same time. They range from really inexpensive plastic models to sleeker, more expensive brushed stainless steel versions.

Root Vegetable Roast

Prep time: 25 minutes/Cook time: 70 minutes

All the root vegetables we interviewed agreed that because they grow slowly and in the dark (underground), they prefer to be cooked slowly and in the dark (close that oven door, please). They respond to this kindness by turning delectably rich and sweet.

3 small white turnips (¾ pound total)
3 small parsnips (½ pound total)
3 medium carrots (½ pound total)
1 small rutabaga (1½ pounds)

⅓ cup olive oil
2 scallions, thinly sliced
¼ cup basil leaves
2 garlic cloves, peeled
¾ teaspoon salt

1. Preheat oven to 400°F.
2. Peel turnips and cut into ½-inch-thick wedges. Peel parsnips, halve lengthwise, and cut into 1-inch lengths. Peel carrots, halve lengthwise, and cut into 1-inch lengths. Peel rutabaga and cut into wedges 1½ inches long by ½ inch thick.
3. In 1-quart saucepan, combine oil, scallions, basil, and garlic and simmer over low heat 5 minutes. Transfer to food processor and process until smooth. Push seasoned oil through fine-meshed sieve into 9 x 13-inch baking pan.
4. Add vegetables to pan and toss to coat with oil. Cover with aluminum foil. Roast 45 minutes. Remove foil and roast 15 to 20 minutes more, or until vegetables are tender and lightly browned. Sprinkle vegetables with salt, toss, and serve hot or at room temperature. *Makes 4 servings/295 cals, 18g fat per serving*

Bean There, Done That

Prep time: 5 minutes plus soaking time/Cook time: 1 hour 45 minutes

Sure, you can use canned beans in most recipes. But taste them side-by-side with dried beans cooked from scratch, and you'll notice a big difference in both taste and texture. So here's the drill for firm, flavorful beans that will improve any bean-based recipe, such as our Huevos Rancheros (page 130). On the other hand, if you want to serve the beans as a side dish right away, use the Savory Beans variation that follows.

8 ounces (1¼ cups) dried red or white kidney beans, pinto beans, or black beans, picked over

1 bay leaf
¼ teaspoon salt, or more to taste

1. If you have the time, soak beans in bowl with cold water to cover by several inches at room temperature overnight. Drain.
2. Place beans (soaked or unsoaked) in 5-quart saucepan, add cold water to cover by 3 inches, and bring to a boil, skimming any foam that rises to surface. Add bay leaf and salt. Reduce to a simmer and partially cover. Cook, checking water level occa-

sionally and adding water if needed to cover beans, about 1½ to 2¼ hours (depending on whether beans have been soaked), or until tender. Use right away in a recipe, or freeze for later (see "Know How" at right). *Makes 3¾ cups/100 cals, .2g fat per ½ cup*

Savory Beans Follow the recipe above, but in step 2, after the beans have come to a boil, add 3 whole peeled garlic cloves and 1 whole peeled onion studded with 3 cloves. Remove the onion and bay leaf before serving, but leave in the garlic. *Makes 3¾ cups/110 cals, .2g fat per ½ cup*

Vegetable Stir-Fry Master Recipe

Prep time: 15 minutes/Cook time: 10 minutes

This is The Recipe that Launched a Thousand Stir-Fries. It gives you the classic components of a stir-fry: The Sauce, The Aromatics, and The Vegetables. Now it's up to you: Switch veggies, add different seasonings, make it your own. Just remember to start cooking dense (hard) vegetables before soft, thin, or leafy ones.

The Sauce:
1 cup chicken broth
1 tablespoon soy sauce
2 teaspoons cornstarch
1 teaspoon sesame oil
1 teaspoon sugar
½ teaspoon salt

The Aromatics:
1 tablespoon vegetable oil
1 tablespoon minced peeled fresh
   ginger

1 medium onion, halved and thickly
   sliced
3 garlic cloves, minced

The Vegetables (6 cups total):
2 tablespoons vegetable oil
3 cups small broccoli florets
2 bell peppers (red, yellow, or
   green), cut into strips
1 cup frozen corn kernels

1. Make The Sauce: In small bowl, whisk together broth, soy sauce, cornstarch, sesame oil, sugar, and salt; set aside.
2. Start with The Aromatics: In wok or 12-inch skillet, heat vegetable oil over medium-high heat. Add ginger and stir-fry 30 seconds. Add onion and garlic, and stir-fry 1 minute.
3. Add The Vegetables (starting with the hard vegetables first): Add vegetable oil and broccoli, and stir-fry 3 minutes. Add the bell peppers and stir-fry 2 minutes. Add the corn and stir-fry 1 minute. The vegetables should be crisp-tender.
4. Whisk The Sauce to recombine. Pour into wok and cook, tossing, 1 minute, or until sauce is slightly thickened and vegetables are coated. *Makes 4 servings/220 cals, 13g fat per serving*

Different Spins

Hey, who said stir-fries have to be Asian? How about an Italian stir-fry? For the sauce: Balsamic vinegar replaces the soy sauce. Omit the sesame oil. For the aromatics: Increase the garlic and ditch the ginger. For the vegetables: Try zucchini, bell peppers, and fresh tomatoes. Season with oregano, basil, red pepper flakes, and sprinkle with grated Parmesan just before serving. Needless to say, you can try Mexican, Thai, and other variations, too.

Madras Lentil Curry

Prep time: 25 minutes/Cook time: 50 minutes

If you think lentils are stodgy stuff, just check out Indian cuisine. With a vegetarian population numbering in the hundreds of millions, India is home to some of the most inventive vegetable dishes in the world, and lentils loom large in these recipes. They supply a sturdy, high-protein foundation for fragrantly spicy dishes. One knock-out example: This vegetable-and-lentil curry jazzed with pungent Madras curry powder. Leftovers? Take them to work to reheat in the microwave.

2 tablespoons olive oil

4 garlic cloves, minced

2 tablespoons minced peeled fresh ginger

1 red bell pepper, cut into ½-inch pieces

1 small cauliflower (2 pounds), cut into florets

¾ pound all-purpose potatoes, peeled and cut into ½-inch chunks

1 cup lentils, picked over and rinsed

2 tablespoons curry powder, preferably Madras

1 teaspoon ground cumin

1 teaspoon ground coriander

2½ cups canned tomatoes, chopped, with their juice

¾ teaspoon salt

¼ teaspoon freshly ground black pepper

1 cup frozen peas, thawed

½ cup plain low-fat yogurt, for serving (optional)

1. In 5-quart Dutch oven or large saucepan with lid, heat oil over low heat. Add garlic and ginger and cook, stirring frequently, 1 minute, or until garlic is tender. Stir in bell pepper and cook, stirring frequently, 5 minutes, or until tender.

2. Stir in cauliflower, potatoes, lentils, curry powder, cumin, and coriander and cook 2 minutes, or until well coated.

3. Add tomatoes, salt, black pepper, and 1¾ cups water and bring to a boil. Reduce to a simmer and cover. Cook 30 minutes, or until lentils are cooked through and vegetables are tender.

4. Stir in peas and cook 1 minute, or until heated through. Divide curry evenly among plates and top each serving with yogurt if desired. *Makes 4 servings/375 cals, 9g fat per serving*

THE **RIGHT** STUFF

In India, cooks prepare a specific spice blend, or *masala*, to complement the ingredients in a particular dish. Curry powder is a sort of westernized, all-purpose version of *masala* that usually contains these ingredients: turmeric, dried chilies, black pepper, fenugreek, coriander, cumin, mustard seeds, cinnamon, and cloves. Madras curry powder is hotter than standard types. Look for a brand that's imported from India.

KNOW HOW

Sometimes, in spite of the most modern processing, Unwanted Things find their way into bags of lentils (and beans). This is why most cookbooks have you "pick over and rinse" beans before you cook them. Usually, the Things are just innocent little shriveled beans that've snuck under the net. But sometimes you'll run across small stones. Pour the beans into a colander and poke through them to check for Things; then rinse the beans under cold water to remove any dirt or chaff.

◀ *The tantalizing flavors of Madras Lentil Curry could turn anyone into a vegetarian.*

Vegetable Couscous Royale

Prep time: 30 minutes/Cook time: 15 minutes

You might call this Moroccan specialty a distant cousin of pasta primavera. It combines the local pasta (couscous) with a variety of vegetables. Couscous absorbs flavors wonderfully well. Stir in a little butter and it tastes super-buttery; top it with braised spiced vegetables and it soaks up the sauce like mashed potatoes. Harissa, a torrid red-pepper sauce (recipe below), is the traditional accompaniment, but is entirely optional, especially if your audience is heat-phobic.

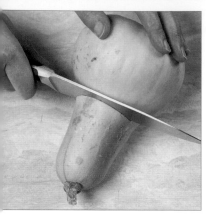

To cut up butternut squash, first cut the squash apart at "waist" level. Use a long, sturdy chef's knife.

Halve the top and bottom parts vertically. Use a rocking motion to cut through the thicker bottom section.

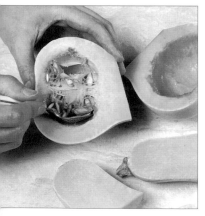

Scoop the seeds out of the squash, then peel the quarters with a vegetable peeler.

Harissa (recipe follows)
1 pound butternut squash
2 carrots
1 yellow squash
1½ cups chicken broth
2 garlic cloves, minced
1 tablespoon paprika
1½ teaspoons turmeric
1 teaspoon salt

½ teaspoon ground ginger
½ teaspoon ground coriander
1 can (19 ounces) chick-peas, rinsed and drained
¼ cup raisins
⅓ cup chopped cilantro
1 tablespoon fresh lemon juice
1½ cups couscous
2 tablespoons unsalted butter

1. Make Harissa, transfer to serving bowl, and set aside.
2. Peel and seed butternut squash (see how-to photos at left). Peel carrots, halve lengthwise, and cut into 1-inch pieces. Halve yellow squash lengthwise and cut into ½-inch lengths.
3. In 3-quart saucepan, combine broth, garlic, paprika, turmeric, ¾ teaspoon salt, ginger, coriander, and 1½ cups water and bring to a boil over medium heat. Add butternut squash and carrots, cover, and simmer 5 minutes. Add yellow squash, chick-peas, and raisins, cover, and simmer 5 minutes, or until yellow squash and butternut squash are tender. Remove pan from heat and stir in cilantro and lemon juice.
4. Meanwhile, in 2-quart saucepan, bring 2 cups water and remaining ¼ teaspoon salt to a boil. Add couscous and butter. Cover and remove pan from heat. Let stand 5 minutes, or until couscous is tender. Fluff with a fork and transfer to large bowl.
5. Spoon vegetables and cooking liquid over couscous. Serve with Harissa. *Makes 4 servings/515 cals, 9g fat per serving without harissa*

Harissa In food processor, combine 1 roasted red pepper (preferably homemade, see page 15), 2 peeled whole garlic cloves, 1 tablespoon tomato paste, 1 tablespoon water, 2 teaspoons red hot pepper sauce, and ¼ teaspoon salt and puree. *Makes about ⅓ cup/10 cals, 0g fat per 1 tablespoon.*

We'll Never *shh* Tell

Vegetables get easier every day. In addition to canned and frozen standbys, there are now bags of shredded, sliced, and diced vegetables in the fresh produce section. Tomato sauce and caponata (an Italian eggplant relish) are the only two *canned* veggies we use—we find most others to be mushy and over-salted. Frozen vegetables, however, are perfect for stylish side-dish purees. Fresh shredded carrots and cabbage go into a pair of warm salads.

Ratatouille à la Minute

In 10-inch skillet, heat 1 tablespoon olive oil over medium heat. Add 1 can (14½ ounces) stewed tomatoes, coarsely chopped, with their juice, and cook 3 minutes. Add 2 jars or cans (15 ounces total) caponata and cook, stirring, 3 minutes. Remove from heat; stir in ¼ cup chopped basil. Serve at room temperature or chilled. Makes 4 servings/270 cals, 18g fat per serving

Moroccan Carrot Salad

In large saucepan, combine ¼ cup fresh lemon juice and ½ teaspoon each of sugar, cinnamon, cumin, coriander, and salt. Add ¼ teaspoon cayenne pepper and bring to a boil. Stir in 10-ounce package shredded carrots and cook 2 minutes. Transfer mixture to large bowl, add ¼ cup raisins, 2 tablespoons olive oil, and 2 tablespoons chopped cilantro, and toss to combine. Cover and refrigerate until serving. Makes 4 servings/125 cals, 7g fat per serving

Hot Sautéed Slaw

In large bowl, whisk 2 tablespoons olive oil, 1 tablespoon each Dijon mustard and lemon juice, and ½ teaspoon salt. In 12-inch skillet, heat 1 tablespoon olive oil. Add 1 minced medium onion and 2 minced garlic cloves and sauté 7 minutes, or until tender. Add 1 package (16 ounces) coleslaw mix and sauté, stirring, 5 minutes, or until wilted. Add to dressing and toss well to combine. Serve hot. Makes 4 servings/145 cals, 11g fat per serving

Vegetable Purees PLUS

For each of these super-simple purees, first cook the frozen vegetable according to the package directions. Drain, reserving some of the cooking liquid, and puree, while still hot, in a food processor, as directed below.

Minty Pea Puree Puree 1 package (10 ounces) cooked frozen peas with ¼ cup reserved cooking liquid, ⅓ cup fresh mint, 2 tablespoons unsalted butter, and ¾ teaspoon salt. Makes 4 servings/110 cals, 6g fat per serving

Sesame Green Bean Puree Puree 1 package (10 ounces) cooked frozen green beans with 2 tablespoons reserved cooking liquid, 2 tablespoons sesame oil, and ½ teaspoon salt. Makes 4 servings/85 cals, 7g fat per serving

Brown-Butter Cauliflower Puree In small skillet, cook 3 tablespoons unsalted butter until it foams and turns a rich brown. Puree 1 package cooked (10 ounces) frozen cauliflower with 2 tablespoons reserved cooking liquid, the browned butter, ½ teaspoon salt, and ¼ teaspoon dried sage. Makes 4 servings/95 cals, 9g fat per serving

Spinach & Garlic Puree Cook 1 package (10 ounces) frozen spinach with 2 garlic cloves. Puree with 3 ounces softened cream cheese, ¼ teaspoon salt, and ⅛ teaspoon each cayenne pepper and ground nutmeg. Makes 4 servings/95 cals, 8g fat per serving

Herbed Lima Bean Puree Cook 1 package (10 ounces) frozen lima beans with ¼ teaspoon each dried thyme and rosemary. Puree with 2 tablespoons reserved cooking liquid, 2 tablespoons unsalted butter, and ½ teaspoon salt. Makes 4 servings/125 cals, 6g fat per serving

Sicilian Bitter Greens Salad

Prep time: 20 minutes/Cook time: 5 minutes

THE **RIGHT** STUFF

Arugula, like fennel, broccoli rabe, and some others, is a vegetable that was everyday fare in Italian communities for years before restaurant chefs discovered it. Arugula's pungent flavor (some call it bitter) goes beautifully with rich flavors like olives and pine nuts; it's great with tomatoes and sharp cheeses, too.

Next time you're serving pasta for dinner, start with this authentic Italian salad. (Or serve the salad as the Italians do—*after* the main dish.) The greens are tossed with orange segments and brine-cured olives. Gaeta olives, which are Italian, would certainly be appropriate for this dish, but Kalamata olives (which are Greek), are much more readily available in supermarkets.

2 tablespoons pine nuts or slivered almonds

4 navel oranges

3 tablespoons extra-virgin olive oil

2 tablespoons balsamic vinegar

1 teaspoon Dijon mustard

½ teaspoon salt

¼ teaspoon crushed red pepper flakes

2 bunches arugula (6 ounces each), well washed

1 bunch watercress (5 ounces)

⅓ cup brine-cured olives, such as Gaeta or Kalamata, pitted and thinly sliced

1. In small skillet, toast nuts over low heat, tossing frequently, 3 minutes, or until golden brown; set aside.
2. With paring knife, slice off ends of oranges. Standing each orange upright, cut off peel and pith beneath in lengthwise strips; discard. Working over a strainer set in a bowl to catch juice, cut between membranes and flesh to separate segments. Squeeze the membranes to extract as much juice as possible. (See technique photos, page 8.)
3. Measure out ¼ cup of the fresh orange juice (reserve remainder for another use) and place in large salad bowl. Whisk oil, vinegar, mustard, salt, and pepper flakes into bowl until dressing is combined.
4. Add arugula, watercress, olives, and orange segments to dressing and toss to coat well. Garnish salad with pine nuts. *Makes 4 servings/240 cals, 17g fat per serving*

Different Spins

The basic vinaigrette is open to variation: For red wine vinegar, substitute balsamic, rice, or Champagne vinegar—or lemon, lime, or grapefruit juice. Replace 1 or 2 tablespoons of the olive oil with sesame, hazelnut, or walnut oil. And feel free to add minced garlic or shallots as well as fresh or dried herbs. Taste as you go.

Neo-Classic Vinaigrette

Prep time: 5 minutes

A classic French vinaigrette proportion is five parts oil to one part vinegar (!!). We've cut that to a two-to-one ratio, which seems more suitable for modern palates. The mustard makes up for the missing oil by thickening the dressing. This recipe makes enough for several salads; refrigerate the unused vinaigrette in a jar or bottle.

⅔ cup red wine vinegar

1 tablespoon Dijon mustard

½ teaspoon salt

1⅓ cups extra-virgin olive oil

Pour vinegar into medium bowl. Whisk in mustard and salt. Slowly whisk in oil, little by little, until dressing is well combined and thickened. *Makes 2 cups/160 cals, 19g fat per 2 tablespoons*

Thai Salad Dressing

Prep time: 15 minutes

The miracle of a Thai-style salad dressing is that it has no oil at all and doesn't even come close to tasting like a nonfat dressing. We think it's the balance of the sour, salty, and sweet that makes it work. Use it on a tossed green salad, or try it on thinly sliced seedless cucumbers, chilled cooked broccoli, or steamed shredded cabbage.

¾ cup fresh lime juice

¼ cup honey

3 tablespoons soy sauce

1½ teaspoons anchovy paste

¼ teaspoon cayenne pepper

½ cup chopped cilantro, basil, or mint

In medium bowl, whisk lime juice, honey, soy sauce, anchovy paste, and cayenne. Stir in cilantro. *Makes about 1 cup/45 cals, .2g fat per 2 tablespoons*

Salade Hâchée

Prep time: 20 minutes

"Chopped salad" certainly sounds better in French, doesn't it? You'll notice that there's not a lot of dressing here; that's because the chopped vegetables take up the dressing more readily than do great big lettuce leaves. And this salad is easier to eat than one of those pretty-on-the-plate, whole-leaf salads where you're forced to try to find an elegant way to stuff a large piece of lettuce into your mouth (without dribbling the dressing down your chin).

¼ cup olive oil

3 tablespoons fresh lemon juice

¼ teaspoon salt

¼ teaspoon freshly ground black pepper

6 cups chopped iceberg lettuce (1 medium head)

2 cups shredded carrots (4 large)

2 scallions, chopped

6 ounces crumbled feta cheese

½ cup finely slivered basil or mint leaves, or ⅓ cup snipped dill

In large bowl, whisk together oil, lemon juice, salt, and pepper until well combined. Add lettuce, carrots, scallions, feta, and basil and gently toss until well coated with dressing. *Makes 4 servings/280 cals, 23g fat per serving*

Different Spins

Our Salade Hâchée is a heartbeat away from being a Cobb salad, and can be nudged in that (main-dish) direction by topping it with shredded chicken, crumbled bacon, diced avocado, chopped hard-cooked eggs, and/or tomatoes—the usual Cobb salad suspects.

Caesar Salad with Frico

Different Spins

In addition to the obvious and ever-popular Chicken Caesar, try topping Caesar salad with chunks of Grilled Swordfish (page 80), or slices of Grilled Flank Steak (page 40). Simply broiled shrimp is good, too.

Prep time: 15 minutes/Cook time: 15 minutes

A New York City restaurateur introduced *frico* (and named his restaurant after them) not long ago. These crisp disks of grated cheese make an ideal salad garnish. If you have trouble getting the fragile disks off the pan in one piece, don't worry: Break them into shards. They'll taste just as good.

Frico (recipe follows)

8 slices Italian bread, ¾ inch thick (4 ounces)

2 garlic cloves, peeled and halved

2 teaspoons plus 2 tablespoons olive oil

3 tablespoons mayonnaise

3 tablespoons fresh lemon juice

1½ teaspoons anchovy paste

¼ teaspoon salt

¼ teaspoon freshly ground black pepper

1 medium head romaine lettuce, torn into bite-size pieces (12 cups)

3 tablespoons grated Parmesan cheese

1. Make Frico and set aside at room temperature.

2. Preheat oven to 350°F.

Dressed to impress: A Caesar salad with toasty garlic croutons and the lacy cheese crisps called frico.

3. Rub both sides of bread with garlic; discard garlic. Brush one side only of slices with the 2 teaspoons oil. Cut bread into ½-inch pieces. Transfer to baking sheet, spreading evenly, and bake, tossing occasionally, 5 to 7 minutes, or until golden. Remove and set aside.

4. In large bowl, whisk mayonnaise, lemon juice, anchovy paste, remaining 2 tablespoons oil, salt, and pepper. Add lettuce, croutons, and Parmesan; toss to combine.

5. Divide salad evenly among serving plates and top each serving with 2 *frico*. *Makes 4 servings/285 cals, 20g fat per serving without frico*

Frico Preheat oven to 400°F. Line large baking sheet with aluminum foil and brush foil with oil. With small strainer, sprinkle 8 rounds of grated Parmesan cheese onto foil (see photo at right), using 1 tablespoon cheese per round. Bake 5 minutes, or until cheese is melted, crisp, and lacy. While rounds are still warm, with thin-bladed spatula, carefully transfer them, one at a time, to a sheet of aluminum foil to cool to room temperature. *Makes 8 frico/25 cals, 2g fat per frico*

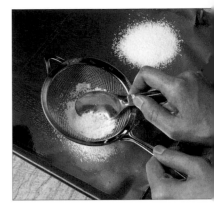

Sift the Parmesan through a strainer to break up any lumps; form rounds about 3 inches in diameter on the pan. After baking, remove the *frico* from the foil while they're still warm, or they may stick.

Sourdough Panzanella

Prep time: 25 minutes/Cook time: 10 minutes
Marinating time: 1 to 8 hours

Panzanella is a rustic Italian salad with *pane*—bread—as the main ingredient. It's one of the many recipes originally devised to use up stale bread (bread pudding and French toast are distant relatives). The cubes of bread are tossed with tomatoes, mozzarella, basil, olives, and dressing, and left to marinate until the bread soaks up all of the delicious flavorings. The traditional bread used in this salad is Tuscan, but we like the added tang of sourdough. You can use any bread you want as long as it's a sturdy bread that won't turn to mush in the dressing.

8 ounces sourdough bread, cut into ½-inch cubes (4 cups)	1 pound plum tomatoes, cut into ½-inch chunks (2½ cups)
¼ cup extra-virgin olive oil	1 large cucumber, peeled, halved, seeded, and sliced ½ inch thick
2 tablespoons balsamic vinegar	8 ounces part-skim mozzarella, cut into ½-inch chunks
½ teaspoon light brown sugar	
½ teaspoon salt	⅓ cup brine-cured olives, such as Kalamata, pitted and slivered
¼ teaspoon freshly ground black pepper	⅓ cup shredded basil leaves

1. Preheat oven to 400°F.

2. Toast bread cubes in even layer on baking sheet, tossing once or twice, 7 minutes, or until lightly browned.

3. In large bowl, whisk together oil, vinegar, sugar, salt, and pepper. Add tomatoes, cucumber, mozzarella, olives, and basil and toss well. Cover and let stand at room temperature for 1 hour or up to 8 hours in the refrigerator before serving. *Makes 4 servings/490 cals, 28g fat per serving*

THE **RIGHT** STUFF

Fresh mozzarella hasn't quite made the leap into supermarket land, where shrink-wrapped (and rubbery) mozzarella still rules. But some companies now offer packages of *bocconcini*—little balls of fresh factory-made mozzarella, packed in whey so they stay moist. So, if you don't have a cheese store, Italian grocery, or other source of fresh mozzarella, use bocconcini in the panzanella recipe.

Endive with Pears & Blue Cheese

Prep time: 20 minutes

Luscious Bartlett pears—be sure they're ripe—are unbelievably good in combination with blue cheese. If you can't get sherry vinegar, white or red wine vinegar will do.

⅓ cup sherry vinegar

3 tablespoons extra-virgin olive oil

2 tablespoons sugar

¼ teaspoon salt

¼ teaspoon freshly ground black pepper

4 ripe Bartlett pears

3 endives, sliced crosswise into ½-inch pieces

½ pound Roquefort cheese, crumbled

¼ cup pecans, toasted and finely chopped

1. In medium bowl, whisk together vinegar, oil, sugar, salt, and pepper.

2. Halve and core the pears and cut each into 12 wedges; set aside.

3. Divide endives among salad plates and drizzle one-fourth of vinaigrette over endive. Arrange pear wedges on endive and drizzle with remaining vinaigrette. Sprinkle Roquefort and pecans evenly over salads and serve. *Makes 4 servings/475 cals, 33g fat per serving*

Green Bean Salad with Hazelnuts

Prep time: 20 minutes/Cook time: 20 minutes/Chilling time: 2 hours

Forget those frozen "frenched" green beans with slivered almonds—this is the real thing, with irresistible sesame-hazelnut flavor. It's a great salad for Christmas dinner: The green beans and bits of red bell pepper fit the holiday color scheme.

½ cup hazelnuts

3 tablespoons rice vinegar or white wine vinegar

2 tablespoons olive oil

1 tablespoon sesame oil

¾ teaspoon salt

1¼ pounds green beans, cut into 1-inch lengths

½ cup sliced water chestnuts, rinsed and cut into thin strips

3 scallions, cut into 2-inch strips

1 red bell pepper, cut into ¼ x 2-inch strips

1. Preheat oven to 400°F.

2. Spread hazelnuts evenly in small baking pan and toast 7 minutes, or until skins begin to crack. Place nuts in kitchen towel and rub until skins loosen and come off (you can never get all the skin off; don't worry). When cool enough to handle, coarsely chop; set aside.

3. In large bowl, whisk together vinegar, olive oil, sesame oil, and salt.

4. In steamer basket set over pan of simmering water, steam beans, covered, 7 to 10 minutes, or until crisp-tender. Add beans to vinaigrette and toss to coat. Add water chestnuts, scallions, and bell pepper and toss to combine.

5. Serve warm or at room temperature. Garnish salad with hazelnuts before serving. *Makes 4 servings/250 cals, 19g fat per serving*

One Potato, Two Potato

Prep time: 25 minutes/Cook time: 20 minutes

Hold the mayo—this is potato salad *à la française*, dressed while warm with a mustard vinaigrette. We've also devised a cool trick to make the dressing thick and creamy: A baking potato is added to the pot when the boiling potatoes are cooked. The baking potato sort of "melts" when it's boiled, and as the salad is tossed the potato particles magically merge with the vinaigrette. Be sure to serve this salad warm or at room temperature; if you *have* to refrigerate it, take it out at least 30 minutes ahead of time and let it stand before serving.

1¼ pounds red potatoes	¼ cup olive oil
1 large baking potato (8 ounces)	1 tablespoon Dijon mustard
1 pound sweet potatoes	1 teaspoon salt
½ cup dry white wine	1 red bell pepper, diced
½ cup minced scallions	1 rib celery, cut into ¼-inch dice
⅓ cup white wine vinegar	

1. Cut red potatoes into ½-inch chunks. Peel baking potato and cut it into ½-inch chunks. Peel sweet potatoes and cut them into ½-inch chunks.

2. In 3-quart saucepan of boiling salted water, combine red potatoes and baking potato and cook about 15 minutes, or until red potatoes are tender (the baking potato will be *very* tender). Meanwhile, in 2-quart saucepan of simmering salted water, cook sweet potatoes about 10 minutes, or until tender.

3. While potatoes cook, in large bowl, combine wine and scallions. Drain white and sweet potatoes and, while they are still hot, add to wine mixture. Toss gently to coat.

4. In small bowl, whisk together vinegar, oil, mustard, and salt until combined. Pour dressing over potatoes, add red pepper and celery, and toss. Serve at once or let cool to room temperature and serve. Do not chill. *Makes 8 servings/195 cals, 7g fat per serving*

In a pinch

So you went to the store and bought everything you needed for the Green Bean Salad . . . except you forgot the water chestnuts. If you have a crisp apple or pear on hand, you're all set. Core and peel the fruit and cut into matchsticks. Toss with a little lemon juice to keep the fruit from browning, and add it to the salad.

Different Spins

This potato salad can go with the flow, according to what tempting seasonal ingredients you choose to add. You can fold in some chopped fresh dill, tarragon, or parsley, for instance. Or chunks of beefsteak tomato, diced fresh fennel, or steamed cubes of zucchini or yellow summer squash.

This unusual pasta salad features rice-shaped orzo pasta, tangy Italian cheese, and a plentiful portion of broiled shrimp.

THE **RIGHT** STUFF

Most of us know ricotta as the fresh, spoonable white cheese layered into lasagna. Ricotta salata is its grown-up relative. It's a salty cheese that when young can be sliced or crumbled, but when aged becomes a grating cheese, like Parmesan. You want the younger cheese for this recipe.

Orzo Salad with
Ricotta Salata & Shrimp

Prep time: 25 minutes/Cook time: 5 minutes
Marinating time: 2 hours or overnight

Pasta salad has come a long way from the mayo-drenched macaroni salad of yesteryear. Try this lightly dressed toss of orzo, corn kernels, oregano-scented shrimp, and sharp Italian cheese.

½ pound orzo or other very small pasta shape

1 cup frozen corn

4 tablespoons extra-virgin olive oil

2 teaspoons grated lemon zest

3 tablespoons fresh lemon juice

1 teaspoon salt

1 pound medium shrimp, shelled and deveined

¼ teaspoon dried oregano

1 red bell pepper, cut into ½-inch pieces

½ pound ricotta salata or feta cheese, crumbled

¼ cup snipped dill

1. In large pot of boiling salted water, cook orzo according to package directions. Add corn during final 10 seconds of cooking. Drain.

2. Meanwhile, in large bowl, whisk together 3 tablespoons oil, lemon zest, lemon juice, and salt. Add orzo and corn and toss to combine.

3. Preheat broiler.

4. In large bowl, toss together shrimp, oregano, and remaining 1 tablespoon oil. Arrange shrimp in single layer on broiler rack and broil 6 inches from heat 1 to 1½ minutes per side, or until just cooked through.

5. Add shrimp, bell pepper, cheese, and dill to orzo mixture and toss. Serve warm, at room temperature or chilled.   *Makes 4 servings/635 cals, 29g fat per serving*

Autumn Rice Salad with Smoked Turkey

Prep time: 20 minutes/Cook time: 50 minutes

Aaaaah, autumn. Golden time of newly harvested pears and wild rice and some major holiday meals with roast turkey. Ease yourself into the season with this hearty salad, which does not call for roasting a big bird—smoked turkey from the deli does the trick. And you can make the whole salad ahead of time.

1 cup chicken broth	3 tablespoons red wine vinegar
½ teaspoon dried tarragon	1 tablespoon Dijon mustard
½ teaspoon salt	4 ounces dried pears, thinly sliced, or 1 cup golden raisins
¼ teaspoon freshly ground black pepper	1 small red bell pepper, diced
3 carrots, halved lengthwise and sliced ¼ inch thick	6 ounces smoked turkey, cut into ¼-inch chunks
½ cup wild rice, rinsed	2 tablespoons coarsely chopped toasted pecans
1 cup brown rice	
3 tablespoons extra-virgin olive oil	

1. In 3-quart saucepan, bring broth, tarragon, ¼ teaspoon salt, pepper, and 2 cups water to a boil over medium heat. Add carrots and cook 2 minutes. Add wild rice, reduce to a simmer, and cover. Cook 7 minutes.

2. Add brown rice and cover. Simmer 35 to 45 minutes, or until brown and wild rices are tender.

3. Meanwhile, in large bowl, whisk together oil, vinegar, mustard, and remaining ¼ teaspoon salt. Add cooked rices and pears and toss well. Cool to room temperature.

4. Add bell pepper and turkey and toss. Garnish with pecans.   *Makes 4 servings/515 cals, 16g fat per serving*

Different Spins

Any small grain or pasta would be good in place of the orzo for this salad. Toss it with cooked couscous, barley, white rice, brown rice—or use bulghur (soaked, not cooked).

THE **RIGHT** STUFF

Although we call it rice, this precious foodstuff is really the seed of a marsh grass native to northern Minnesota and environs. To prepare wild rice for cooking, place it in a large strainer and rinse under cold running water to remove any dirt or chaff.

Make the Grilled Summer Vegetable Salad the centerpiece of an outdoor buffet. Throw a couple of flank steaks on the barbie (try more than one marinade, see pages 40 and 41), and maybe offer one more salad, like One Potato, Two Potato (page 107). Add a big basket of thickly sliced French bread, pitchers of iced tea and coffee, and, for dessert, Plum-Berry Cobbler (page 148).

Don't stop with the vegetables listed above. Get creative. Lots of vegetables are good grilled (though skinny ones like asparagus will certainly require a grill topper). For vegetable grilling times, see Vegetable Cooking Chart (page 171).

Grilled Summer Vegetable Salad

Prep time: 20 minutes/Soaking time: 30 minutes/Cook time: 30 minutes

You can make a meal of this salad, or serve it alongside something meaty (like beef or chicken) cooked over the same fire. If you often grill small-scale or delicate foods, such as vegetables, you might want to pick up a grill topper at the housewares store. It's a sturdy, flat metal sheet perforated with holes to let the smoke through. With one of these, it's a lot easier to cook (and especially to turn) cut-up vegetables and fragile items like shrimp.

3 ears corn, unhusked

4 tablespoons olive oil

1 teaspoon chili powder

4 portobello mushrooms (6 ounces each), stems removed

2 yellow squash, cut lengthwise into ¼-inch-thick slices

1 large red onion (12 ounces), cut crosswise into 4 slices

2 poblano or green bell peppers, quartered lengthwise

1 medium tomato, finely chopped

2 tablespoons balsamic vinegar

¾ teaspoon salt

1. Peel back husks on corn and remove corn silk. Replace husks to cover ears and put ears in large bowl with water to cover; soak 30 minutes.

2. Meanwhile, preheat grill to medium. In small bowl, stir together 2 tablespoons oil and chili powder. Brush mushrooms, squash, and onion with seasoned oil.

3. Drain corn, transfer to grill, and grill about 15 minutes, turning after 7 minutes, or until husks start to char. Remove and let cool.

4. Add remaining vegetables to grill in batches. Arrange peppers, skin side down; add mushrooms, squash, and onion slices and grill, turning, 7 minutes, or until tender. As the vegetables are done, transfer them to a platter to cool. Peel peppers if desired.

5. In large bowl, whisk together tomato, vinegar, salt, and remaining 2 tablespoons oil. Scrape corn kernels from ears into bowl. Cut peppers and mushrooms into ¼-inch-thick slices; add to bowl. Cut squash into 1-inch lengths, halve onion slices, and add to bowl. Toss well to combine and serve. Or cover with plastic wrap, refrigerate, and serve chilled.   *Makes 4 servings/265 cals, 15g fat per serving*

Broiled Vegetable Salad You can make this salad under the broiler, too. Follow recipe through step 2. Preheat broiler. Drain corn, arrange on broiler rack 8 inches from heat, and broil 15 minutes, turning midway. Add peppers, mushrooms, squash, and onion in batches and broil, turning as needed, about 7 minutes per batch. As the vegetables are done, transfer them to a platter to cool. Peel peppers if desired and continued with step 5 above.

pasta
& grains

Spaghetti Caprese

Prep time: 15 minutes/Cook time: 20 minutes

It's a lovely image, the devoted cook tirelessly stirring a huge kettle of marinara or bolognese—but really, who in their right mind wants to spend a whole day making spaghetti sauce? Especially when bottled pasta sauces have made such an effort unnecessary. But then there are the sauces you cannot buy at the store, like this classic combination of fresh tomatoes, mozzarella, and basil.

12 ounces spaghetti

2 pounds tomatoes

3 garlic cloves, peeled

¼ cup extra-virgin olive oil

1 teaspoon salt

½ pound part-skim mozzarella, cut into ¾-inch chunks

½ cup basil leaves, slivered

1. Bring large pot of salted water to a boil. Add spaghetti and cook according to package directions until al dente.

2. Meanwhile, in saucepan of boiling water, blanch tomatoes 10 seconds to loosen skins. With slotted spoon, remove and rinse under cold water to stop cooking and cool. Add garlic to boiling water and cook 2 minutes; drain.

An uncooked sauce is ideal on a hot day: The warm pasta melds the flavors of the tomatoes, garlic, basil, mozzarella, and olive oil.

3. Peel tomatoes and coarsely chop. Mince garlic. In large bowl, combine tomatoes and garlic, add oil and salt, and toss to combine. Add mozzarella and basil and toss well.

4. Drain pasta, reserving ¼ cup cooking liquid. Add hot pasta and reserved pasta cooking liquid to bowl and toss well. *Makes 4 servings/630 cals, 25g fat per serving*

Linguine with White Clam Sauce

Prep time: 20 minutes/Cook time: 20 minutes

Some people firmly believe that Italians *never* use cheese on or in any pasta dish that contains seafood. But that's not an unbreakable rule, and when the cheese works as perfectly as the Parmesan in this recipe—well, rules were made to be broken. To do it justice, this white clam sauce really has to be made with fresh clams. And if you can get them (and afford them), Manila clams, a West Coast variety, are even sweeter and more tender than littlenecks.

12 ounces linguine

1 tablespoon olive oil

¼ cup minced onion or shallots

4 garlic cloves, minced

1 cup dry white wine

3 dozen littleneck clams, well scrubbed

½ teaspoon salt

2 tablespoons unsalted butter, in pieces

⅓ cup chopped parsley

⅓ cup grated Parmesan cheese

1. Bring large pot of salted water to a boil. Add linguine and cook according to package directions until al dente.

2. Meanwhile, in 5-quart Dutch oven or large flameproof casserole, heat oil over low heat. Add onion and garlic and cook, stirring frequently, 4 minutes, or until tender. Add wine, bring to a boil, and boil 2 minutes.

3. Add clams, cover, and cook 4 to 5 minutes. Check occasionally and transfer clams to a bowl as they open. When clams are cool enough to handle, remove from shells and coarsely chop. Discard shells and any unopened clams in pan.

4. Return wine mixture to a boil, stir in salt, and remove pan from heat. Add chopped clams, butter, and parsley, stirring to combine.

5. Drain linguine. Add to clam sauce and toss well. Add Parmesan and toss well again. *Makes 4 servings/570 cals, 14g fat per serving*

KNOW HOW

"Knock knock."

"Who's there?"

"Live clams."

Sorry, there's no punchline—but knocking on a clam shell is how you tell if clams are really alive before you cook them (and they *do* have to be alive). Clams that are tightly closed are definitely alive. But if any have open shells, pick them up and tap them on the counter. If the little guy inside is alive, the shell will snap shut. If the shell stays open, toss it. On the other hand, after cooking, the reverse is true: The *open* clams are good, and any that stay shut should be tossed out.

Wild Mushroom Lasagna

Prep time: 40 minutes/Cook time: 1½ hours

Trust us on this one: Lasagna does not need tomato sauce, mozzarella, or even meat to be delicious. Consider this "white lasagna" made with three kinds of mushrooms, a buttery *balsamella* (that's a rich white sauce), and meltingly rich Fontina cheese. Layer these with lasagna noodles and you get a meal to make strong men weep.

½ cup dried shiitake or porcini mushrooms (½ ounce)

12 lasagna noodles (about 10 ounces)

1 tablespoon olive oil

1 small onion, minced

½ pound fresh shiitake mushrooms, stems discarded, caps thinly sliced

1 pound button mushrooms, thinly sliced

1 teaspoon salt

½ teaspoon freshly ground black pepper

3 tablespoons unsalted butter

3 tablespoons flour

2½ cups milk

⅛ teaspoon ground nutmeg

½ pound Italian Fontina cheese, shredded

⅓ cup grated Parmesan cheese

1. In medium bowl, combine dried mushrooms and 1 cup boiling water. Let stand 20 minutes, or until mushrooms are softened. With fingers, scoop out mushrooms. Strain soaking liquid into bowl through fine-meshed sieve or sieve lined with paper towel; set aside. Rinse mushrooms and coarsely chop.

2. Meanwhile, in large pot of boiling salted water, cook lasagna noodles according to package directions; drain. Transfer noodles to bowl of cool water to prevent them from sticking together.

3. In 12-inch nonstick skillet, heat oil over low heat. Add onion and cook, stirring frequently, 7 minutes, or until tender. Add fresh and chopped dried shiitakes and cook, stirring frequently, 5 minutes, or until they begin to soften. Add button mushrooms and season with ½ teaspoon salt and pepper. Measure out ½ cup of mushroom soaking liquid and set aside; add any remaining liquid to skillet and cook, stirring frequently, 7 minutes, or until mushrooms are tender.

4. In 3-quart saucepan, melt butter over low heat. Whisk in flour until well combined. Cook, whisking frequently, 3 minutes, or until flour is cooked. Whisk in reserved ½ cup mushroom soaking liquid and cook, whisking frequently, 4 minutes, or until slightly thickened. Gradually whisk in milk. Cook, whisking frequently, 5 minutes, or until sauce is thick enough to coat back of spoon. Stir in nutmeg and remaining ½ teaspoon salt.

5. Preheat oven to 375°F.

6. In 9 x 13-inch glass baking dish, arrange 3 noodles in single layer. Top with one-third of mushroom filling, one-fourth of sauce, and one-third of Fontina. Make 2

In a pinch

If you want to make this lasagna without scurrying around trying to find wild mushrooms and Italian cheese, do this: Use all button mushrooms (1¼ pounds total), supermarket dried mushrooms (usually found near the canned mushrooms), and Muenster cheese (instead of the Fontina).

KNOW HOW

When you soak dried mushrooms, sometimes a little bit of grit collects in the bottom of the bowl. You don't want this stuff to end up in your meal, so gently lift the mushrooms out of the liquid (rather than dumping the whole thing into a strainer) and then strain the soaking liquid separately.

THE **RIGHT** STUFF

The original (and still the best and most expensive) Fontina is a cheese called Fontina Val d'Aosta, made in a part of Italy that borders on Switzerland. But other Italian Fontinas are nearly as good, and versions of this cheese are made in Denmark and Sweden, too. Any of these is fine for cooking.

more layers in same manner. Top with a final layer of noodles and the remaining sauce. Sprinkle Parmesan over top and cover with aluminum foil.

7. Bake lasagna 15 minutes. Remove foil and bake 15 minutes more, or until top is golden brown and bubbly. Let lasagna stand 5 to 10 minutes before serving. *Makes 8 servings/400 cals, 19g fat per serving*

Pasta Picadillo

Prep time:15 minutes/Cook time: 20 minutes

Picadillo (not to be confused with peccadillo, which is a small sin) is a ground meat mixture that roughly translates from the Spanish as hash. Found in a number of Spanish-speaking countries, picadillo varies according to local custom; but in all cases the meat is chopped or minced (as in a hash). And in most picadillos, the seasonings lean toward the sweet: For example, raisins are a common ingredient, as are sweet spices, such as cinnamon. Sometimes picadillo is served as a stew, over rice; sometimes it is used as a stuffing mixture. To our knowledge, using it as a pasta sauce is entirely our invention.

1 pound ground sirloin	1 teaspoon salt
1 onion, chopped	½ teaspoon freshly ground black pepper
1 garlic clove, minced	
1 can (14 ounces) tomatoes, chopped, with their juice	¼ teaspoon ground cinnamon
1 Golden Delicious apple, peeled and chopped	1 can (8 ounces) tomato sauce
	8 ounces orzo or elbow macaroni
⅓ cup raisins	⅓ cup slivered almonds, toasted (optional)
¼ cup pimiento-stuffed green olives, chopped	

1. Crumble beef into 12-inch nonstick skillet and cook over medium-high heat, breaking meat up with a spoon, 5 minutes, or until no longer pink. Add onion and garlic and cook, stirring, 4 to 5 minutes, or until onion is tender. Stir in tomatoes, apple, raisins, olives, salt, pepper, cinnamon, and tomato sauce and bring to a boil. Cover, reduce heat to low, and simmer, stirring occasionally, 20 minutes.

2. Meanwhile, bring large pot of salted water to a boil. Add pasta and cook according to package directions until al dente. Drain and keep warm, loosely covered.

3. Divide pasta among pasta bowls and top with picadillo. Garnish with almonds. *Makes 4 servings/575 cals, 20g fat per serving*

KNOW HOW

Though lasagna fails in the throw-the-meal-together-at-the-last-minute category, it more than compensates in the make-ahead category. You have two options for making the lasagna ahead of time, depending on your schedule. You can fully assemble the lasagna, cover it tightly with foil, freeze, and then bake—unthawed and covered—in a 350°F oven until hot throughout (start checking after 45 minutes). Or, you can bake the lasagna, cover, refrigerate, and then reheat in a 350°F oven (start checking after 30 minutes).

Lighten Up!

If you make the Pasta Picadillo with lean ground turkey breast instead of ground sirloin, you can cut the fat grams more or less in half—though you *will* have to add back a little fat in the form of 1 or 2 teaspoons of oil in the skillet to keep the turkey from sticking.

Creamy Spinach-Pepper Pasta

Prep time: 25 minutes/Cook time: 15 minutes

THE RIGHT STUFF

Fresh pasta used to be touted as far superior to dried pasta, but the truth is that it's not better, just different. The main thing you need to know is that fresh pasta cooks much faster than dried—fresh fettuccine in 3 to 5 minutes, as opposed to 9 minutes or longer for dried fettuccine. Whatever kind of pasta you're cooking, check it frequently for doneness, letting your teeth be your guide: *Al dente* means that the pasta offers some resistance when you bite a piece. Drain the pasta immediately when your tooth-o-meter reads "done."

Different Spins

The tang of goat cheese is not to everyone's liking. So you can make this instead with a half pound of feta cheese. Or try it with cream cheese, but use only 6 ounces and throw in 6 or 7 tablespoons of grated Parmesan cheese for flavor (cream cheese by itself is too mild).

Did we just hear someone muttering "where's the Alfredo"? Well, not that we're counting fat grams or anything, but a serving of Alfredo has 128 of them (the equivalent of eating 1½ sticks of butter). So we came up with a pasta sauce to satisfy your "Alfredo tooth." We used goat cheese because it melts into a rich and silky sauce, but has way less fat. (Though make no mistake, this is *not* a diet dish.)

1 tablespoon olive oil
6 scallions, thinly sliced
2 garlic cloves, minced
1 large red bell pepper, diced
1 small red or green jalapeño pepper, seeded and minced
½ cup chopped frozen spinach, thawed and squeezed dry
1½ cups chicken broth

¼ teaspoon salt
¼ teaspoon freshly ground black pepper
⅛ teaspoon ground nutmeg
1 package (9 ounces) fresh spinach fettuccine
½ pound soft goat cheese, crumbled

1. In 10-inch skillet, heat oil over low heat. Add scallions and garlic and cook, stirring occasionally, 2 minutes, or until scallions are tender. Add bell pepper and jalapeño pepper, raise heat to medium, and cook, stirring frequently, 4 minutes, or until bell pepper is crisp-tender. Add spinach and cook, stirring, 4 minutes, or until heated through.

2. Add broth, salt, black pepper, and nutmeg and bring to a boil. Boil 4 to 5 minutes, or until reduced by one-third. Pour pepper sauce into large bowl.

3. Meanwhile, bring large pot of salted water to a boil. Add fettuccine and cook according to package directions until al dente.

4. Drain pasta and transfer to bowl with pepper sauce. Add goat cheese and toss until cheese has melted and sauce is creamy. *Makes 4 servings/400 cals, 17g fat per serving*

Melted goat cheese makes a rich "cream" sauce for spinach pasta and vegetables. ▶

Different Spins

The pesto recipe at right makes only a modest amount, but you can easily double, triple, quadruple (stop us) the recipe, especially when basil is abundant and cheap. Just store your batch of pesto in the freezer in whatever amounts you think you'll need. Then you can pull a "pesto change-o" on some of your favorite foods. Spread pesto on chicken or fish before grilling; toss hot cooked vegetables with a spoonful of the sauce; or spread pesto on sandwich bread in place of mayo.

In a pinch

You may not have tequila on hand if you aren't in the habit of mixing up margaritas at home. You can revert to vodka, of course, or make *penne al vino* with a few ounces of dry white wine.

Fettuccine with Pesto

Prep time: 20 minutes/Cook time: 20 minutes

Who came up with this wacky idea of serving pasta with potatoes? Actually, the same folks who invented pesto—and you know how incredible *that* is! This is the traditional Ligurian way to serve *pasta al pesto.*

Pesto (recipe follows)

12 ounces dried fettuccine or linguine

¾ pound all-purpose potatoes, peeled and cut into chunks

3 tablespoons heavy or whipping cream

1. Make Pesto; set aside at room temperature.
2. Bring large pot of salted water to a boil. Add pasta and cook according to package directions until al dente.
3. Meanwhile, in medium saucepan of boiling salted water, cook potatoes 7 minutes, or until tender. Drain, reserving ¾ cup cooking liquid. Transfer potatoes to large bowl.
4. Drain pasta. Transfer to bowl with potatoes. Add pesto, reserved potato cooking liquid, and cream and toss well to combine thoroughly. *Makes 4 servings/405 cals, 6g fat per serving*

Pesto In small saucepan of boiling water, cook 3 peeled garlic cloves 2 minutes; drain. Transfer garlic to food processor and add 2 cups fresh basil leaves, ¼ cup extra-virgin olive oil, 2 tablespoons pine nuts, and 1¼ teaspoons salt. Process until smooth. Remove sauce to bowl and stir in ½ cup grated Parmesan cheese. *Makes ¾ cup/205 cals, 20g fat per 3 tablespoons*

Penne alla Tequila

Prep time: 10 minutes/Cook time: 20 minutes

Penne alla vodka is a big hit even though its rosy tomato-cream sauce barely hints at the spirits it contains. We've pulled a Mexican switch by substituting fiery tequila, but we couldn't bear to give up the traditional smoked salmon and sour cream.

12 ounces penne or ziti

2 teaspoons unsalted butter

2 scallions, white part only, minced

⅓ cup tequila

¾ cup heavy or whipping cream

½ teaspoon salt

1 tablespoon tomato paste

¼ pound smoked salmon, cut into thin strips

3 tablespoons sour cream

3 tablespoons snipped chives or scallion greens

1. Bring large pot of salted water to a boil. Add penne and cook according to package directions until al dente.

2. Meanwhile, in 10-inch nonreactive (i.e., not unlined aluminum or cast iron) skillet, melt butter over low heat. Add scallion whites and cook, stirring frequently, 3 minutes, or until tender. Remove pan from heat and add tequila. Return pan to heat, raise heat to high, and cook 1 minute. Add heavy cream and salt and boil 2 minutes, or until slightly thickened. Whisk in tomato paste until combined.

3. Reduce heat to low. Add smoked salmon and cook sauce just until heated through.

4. Drain penne and transfer to large bowl. Pour sauce over pasta, add sour cream and chives, and toss well to combine. *Makes 4 servings/600 cals, 23g fat per serving*

Radiatore Cacciatore

Prep time: 20 minutes/Cook time: 30 minutes

The tomato-infused chicken and mushrooms of chicken cacciatore—hunter's-style chicken—make a wonderful pasta sauce. We liked the tongue-twisting title, but you can use any small pasta shape in place of the radiatore. Go for something like pasta twists or medium shells to catch all of the delicious sauce.

1 tablespoon olive oil	⅓ cup chicken broth
1 pound skinless, boneless chicken thighs, cut into ½-inch chunks	⅓ cup brine-cured olives, such as Gaeta or Kalamata, pitted and coarsely chopped
1 medium onion, finely chopped	1 teaspoon grated orange zest
3 garlic cloves, minced	½ teaspoon salt
½ pound small button mushrooms, quartered	⅛ teaspoon cayenne pepper
1½ cups canned crushed tomatoes	12 ounces radiatore pasta

1. In 10-inch nonstick skillet, heat oil over medium-high heat. Add chicken and cook, turning, 5 minutes, or until lightly brown all over. With slotted spoon, transfer chicken to bowl.

2. Add onion and garlic to pan and cook, stirring frequently, 7 minutes, or until onion is tender. Add mushrooms and cook, stirring frequently, 5 minutes, or until crisp-tender. Add tomatoes, broth, olives, orange zest, salt, and cayenne and bring to a boil.

3. Return chicken to pan, reduce to a simmer, and cover. Cook 10 minutes, or until chicken is cooked through and sauce is flavorful.

4. Meanwhile, bring large pot of salted water to a boil. Add radiatore and cook according to package directions until al dente. Drain. Transfer to large bowl, add sauce, and toss. *Makes 4 servings/570 cals, 13g fat per serving*

THE **RIGHT** STUFF

The devices that heat your home probably do not resemble the pasta shown here, but an Italian designer was inspired by the shape of a typically *Italian* radiator to create the ruffly, convoluted *radiatore*. They're singularly mouth-filling and chewy, and are a perfect match for chunky sauces.

Different Spins

For a distinctly Asian twist, try this lamb sauce with cellophane noodles instead of pasta. Cellophane noodles, because they're made from vegetable starch (usually bean starch), rather than wheat flour, are clear and shimmery. That's why they're called (in additional to "cellophane") shining noodles, glass noodles, silver noodles, or transparent noodles. Cook the noodles according to package directions.

Linguine with Lamb & Peanut Sauce

Prep time: 30 minutes/Cook time: 20 minutes

Go with this warming dish sometime when snow-shoveling, sledding, ice-skating, or cross-country skiing has been the order of the day. You can also make this with strips of flank steak (see variation below), pork loin, or boneless chicken thighs.

1 cup chicken broth

4 tablespoons smooth peanut butter

1 tablespoon soy sauce

2 teaspoons cornstarch

2 teaspoons sugar

½ teaspoon crushed red pepper flakes

6 teaspoons olive oil

3 scallions, cut into 1-inch pieces

3 garlic cloves, minced

2 tablespoons minced peeled fresh ginger

2 bell peppers (red, green, or yellow), cut into ¼ x 2-inch strips

12 ounces linguine

1 pound well-trimmed boneless leg of lamb, cut into ¼ x 2-inch strips

¼ teaspoon salt

1. In small bowl, whisk together broth, peanut butter, soy sauce, cornstarch, sugar, and red pepper flakes.

2. In 12-inch nonstick skillet, heat 2 teaspoons oil over medium heat. Add scallions, garlic, and ginger and cook, stirring frequently, 5 minutes, or until scallions are tender. Add 2 teaspoons oil and bell peppers and cook, stirring frequently, 5 minutes, or until crisp-tender. With slotted spoon, transfer vegetables to plate.

3. Meanwhile, bring large pot of water to a boil. Add linguine and cook according to package directions until al dente. Drain.

4. Add remaining 2 teaspoons oil and lamb to skillet. Increase heat to high and cook, stirring constantly, about 3 minutes, or until lightly browned. Sprinkle with salt.

5. Return vegetables to pan. Stir peanut butter mixture, add to pan, and cook, tossing, 2 minutes, or until sauce is lightly thickened and coats back of spoon.

6. Divide linguine among pasta bowls and top with the lamb and peanut sauce.
Makes 4 servings/655 cals, 22g fat per serving

Linguine with Beef & Peanut Sauce Follow directions for lamb recipe, but substitute 1 pound well-trimmed flank steak. To prepare the flank steak for stir-fry, halve it lengthwise with the grain. Then cut it across the grain into ¼-inch-thick strips. (See meat-cutting technique on page 14.) *Makes 4 servings/695 cals, 26g fat per serving*

We'll Never *shh* Tell

Pasta always cooks quickly, and the incredible variety of bottled tomato (and other) sauces out there make it a no-brainer dinner. But we've tried to take the art of quick and easy pasta meals to a new (and better) height. To begin with, you can up the ante by using a stuffed pasta—tortellini (see Rich Tortellini, at right), ravioli, pierogi, and their kin. Sold fresh or frozen in supermarkets, these pasta packets are the start of many a hearty dinner. And we just couldn't resist a new take on macaroni and cheese (in heaven they serve it every day, *sans* calories) made with Monterey Jack and salsa. Now for our sauce picks: Garlic fans will go for Pasta Agliata (garlicky pasta) with a creamy spinach sauce. Salsa di Boccale is a little number you won't find in an Italian restaurant: *Boccale* means "jar," and nearly all the ingredients come packed in glass (you should find them in the supermarket wherever Italian-style ingredients such as marinated artichokes or tapenade are located).

Pasta Agliata

In 10-inch skillet, cook 6 minced garlic cloves in 3 tablespoons olive oil over low heat 7 minutes, or until very soft.

Add 1 package (10 ounces) chopped frozen spinach, thawed and squeezed dry, and ¾ teaspoon each of grated lemon zest and salt and cook 5 minutes, or until spinach is very tender. Meanwhile, in large pot of boiling salted water, cook 12 ounces pasta according to package directions until al dente. Drain, reserving ¼ cup pasta cooking liquid. Place pasta in large bowl and cooking liquid in food processor. Add spinach mixture and ⅓ cup heavy or whipping cream and process until smooth. Pour sauce over pasta, add ¼ cup grated Parmesan cheese, and toss well to combine. Makes 4 servings/520 cals, 21g fat per serving

Rich Tortellini

In large pot of boiling salted water, cook 1 package (15 ounces) frozen cheese tortellini according to package directions until al dente. Drain and transfer to large bowl. Meanwhile, in 10-inch skillet, bring 1 jar (14 ounces) marinara sauce to a simmer over low heat. Stir in ⅓ cup heavy or whipping cream and ¼ cup chopped fresh basil, bring to a simmer, and simmer 5 minutes to blend flavors. Pour sauce over tortellini and toss to combine. Makes 4 servings/395 cals, 11g fat per serving

Mac & Jack

Preheat oven to 350°F. In large pot of boiling salted water, cook 12 ounces elbow macaroni according to package directions until al dente. Drain, transfer to large bowl, and add 1 jar (16 ounces) salsa, 1 cup thawed frozen corn kernels, 3 ounces cream cheese, cut up, 1½ cups grated Monterey Jack cheese, 1½ teaspoons chili powder, and 1 teaspoon salt; toss well to combine. Transfer mixture to 11 x 7-inch glass baking dish, spreading it in an even layer, and cover with foil. Bake 15 minutes. Remove foil and bake 10 minutes more, or until piping hot. Makes 4 servings/625 cals, 22g fat per serving

Salsa di Boccale

In large pot of boiling salted water, cook 12 ounces pasta according to package directions until al dente. Drain, reserving ½ cup cooking liquid. Meanwhile, in large bowl, toss together 1 jar (6½ ounces) marinated artichokes, chopped but not drained, ⅓ cup finely chopped, drained oil-packed sun-dried tomatoes, ¼ cup tapenade (olive paste), and ½ teaspoon crushed red pepper flakes. Add hot pasta, reserved pasta cooking liquid, and ½ cup grated Parmesan cheese and toss well to combine. Makes 4 servings/495 cals, 15g fat per serving

1 2 1

Pumpkin "Ravioli" with Sage Butter Sauce

Prep time: 35 minutes/Cook time: 20 minutes

Different Spins

For a really quick meal, cook up a pound of frozen cheese ravioli and serve them with the Sage Butter Sauce. You might even get lucky and find fresh or frozen ravioli with a traditional Italian pumpkin filling.

This is most certainly not your everyday dish—but it's a real knockout. Although it is somewhat labor-intensive, it is not at all difficult. In fact, if you can, draft a couple of kids into ravioli-assembling service; they really won't be able to mess up much (at the worst you'll have some slightly misshapen ravioli, but that's charming, right?) The only ticklish moment is after cooking the ravioli: You have to scoop them out of the cooking water rather than draining them into a colander so they won't stick together. If this recipe strikes you as too time-consuming, you should at least try the really easy Sage Butter Sauce over cooked pasta (see "Different Spins," at left).

½ cup natural (unblanched) almonds, toasted

⅔ cup grated Parmesan cheese

1 cup canned unsweetened solid-pack pumpkin

2 tablespoons mango chutney, finely chopped

1 teaspoon Dijon mustard

1 teaspoon sugar

½ teaspoon salt

¼ teaspoon freshly ground black pepper

40 wonton skins (each 3¼ inches square)

Sage Butter Sauce (recipe follows)

Spoon a good-sized mound of pumpkin filling onto the center of each wonton skin. Then dip your finger in water and moisten the edges of the wonton skin.

1. In mini food processor, process toasted almonds until finely ground (or by hand, very finely chop). Transfer to medium bowl and stir in Parmesan, pumpkin puree, chutney, mustard, sugar, salt, and pepper until combined.

2. Remove 10 wonton skins at a time, keeping remainder covered with plastic wrap. Spoon a generous tablespoonful of the pumpkin filling onto center of each square. Moisten edges with water, top with another wonton skin, and press edges together to seal (see photos at left). Place filled ravioli on platter and cover with plastic wrap to keep from drying out. Make ravioli with remaining wonton skins and pumpkin filling in same manner.

3. Bring 2 large pots of salted water to a boil. Add 10 ravioli to each pot and cook 5 to 7 minutes, or until tender. Stir gently to keep the ravioli separate.

4. Meanwhile, make the Sage Butter Sauce; cover loosely to keep warm.

5. With a slotted spoon, scoop the ravioli out of the pot and transfer to pasta bowls. Top with the Sage Butter Sauce. *Makes 4 servings/445 cals, 14g fat per serving without sauce*

Place a second wonton skin on top, align the edges, and press firmly together to seal.

Sage Butter Sauce In small bowl, blend 1 teaspoon cornstarch with 1 tablespoon cold water. In 10-inch skillet, heat 1 cup chicken broth over high heat and cook 3 minutes, or until slightly reduced. Add 2 teaspoons dried sage and cornstarch mixture and boil 1 minute. Remove pan from heat and swirl in 3 tablespoons butter (cut in pieces) until melted. *Makes 1 cup/85 cals, 9g fat per ¼ cup*

Orecchiette with Broccoli & Hot Italian Sausage

Prep time: 20 minutes/Cook time: 35 minutes

For some unknown reason, the cup-shaped pasta called *orecchiette* (which means "little ears") is often served with greens: cabbage or broccoli—or broccoli's assertive Italian cousin, ruffly broccoli rabe (see variation below). Obviously you can make this dish with any old pasta, though a small, shaped pasta (like small or medium shells) would be best.

1 bunch broccoli (about 1 pound)
10 ounces hot Italian sausages
2 tablespoons olive oil
3 garlic cloves, minced
¼ teaspoon salt

12 ounces orecchiette or small shell pasta
¾ cup chicken broth
⅓ cup grated Parmesan cheese

1. Cut tops of broccoli into ½-inch florets. Peel the stems and halve them lengthwise, then cut crosswise into ½-inch pieces.

2. Prick sausages in several places with fork. Place them in 10-inch nonstick skillet with ¼ inch water and cook over medium heat until cooked through, 10 to 15 minutes. Pour fat out of skillet. Set sausages aside to cool, then cut into ¼-inch slices.

3. In same skillet, heat oil over low heat. Add garlic and cook 2 minutes, or until tender. Add broccoli, cooked sausage, and salt and cook, stirring frequently, 20 minutes, or until broccoli is very tender.

4. Meanwhile, bring large pot of salted water to a boil. Add orecchiette and cook according to package directions until al dente. Drain, reserving ⅓ cup cooking liquid. Keep pasta warm.

5. Add broth to broccoli mixture and bring to a boil. Cook 5 minutes, or until lightly thickened. Transfer mixture to large bowl, add pasta, Parmesan cheese, and reserved pasta cooking liquid, and toss well. *Makes 4 servings/610 cals, 24g fat per serving*

Pasta with Broccoli Rabe & Chorizo In place of broccoli, use 1 pound broccoli rabe. Trim off and discard tough ends of stems. Rinse well, pat dry, and cut into ½-inch-long pieces. In place of Italian sausages, use ½ pound *chorizo* (a spicy Latin American sausage; be sure to get the fully cooked *chorizo*, not the fresh, uncooked). Halve the *chorizo* lengthwise and then thinly slice crosswise. This variation on the recipe is prepared just like the above broccoli and Italian sausage version, except since the *chorizo* is already cooked you can omit step 2. *Makes 4 servings/690 cals, 32g fat per serving*

Lighten Up!

For a leaner pasta dish, substitute strips of smoked turkey for the sausage (add it in step 3). Or leave the meat out altogether, but if you do this, you'll want to up the seasonings a bit. (Not the Parmesan, though, or "Lighten Up" will no longer apply.)

THE **RIGHT** STUFF

Broccoli rabe by any other name (and it has many, including broccoli raab, broccoli de rabe, rapini, and rape) is an exceptionally tasty leafy vegetable. It has small clusters of flower buds that hint at its kinship with broccoli. Once confined to Italian neighborhoods, broccoli rabe is now a common sight in supermarkets.

Golden Couscous

Prep time: 10 minutes/Cook time: 10 minutes

If couscous is news to youse, this recipe is a good basic introduction. If you like it, then try it as a main course (see Vegetable Couscous Royale, page 100).

1½ cups canned carrot juice

1½ cups chicken broth

½ teaspoon salt

¼ teaspoon freshly ground white or black pepper

1½ cups couscous

2 carrots, shredded

2 tablespoons unsalted butter

½ cup chopped mint or basil

½ cup golden raisins

½ cup pecans, toasted and coarsely chopped

1. In 3-quart saucepan, combine carrot juice, broth, salt, and pepper over medium heat and bring to a boil. Add couscous, carrots, butter, and mint and stir to combine. Remove pan from heat, cover, and let stand 5 minutes, or until liquid has been absorbed. Fluff with fork to separate grains.

2. Add raisins and toasted pecans and fluff to combine. *Makes 4 servings/520 cals, 16g fat per serving*

In a pinch

Although the carrot juice is responsible for both the rich, golden look of the couscous, as well as for a wonderful, slightly sweet flavor, you can certainly make this recipe without it. Just double up on the chicken broth called for and add 1 more shredded carrot.

THE **RIGHT** STUFF

There's not a great difference in flavor, texture, or nutritional value between yellow and white cornmeal; the two kinds of meal are simply ground from different varieties of corn. But some cooks are very particular about using one or the other: Southern cooks seem to prefer white meal, while polenta (see opposite page) is traditionally made with yellow.

Spoonbread Southwestern Style

Prep time: 20 minutes/Cook time: 30 minutes

The operative word here is "spoon," not bread. You can't slice spoonbread or make sandwiches with it. It's really more of a cornmeal pudding/soufflé that you *spoon* out of the baking dish. Serve it as a side dish, the way you would rice. This would be a great accompaniment to our Kansas City BBQ'd Ribs (page 45).

2 cups milk

⅔ cup white or yellow cornmeal

2 teaspoons sugar

1½ teaspoons chili powder

1 teaspoon ground cumin

1 teaspoon baking powder

½ teaspoon salt

½ teaspoon dried oregano

3 large eggs

¼ pound shredded Monterey Jack cheese (1 cup)

2 pickled jalapeño peppers, seeded and minced (1 tablespoon)

1. Preheat oven to 400°F. Lightly butter 9-inch square glass baking dish.

2. In small bowl, stir together ½ cup milk and cornmeal until well combined.

3. In 2-quart saucepan, heat remaining 1½ cups milk over medium heat until hot and almost boiling. Gradually stir in soaked cornmeal and cook, stirring constantly, 3 minutes, or until thick. Remove pan from heat and stir in sugar, chili powder, cumin, baking powder, salt, and oregano until combined.

4. In large bowl, beat eggs together lightly. Whisking constantly, add a little of hot cornmeal mixture to eggs and whisk until combined. Whisk in remaining cornmeal mixture, cheese, and pickled jalapeños.

5. Spoon batter into baking dish, levelling top, and bake 22 to 25 minutes, or until top is golden brown and center is soft but not dry. (Toothpick inserted in center should come out with crumbs clinging to it.) Serve hot. *Makes 4 servings/335 cals, 17g fat per serving*

Polenta with Tomato-Porcini Sauce

Prep time: 35 minutes/Cook time: 50 minutes

In Italy, polenta, a versatile cornmeal dish, is treated much like pasta. If you bake it with tomato sauce and cheese (à la lasagna), you have a substantial main course.

½ cup dried porcini mushrooms (½ ounce)	1½ cups canned crushed tomatoes
¼ pound bacon (4 slices)	1¼ teaspoons salt
1 small red onion, minced	½ teaspoon freshly ground black pepper
2 garlic cloves, minced	1 cup yellow cornmeal
¼ pound fresh shiitake or button mushrooms, trimmed and thinly sliced	1 cup grated Parmesan cheese

1. In small bowl, combine dried porcini and 1 cup boiling water. Let stand 20 minutes, or until porcini are softened. With fingers, scoop out mushrooms. Strain soaking liquid into bowl through fine-meshed sieve or sieve lined with paper towel; reserve. Rinse mushrooms and coarsely chop.

2. Meanwhile, in 10-inch skillet, cook bacon over medium heat 7 minutes, or until crisp. With slotted spoon, transfer to paper towels to drain. Crumble; set aside.

3. Add onion and garlic to pan and cook, stirring frequently, 7 minutes, or until onion is tender. Add fresh and dried mushrooms and cook, stirring frequently, 5 minutes, or until mushrooms are tender. Add reserved soaking liquid and bring to a boil over high heat. Cook 5 to 7 minutes, or until liquid has been absorbed. Add tomatoes, ¼ teaspoon salt, and pepper and bring to a boil. Reduce to low and simmer 15 minutes, or until sauce is richly flavored. Remove from heat.

4. Preheat oven to 350°F.

5. Meanwhile, in medium bowl, stir together cornmeal and 2 cups cold water until well combined. In 3-quart saucepan, bring 2 cups water and remaining 1 teaspoon salt to a boil over medium heat. Whisk in cornmeal mixture and reduce heat to low. Cook, stirring constantly, about 15 minutes, or until quite thick. Stir in ¾ cup Parmesan and reserved bacon.

6. Spoon polenta into 11 x 7-inch glass baking dish and top with sauce. Sprinkle remaining ¼ cup Parmesan over top. Bake 20 minutes, or until bubbly. Let stand 5 to 10 minutes before serving. *Makes 4 servings/415 cals, 23g fat per serving*

KNOW HOW

Adding any dry ingredient—be it flour, cornstarch, or cornmeal—to water usually means that you'll soon be dealing with an annoyingly lumpy mixture. To avoid this problem for both the spoonbread and the polenta, we first combine the cornmeal with cold liquid (such as milk or water) before stirring it into a boiling liquid.

In a pinch

Heat up a jar of good-quality mushroom-marinara sauce instead of making the Tomato-Porcini sauce. You can even buy ready-to-eat polenta, which comes in a chubby sausage-like form and can be found in the dairy case. Cut the polenta into slices and layer in the baking dish as directed. Sprinkle the polenta with the crumbled bacon and Parmesan and bake as directed.

Roasted Pepper Tabbouleh

Prep time: 30 minutes/Soak time: 30 minutes

THE **RIGHT** STUFF

Bulghur (also spelled bulgur) is the basis for tabbouleh, a favorite Middle-Eastern salad. Bulghur is wheat kernels that have been steamed, dried, and crushed. The steaming and crushing allow the wheat to "cook" by fairly brief steeping in boiling water. Look for bulghur near the rice in the super-market. If you have a choice of several granulations, buy fine bulghur for tabbouleh.

This is one of the few recipes in which parsley is not just a pretty face, but a major flavor component. Lemon juice and mint provide refreshing reinforcement.

8 ounces bulghur (1 ⅓ cups)
1 teaspoon grated lemon zest
½ cup fresh lemon juice
¼ cup extra-virgin olive oil
¾ teaspoon salt
½ teaspoon freshly ground black pepper
⅛ teaspoon ground allspice (optional)

1 cup chopped parsley
⅓ cup chopped mint or basil
3 green bell peppers, roasted and peeled (page 15), cut into ½-inch squares
1 cup canned chick-peas, rinsed and drained
1 large tomato (8 ounces), seeded and cut into ½-inch chunks

1. In large bowl, combine bulghur and 3½ cups boiling water. Let stand at room temperature 30 minutes, or until softened. Pour into large strainer lined with kitchen towel and squeeze bulghur dry.

Roasted green peppers, chunks of tomato, and chick-peas add substance to this hearty grain-based salad.

2. Meanwhile, in large bowl, whisk together lemon zest, lemon juice, oil, salt, pepper, and allspice. Stir in parsley and mint.

3. Add bulghur and toss to combine. Add roasted peppers, chick-peas, and tomato and toss again. Serve chilled or at room temperature. *Makes 4 servings/405 cals, 16g fat per serving*

Risotto Semplice*

Prep time: 10 minutes/Cook time: 45 minutes

Risotto, though fundamentally an uncomplicated dish, has an intimidating reputation. Traditional recipes are so finicky and fanatical about technique that you don't dare even try them. And the ingredients can be daunting, too—a true *risotto milanese* calls for beef marrow and saffron. Our recipe has simplified this rich, creamy rice dish (you'll *never* miss that beef marrow). And we've also pared down the method: The classic recipe calls for constantly stirring the rice as you add the broth in tiny increments (about 45 minutes chained to the stove); here you add the broth in two batches. (*Semplice* means simple in Italian.)

3 tablespoons unsalted butter	½ teaspoon salt
1 medium onion, minced	½ cup grated Parmesan cheese
1½ cups Arborio rice	½ teaspoon freshly ground black
½ cup dry white wine	pepper
2½ cups chicken broth	

1. In heavy-bottomed 3-quart saucepan, melt 1 tablespoon butter over low heat. Add onion and cook, stirring frequently, 10 minutes, or until soft and golden brown. Do not let onion burn. Add rice and stir to coat. Add wine and cook 4 minutes, or until absorbed.

2. Meanwhile, in medium saucepan, heat broth and 1½ cups water over medium heat until warm; keep warm while making risotto.

3. Pour 2 cups warm broth mixture into rice and cook over low heat, stirring occasionally, 15 minutes, or until liquid has been completely absorbed.

4. Add remaining 2 cups warm broth mixture and salt and cook over low heat, stirring frequently, another 15 minutes, or until almost all liquid has been absorbed. Rice should be tender (not mushy) and there should be a creamy "sauce" coating the rice.

5. Remove pan from heat, and stir in Parmesan, pepper, and remaining 2 tablespoons butter. Serve hot. *Makes 4 servings/400 cals, 13g fat per serving*

THE **RIGHT** STUFF

You'll notice that Risotto Semplice does require one special ingredient: Arborio rice. A variety grown in the Po Valley of Italy, Arborio plumps up in cooking without bursting; its starchy coating cooks to a creamy "sauce" while the grain itself remains al dente.

In a pinch

If your "market research" turns up nary a grain of Arborio rice, you can make the risotto with regular long-grain white rice. Just be sure not to use converted rice, which won't yield the slightest bit of creaminess (converted rice is designed to turn out grains that are fluffy and separate).

Rice Above It

How to Cook White Rice This might seem like a no-brainer, but it isn't. To begin with, we find the rice-cooking instructions on the box of rice inadequate. But, in any case, we use a completely different method. Try this and see if it works for you: Start by measuring 1¾ cups of water into a 3-quart saucepan. The size of the pan matters—in a small pan, the rice will boil over. Add 1 cup uncooked long-grain rice and ½ teaspoon salt. Bring to a boil (uncovered) over high heat. Reduce heat to a simmer (if you have an electric stove, have a second burner ready), cover, and cook for 15 minutes. If you like rice a little drier, cook for another 3 minutes. Let stand covered and off the heat for a couple of minutes. To serve, fluff with a fork to separate the grains. *Makes 3 cups/115 cals, .2g fat per ½ cup*

How to Cook Brown Rice The same general rules apply for cooking method, size of pot, and amount of rice and salt, but use 2 cups of water and cook for 45 minutes. *Makes 3 cups/115 cals, .9g fat per ½ cup*

Barley Pilaf with Caramelized Onions

Prep time: 20 minutes/Cook time: 40 minutes

A pilaf is technically rice that has been cooked in broth (often with bits of meat or poultry), but barley makes an especially hearty stand-in. We've kept this side dish meatless, using caramelized onions, toasted almonds, and bits of dried apricots to add flavor. Of course other fruits and nuts would be great here. Try one of these combinations: pecans & dried cherries, walnuts & dried cranberries, or pine nuts & minced dried pears. (P.S. The parsley is just for color. Omit it if you don't have any.)

2 ounces (⅓ cup) natural (unblanched) whole almonds	¾ cup (6 ounces) dried apricots, coarsely chopped
2 tablespoons olive oil	¾ teaspoon salt
2 large onions, minced	½ teaspoon dried sage
2 garlic cloves, minced	½ teaspoon freshly ground black pepper
1 cup (7 ounces) pearl barley	
1½ cups chicken broth	¼ cup chopped parsley

1. Preheat oven to 350°F. Spread almonds on baking sheet and toast 7 minutes, or until fragrant and crisp. Cool, coarsely chop, and set aside. Leave oven on.
2. Meanwhile, in 5-quart Dutch oven or large flameproof casserole, heat oil over medium heat. Add onions and garlic and cook, stirring frequently, 10 minutes, or until onions are golden brown.
3. Add barley and stir to coat. Add broth, apricots, salt, sage, pepper, and 1 cup water and bring to a boil. Cover and transfer pan to oven.
4. Bake pilaf 25 to 30 minutes, or until barley is tender and all liquid has been absorbed. Stir in almonds and parsley. *Makes 4 servings/475 cals, 16g fat per serving*

Different Spins

Try one of these simple variations on plain old rice:
<u>*Green Rice:*</u>
Add 2 minced garlic cloves and 2 sliced scallions to the rice at the beginning. At the end, stir in ½ cup chopped cilantro (or parsley) and 1 tablespoon lime or lemon juice.
<u>*Coconut Rice:*</u>
After rice has cooked 12 minutes, stir in ½ cup flaked coconut. For extra flavor, toast the coconut lightly before adding.

THE **RIGHT** STUFF

Pearl barley (in addition to being a great name for a nightclub singer) is the most common type of barley found. Barley that has been "pearled" has had its three-layered husk milled away, making the grain look like little oval pearls. "Quick-cooking" barley, which has been crushed (kind of like oats are crushed into flakes for making oatmeal), is great when you're short on time, but don't use it in this recipe or you'll end up with mush.

breakfast
brunch
&breads

Huevos Rancheros

Prep time: 15 minutes/Cook time: 10 minutes

When you need some serious sustenance (before a fall weekend frisbee game . . . or maybe just a strenuous trip to the mall), these Tex-Mex ranch-style eggs are guaranteed to get you through the morning—and a good part of the afternoon. What we've got here is a corn tortilla covered with refried beans, topped with an egg, and spiced up with tomato sauce. The eggs are cooked "over easy," which means fried on one side, then carefully turned and cooked until done.

Spicy Fresh Tomato Sauce (recipe follows)

Refried Beans (recipe follows)

2 tablespoons olive oil

4 corn tortillas (6 inches in diameter)

4 eggs

1. Make Spicy Fresh Tomato Sauce and Refried Beans and keep both warm.
2. In 12-inch nonstick skillet, heat 1 tablespoon oil over medium heat. Add tortillas, 1 or 2 at a time, cook 5 seconds per side, or until just soft, and remove to serving plates. Spread Refried Beans over tortillas.
3. Add remaining 1 tablespoon oil to pan. Add eggs, 1 at a time, to pan and fry 2 to 3 minutes per side, or until cooked "over easy." Place 1 fried egg on each serving of refried beans and top with tomato sauce. Serve hot. *Makes 4 servings/400 cals, 20g fat per serving*

Spicy Fresh Tomato Sauce In 10-inch nonreactive (i.e., not unlined aluminum or cast iron) skillet, heat 1 tablespoon olive oil over low heat. Add 1 minced small onion and cook, stirring frequently, 4 minutes, or until soft. Add 2 medium peeled, seeded, and chopped tomatoes, ½ teaspoon salt, and ⅛ teaspoon cayenne pepper and cook, stirring frequently, 7 minutes, or until sauce is thick and dry. Remove pan from heat and stir in 2 tablespoons chopped cilantro. *Makes generous 1 cup/55 cals, 4g fat per ¼ cup*

Refried Beans In 10-inch skillet, heat 1 tablespoon olive oil over medium heat. Add 1 small minced onion and 1 minced garlic clove and cook, stirring frequently, 4 minutes, or until onion is tender. Add 2 cups cooked pinto beans—either homemade (see Bean There, Done That, page 96) or canned, rinsed and drained. Mash beans lightly with potato masher or large spoon until slightly lumpy and stir in ½ teaspoon salt. Cook, stirring frequently, 5 minutes, or until beans are heated through. *Makes about 2 cups/160 cals, 4g fat per ½ cup*

KNOW HOW

When dropping an egg into a pan to cook—whether to fry or poach it—first break the egg into a cup or small bowl and *then* slide it into the pan. This way if the yolk breaks or you get some shell in the egg, you can start over.

In a pinch

When there's no time for "from scratch," open a can of refried beans and another can of seasoned tomato sauce, and serve up some Huevos Rancheros Muy Prontos.

KNOW HOW

To make a dense, tomato-rich sauce from fresh tomatoes, it's best to seed them first to get rid of some of the liquid. There are a couple of schools of thought on how to do this. After you peel the tomatoes (see technique, page 12), halve them horizontally. Then, you can either squeeze the seeds out of the tomatoes (as you would, say, a lemon half), or you can take the more direct approach and use a thumb or finger to scoop them out—or, if you're in a dainty mood, you can use a teaspoon.

Brighten a plate of Huevos Rancheros with a fresh fruit "kebab" of melon, banana, and grapes.

The Modern Omelet

Prep time: 5 minutes/Cook time: 5 minutes

Omelets are traditionally made one at a time, so the recipe here is for a single serving; this also lets you customize each omelet with a favorite filling. Some basic suggestions for fillings follow—you can take it from there, mixing, matching, and making it up as you go along. Possible omelet fillings (use about 3 tablespoons of filling for each omelet): shredded cheese • minced cooked vegetables (potatoes, green beans, asparagus, artichoke hearts) • chopped ham or smoked turkey • salsa & shredded cooked chicken • chopped beefsteak tomatoes & slivered basil • sautéed mushrooms • slivered smoked salmon & sour cream • herbed cottage cheese.

Just before the eggs are done, sprinkle or spoon the filling onto one side of the omelet.

2 eggs	2 teaspoons unsalted butter
2 egg whites	3 tablespoons filling (optional)
½ teaspoon salt	

1. In medium bowl, whisk together eggs, egg whites, salt, and 1 tablespoon water.
2. In a 6-inch omelet pan or nonstick skillet, melt butter over medium heat, rotating pan to cover entire surface. Let butter foam and when it has stopped foaming, pour egg mixture into pan. Cook, without stirring, 10 seconds. When edges begin to set, pull them into center using rubber spatula or wooden spoon. Cook, continuing to pull edges into center as they set, about 2 minutes, or until eggs are no longer runny.
3. Sprinkle filling (if using) over one side of omelet. Slide the filling-covered half of omelet onto a plate and use pan to fold the other half of omelet on top. *Makes 1 serving without filling/250 cals, 18g fat per serving*

As you slide the eggs onto a plate, tip the pan to fold the omelet in two.

Lighten Up!

Though health experts seem to vacillate on the topic of eggs (they are currently in favor), we've opted for an everything-in-moderation approach by creating our omelet and frittata with fewer egg yolks. The results are nearly indistinguishable from their classic antecedents.

Freestyle Frittata

Prep time: 15 minutes/Cook time: 20 minutes

The frittata—a distant Italian relative of the omelet—is a wonderfully forgiving dish (it's really hard to mess it up). Here's the basic idea: You use beaten eggs to bind a bunch of ingredients together into a savory skillet "cake" (in fact, it's traditionally served in wedges). Use the following recipe as a template for any frittata, but keep the amounts of Egg Mixture and Filling the same.

Egg Mixture:
5 eggs
4 egg whites
⅓ cup grated Parmesan cheese
½ teaspoon salt
¼ teaspoon freshly ground black pepper
1 tablespoon olive oil

Filling (3 cups total):
2 cups cut-up (1-inch pieces) cooked asparagus (½ pound)
½ cup chopped baked ham
½ cup shredded Manchego or Cheddar cheese (2 ounces)

1. Make Egg Mixture: In large bowl, whisk together whole eggs, egg whites, Parmesan, salt, and pepper.

2. In 10-inch broilerproof skillet, heat oil over medium heat. Add egg mixture. Sprinkle on the asparagus and ham. Reduce heat to low and cook without stirring, about 15 minutes, or until sides are set and center is still slightly wet.

3. Meanwhile, preheat broiler.

4. Sprinkle Manchego cheese evenly over top of frittata. Broil in pan 6 inches from heat 2 minutes, or until frittata is set and top is golden brown. Slice into wedges and serve hot from pan. Or let cool and serve at room temperature.   *Makes 6 servings/180 cals,12g fat per serving*

Cloud 9 Pancakes

Prep time: 10 minutes/Cook time: 20 minutes

You'll never get pancakes as heavenly as these from a packaged mix. Their cloudlike lightness arises from well beaten egg whites; cottage cheese is the secret to their moist richness.

1 pound low-fat (1%) cottage cheese, well drained	1 teaspoon vanilla
3 eggs, separated	3 tablespoons unsalted butter
⅓ cup flour	Raspberry Sauce (page 153; optional)
¼ cup plus 1 teaspoon sugar	

1. In medium bowl, stir together cottage cheese, egg yolks, flour, the ¼ cup sugar, and vanilla.

2. In large bowl, with electric mixer at medium speed, beat egg whites with the remaining 1 teaspoon sugar to soft peaks. Gently fold whites into cottage cheese mixture. Do not overblend; some streaks of white may remain.

3. Preheat oven to 250°F.

4. In 10-inch nonstick skillet, heat 1 tablespoon butter over medium heat until melted and foamy. Make pancakes in 3 batches, cooking 4 pancakes at a time: Drop batter by scant ¼ cupful into hot skillet and cook 2 minutes, or until set. Turn pancakes and cook 1 minute, or until cooked through. Transfer to large cookie sheet. Make 2 more batches in same manner, using 1 tablespoon of remaining butter per batch and transferring pancakes as they are done to cookie sheet (keep in single layer). You should have 12 pancakes.

5. Bake pancakes 3 to 5 minutes, or until heated through. Serve at once with Raspberry Sauce if desired.   *Makes 4 servings/305 cals, 14g fat per serving*

Different Spins

A frittata is a virtual canvas for creativity. Try some of the following combinations, or make up your own (using 3 cups total): cut-up cooked green beans, smoked turkey & cubed cooked sweet potatoes; sautéed red onion, peas & Gruyère cheese; spinach, cubed cooked new potatoes & smoked trout; feta cheese, cooked shrimp & dill; crumbled bacon, plum tomatoes & goat cheese.

KNOW HOW

The pancake recipe says to beat the egg whites to "soft peaks." What are those? Well, as you begin beating, the whites will become foamy, but soon they'll turn opaque. Keep going—they'll gradually increase in volume and density until, when you scoop some up in a spoon, the top of the egg-white mound will droop over gently. At this point, STOP! or the egg whites will be too dry.

KNOW HOW

You can mix up the herb-and-spice mixture and rub it into the bacon the night before. Refrigerate the bacon in a covered bowl until you're ready to bake it.

Glazed Bacon

Prep time: 5 minutes/Bake time: 25 minutes

Don't worry about waking up the rest of the family—the scent of these spicy glazed bacon strips is more effective (and a whole lot more pleasant) than any alarm clock.

¼ cup packed light brown sugar	½ teaspoon salt
1½ teaspoons freshly ground black pepper	¼ teaspoon ground allspice
1½ teaspoons dried thyme	1 pound thick-sliced bacon (about 12 slices)
½ teaspoon dried sage	

1. In shallow bowl or pie plate, stir together brown sugar, pepper, thyme, sage, salt, and allspice. Add bacon and dredge slices on both sides in spice mixture, then rub it in. Refrigerate bacon until ready to cook.

2. Preheat oven to 400°F. Line jelly-roll pan with aluminum foil.

3. Arrange slices in one layer in pan and bake, turning, 25 minutes, or until bacon is golden brown and sugar mixture has caramelized. Serve hot. *Makes 4 servings/240 cals, 16g fat per serving*

To make a pocket, cut a deep horizontal slit into bottom edge of each slice of bread.

Stuffed French Toast

Prep time: 20 minutes/Cook time: 10 minutes

Basic French toast is so simple to make, a child can do it. And this special-Sunday version, with its deluxe "cheese Danish" filling, requires only a little extra effort. In fact, why not teach your kids how simple it is so that on your birthday, you can request Stuffed French Toast for breakfast—in bed, naturally! You might also drop a hint that raisins, currants, or dried cherries can be stirred into the filling . . .

1 cup part-skim ricotta cheese	Four 1½-inch-thick slices challah bread (cut from 12 x 6-inch loaf)
6 tablespoons sugar	2 eggs
½ cup pecans or walnuts, toasted and coarsely chopped	1 cup milk
⅓ cup raisins	1 tablespoon unsalted butter
1 teaspoon vanilla	1 tablespoon vegetable oil

Spoon some ricotta filling into the pocket, then gently press the sides of the bread together.

1. In medium bowl, stir together ricotta, 3 tablespoons sugar, nuts, raisins, and vanilla until combined.

2. With small, sharp knife, make a pocket in each piece of bread by cutting a horizontal slit along the bottom edge of each piece (see photo at left).

3. Spoon ricotta filling into pockets, dividing it evenly; press edges of bread together gently to enclose filling.

4. In large, shallow bowl, lightly beat eggs and milk together. Dip stuffed bread into egg mixture, coating sides completely and absorbing all egg mixture.

5. In 12-inch skillet, heat butter and oil over medium-low heat. Add stuffed bread and cook 4 minutes per side, or until golden brown all over. Sprinkle with remaining 3 tablespoons sugar and serve hot. *Makes 4 servings/760 cals, 32g fat per serving*

Sunday Morning Hash Browns

Prep time: 15 minutes/Cook time: 50 minutes

The local diner's not the only place to tuck into a plate of perfect hash browns. And if you cook and peel the potatoes the night before, you don't have to get up at the crack of dawn to make these for breakfast.

1½ pounds small all-purpose potatoes	¼ teaspoon freshly ground black pepper
3 tablespoons olive oil	1 green bell pepper, cut into ½-inch pieces
1 large onion, cut into ½-inch cubes	1 red bell pepper, cut into ½-inch pieces
¾ teaspoon salt	

1. In large pot of boiling water, cook potatoes 25 minutes, or until tender but not falling apart. Drain. When cool enough to handle, peel and cut into ½-inch cubes.
2. In 12-inch skillet, heat 2 tablespoons oil over medium heat. Add onion, potatoes, salt, and pepper and cook, stirring frequently, 10 minutes, or until onion is golden brown.
3. Add remaining 1 tablespoon oil and bell peppers and cover. Cook, stirring frequently, 10 minutes, or until peppers are tender. Remove cover and cook 5 minutes more, or until potatoes are golden brown and crusty on edges. Serve hot. *Makes 4 servings/255 cals, 10g fat per serving*

Jalapeño Hash Browns Prepare the Sunday Morning Hash Browns, but add ½ teaspoon ground cumin when you add the salt and black pepper. Add 2 minced pickled jalapeño peppers when you add the bell peppers. Sprinkle the hash browns with chopped cilantro before serving. *Makes 4 servings/260 cals, 11g fat per serving*

THE **RIGHT** STUFF

Challah is a fine-textured, egg-enriched white bread traditionally served on the Jewish sabbath and holidays. It's usually braided into a long loaf, but for some holidays is baked in a round coil shape.

Different Spins

Hash is hardly haute cuisine, so you can mess around with the recipe if you like (we've given you a head start with Jalapeño Hash Browns). Stir in some crumbled bacon, diced ham, roast beef, or cut-up cooked chicken. Use leftover sweet potatoes in place of some or all of the white potatoes. Or—this one's a classic—top each serving of hash with a fried egg.

Country White Bread . . . and Beyond

Prep time: 30 minutes/Rise time: 2 hours/Bake time: 30 minutes

The time will come in your cooking career when you are tempted to make your first loaf of fresh bread. Then, if you are seduced by the fragrance of yeast dough, and if you find the gentle art of kneading therapeutic, you'll probably become a lifetime bread baker. This white bread is a perfect starter recipe, and once you sample a thick slice, still warm and spread with sweet butter and honey, you'll be hooked. From there you can forge ahead with our variations: Focaccia (below), Cinnamon Raisin Bread (opposite), and Sticky Buns (page 139).

1 package active dry yeast
3 teaspoons sugar
1 cup plus 2 tablespoons warm water (105° to 115°F)
3¾ cups flour
¼ cup vegetable or olive oil
2 teaspoons salt

1. In small bowl, sprinkle yeast and 1 teaspoon sugar over ¼ cup warm water and whisk to dissolve. Let stand at room temperature for 5 minutes until foamy.

2. Place 2 cups flour in large bowl and make a well in the center. Add oil, yeast mixture, salt, remaining 2 teaspoons sugar, and remaining warm water (¾ cup plus 2 tablespoons). Stir to combine. Stir in 1 cup flour.

3. Transfer dough to floured work surface and knead enough of remaining ¾ cup flour until dough is smooth and elastic. Transfer dough to large oiled bowl. Turn dough over to coat both sides with oil. Cover with dampened kitchen towel and let stand to rise 1 hour, or until doubled in size.

4. Punch down dough, cover with dampened kitchen towel, and let stand 10 minutes. Shape into 8-inch round ball and flatten slightly. Place on ungreased cookie sheet, cover with dampened kitchen towel, and let stand to rise 30 to 45 minutes, or until doubled in size.

5. Preheat oven to 400°F.

6. With razor (see "The Right Stuff," at left) or sharp knife, gently make several shallow slashes in top of dough. Place cookie sheet on middle rack of oven. Bake loaf 30 minutes, or until crusty and loaf sounds hollow when thumped on bottom. Transfer loaf to wire rack to cool. *Makes 1 loaf, 12 servings/190 cals, 5g fat per serving*

Focaccia Make dough as directed above with the following changes: Use olive oil (not vegetable oil) and reduce sugar to 1 teaspoon (add to yeast mixture). Follow directions through first part of Step 4. Meanwhile, preheat oven to 450°F. After dough has rested 10 minutes, roll it into rough 14 x 10-inch rectangle. Transfer to lightly greased jelly-roll pan and press dough into corners. Using your fingertips (or thumb), make dimples all over dough (see photo, at left). Sprinkle surface of dough with 2 tablespoons olive oil and one of following: 2½ teaspoons coarse (kosher) salt, or 2 tablespoons chopped herbs (such as sage or rosemary), or ¼ cup Parmesan cheese. Bake on bottom rack of oven 20 minutes, or until bottom is golden brown and crisp. Serve warm or at room temperature. *Makes 12 servings/210 cals, 8g fat per serving*

Make rows of shallow, evenly spaced dents in the dough to form the characteristic "dimples" on the focaccia.

Cinnamon Raisin Bread Make dough as directed in Country White Bread. On floured work surface, roll dough out into 14 x 10-inch rectangle. In small bowl, stir together ⅓ cup sugar and 1½ teaspoons ground cinnamon. Brush surface of dough with 2 tablespoons melted unsalted butter. Sprinkle cinnamon sugar over dough and scatter ½ cup raisins over it, patting them into dough. Starting with short end, roll dough up into log; pinch seam to seal. Transfer, seam side down, to greased 9 x 5 x 3-inch loaf pan and cover with dampened kitchen towel. Let stand to rise 30 to 45 minutes, or until doubled in size. Brush top of loaf with 2 tablespoons milk. Bake 30 to 40 minutes, or until loaf sounds hollows when thumped on the bottom. *Makes 1 loaf, 12 servings/250 cals, 7g fat per serving*

Breakfast Bread Pudding

Prep time: 30 minutes/Bake time: 35 minutes

Lots of people think that desserts make divine breakfast foods. And although you might (or might not) draw the line at a morning meal of chocolate mousse, most people consider homey sweets like coffee cake and baked apples perfectly legitimate A.M. fare. If you need further justification, this fragrant fruit pudding—made with bread, apples, cottage cheese, milk, and eggs—covers a respectable number of food groups. If you can stand to make it any more healthful, top the pudding with a spoonful of vanilla yogurt.

3 tablespoons sugar	12 slices cinnamon-raisin bread (12 ounces total), lightly toasted
1 cup low-fat (1%) cottage cheese	1⅓ cups milk
2 tablespoons unsalted butter	3 large eggs
2 Golden Delicious apples, peeled, quartered, and thinly sliced	1 teaspoon vanilla
1 tablespoon fresh lemon juice	¼ teaspoon salt
½ teaspoon ground cinnamon	

1. Preheat oven to 350°F. Lightly butter 8-inch square glass baking dish.
2. In small bowl, stir 2 tablespoons sugar into cottage cheese; set aside.
3. In 10-inch skillet, melt 1 tablespoon butter over medium heat. Add apples, remaining 1 tablespoon sugar, lemon juice, and cinnamon and sauté, tossing occasionally, 5 minutes, or until apples are softened.
4. Fit 4 bread slices over bottom of baking dish. Top with half of cottage cheese and half of sautéed apples. Top with 4 bread slices, remaining cottage cheese, and remaining apples. Top with remaining 4 bread slices.
5. In medium bowl, whisk together milk, eggs, vanilla, and salt. Pour mixture over pudding and let stand 10 minutes; with spatula, press down on bread so top layer will soak up some of egg mixture. Dot with remaining 1 tablespoon butter.
6. Bake 30 minutes, or until bread pudding is set and top is golden brown and lightly puffed. Serve hot or at room temperature. *Makes 6 servings/345 cals, 12g fat per serving*

It's a short hop from focaccia (opposite page) to pizza: Spread the dough in a jelly-roll or pizza pan and cover it with tomato sauce, your favorite pizza toppings, and shredded mozzarella.

THE RIGHT STUFF

If you get into baking, you might want to consider getting a heavy-duty stand mixer with a dough hook attachment. It takes a lot of the work out of making yeast doughs (although some bakers find that working the dough by hand is the most satisfying part of the process).

Take this bread pudding and make it your own. First, try a different bread: Challah is great! Try ripe pears or nectarines. Toss in some toasted chopped nuts (like pecans or almonds). Add 1 tablespoon of rum or bourbon to the egg mixture.

The Crumbiest Coffee Cake

Different Spins

Here's another way to use this buttery coffee cake topping. Cut up enough apples to fill a 9 x 13-inch glass baking dish almost to the top. Sprinkle with ½ cup sugar as you layer the apples in. Cover with the coffee cake topping and bake at 400°F until the topping is crisp and the apples are bubbly (about 25 minutes).

Prep time: 25 minutes/Bake time: 50 minutes

We don't know about you, but most of our friends eat one piece of coffee cake and then spend the rest of the time picking more topping off the rest of the cake. Well, this recipe is for all of them (and all of you), because we have more or less doubled the normal amount of nutty crumb topping.

Cake:

2 cups flour

2 teaspoons baking powder

½ teaspoon baking soda

1½ teaspoons ground cinnamon

½ teaspoon salt

1¾ sticks (14 tablespoons) unsalted butter, at room temperature and cut up

⅔ cup granulated sugar

⅓ cup packed light brown sugar

2 eggs

2 teaspoons vanilla

1 cup sour cream

Topping:

1½ cups sugar

¾ cup flour

1 stick (8 tablespoons) unsalted butter, cut up

2½ teaspoons ground cinnamon

1½ cups pecans or walnuts, finely chopped

Bet you can't eat just one caramel-drenched Sticky Bun. But do pause to make a fresh pot of coffee before starting on the second one.

1. Preheat oven to 350°F. Grease and flour 13 x 9 x 2-inch metal baking pan.
2. Prepare Cake: In bowl, stir together flour, baking powder, baking soda, cinnamon, and salt.
3. In large bowl, with electric mixer, cream butter with both sugars on medium speed until light and fluffy. Beat in eggs, 1 at a time, beating well after each addition. Beat in vanilla.
4. Alternately fold dry ingredients and sour cream into batter, beginning and ending with dry ingredients. Scrape batter into pan and smooth top.
5. Make Topping: In medium bowl, with pastry blender or 2 knives, cut together sugar, flour, butter, and cinnamon until mixture resembles coarse crumbs. Stir in nuts. Sprinkle topping evenly over batter.
6. Bake 45 to 50 minutes, or until toothpick inserted in center comes out just clean (it's OK if there are some crumbs clinging to the toothpick; you don't want the cake to be too dry). Cool in pan on wire rack. Store, covered, in refrigerator up to 3 days.
Makes 16 servings/455 cals, 27g fat per serving

Sprinkle dough with nuts.

Sticky Buns

Prep time: 1½ hours/Rise time: 30 minutes/Bake time: 35 minutes

You probably don't know anybody who makes their own gooey, nutty, buttery sticky buns at home. So shock your friends and family by being the first one in your crowd to revive this old-fashioned art. (P.S. It's wa-a-a-y easier than it looks.)

Country White Bread (page 136)

1 stick (8 tablespoons) unsalted butter, melted

2 tablespoons granulated sugar

1½ cups chopped pecans, toasted

1½ cups packed light brown sugar

⅓ cup heavy or whipping cream

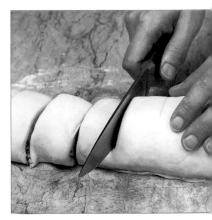

Use a sharp knife to cut dough cylinder into 12 pieces. If your knife isn't sharp enough and is compressing the dough, switch to a serrated knife and cut the dough with a gentle sawing motion.

1. Prepare Country White Bread through step 3.
2. Punch down dough, cover with dampened kitchen towel, and let stand 10 minutes. On floured work surface, roll dough out into 14 x 10-inch rectangle. Brush surface of dough with 2 tablespoons melted butter and sprinkle with granulated sugar and 1 cup pecans. Starting at one long side, roll dough into tight cylinder; pinch seam to seal.
3. Using sharp knife, cut cylinder into 12 equal pieces. In bottom of 13 x 9 x 2-inch metal baking pan, combine brown sugar, remaining 6 tablespoons melted butter, and heavy cream; spread to cover bottom. Sprinkle with remaining ½ cup pecans. Arrange dough spirals, cut side down, on mixture, leaving ¼ inch between pieces. Cover with dampened kitchen towel and let stand to rise 30 minutes, or until doubled in size.
4. Meanwhile, preheat oven to 375°F. Bake buns 30 to 35 minutes, or until puffed and golden brown. While still hot, invert buns onto platter, leaving baking pan in place for a minute so caramel mixture drips onto buns. Carefully lift off baking pan. Serve warm or at room temperature. *Makes 12 sticky buns/480 cals, 24g fat per bun*

Place the cut pieces directly on top of the caramel mixture in the pan. Space the buns about ¼ inch apart.

Cream Scones

Prep time: 15 minutes/Bake time: 30 minutes

For a truly sublime experience, sample a scone while it's still warm, with jam. You might also want to try the scones in Strawberry Scone Cakes (page 150).

(page 150)

2 cups flour

3 tablespoons sugar

2½ teaspoons baking powder

¼ teaspoon salt

6 tablespoons cold unsalted butter, cut up

1 cup dried cranberries, dried cherries, or raisins (4 ounces)

¾ cup heavy or whipping cream

1 large egg, separated

1. Preheat oven to 375°F.

2. In large bowl, stir together flour, 2 tablespoons sugar, baking powder, and salt until well combined. With pastry blender or 2 knives, cut in butter until mixture resembles coarse meal. Stir in dried fruit.

3. In small bowl, whisk together cream and egg yolk. In another small bowl, make the egg wash: Whisk together egg white and 1 tablespoon water; set egg wash aside.

4. Make well in center of dry ingredients, pour in cream mixture, and stir just until dry ingredients are moistened. Transfer dough to lightly floured surface and knead 5 or 6 times until it just holds together.

5. Transfer dough to large ungreased baking sheet. With lightly floured hands, pat dough out into 8-inch round. With sharp knife, cut into 12 wedges; cut all the way through, but do not pull wedges apart or separate them. Brush dough with egg wash and sprinkle with remaining 1 tablespoon sugar.

6. Bake 25 to 30 minutes, or until top is golden brown and toothpick inserted in center comes out clean. Separate scones and transfer to wire rack. Serve warm or at room temperature. *Makes 12 scones/230 cals, 12g fat per scone*

Philpy

Prep time: 15 minutes/Bake time: 25 minutes

"Philpy" is the traditional but inexplicable name for this Southern rice quick bread. Cooked rice in the batter keeps philpy wonderfully moist; there's shredded cheese in this version, too. Serve the bread warm, straight from the pan, slathered with butter.

1 cup flour

1 teaspoon baking powder

¾ teaspoon salt

1 cup cooked white rice (about ⅓ cup uncooked)

¾ cup half-and-half or light cream

1 large egg

1 cup shredded Cheddar or Monterey Jack cheese (4 ounces)

1. Preheat oven to 425°F. Grease 8-inch cast-iron skillet, deep 8-inch cake pan, or 9-inch deep-dish pie plate and place in oven to heat while making batter.

Different Spins

Scones can also be baked in rounds, like biscuits. Pat the dough out ½ inch thick and cut it with a biscuit cutter or the rim of a glass (see opposite page). Reduce baking time to about 15 minutes.

KNOW HOW

Why do most baking recipes call for butter (or shortening) to be cold before you "cut" it into flour? Well, cutting chilled fat into the dry ingredients is the key to perfect pastry. The bits of shortening shouldn't be totally blended into the flour—just distributed throughout it. When these morsels of fat melt in the oven's heat, they create tiny pockets of steam, which make the pastry flaky.

2. In small bowl, stir together flour, baking powder, and salt.

3. In large bowl, with potato masher or wooden spoon, mash rice until almost smooth. Stir in half-and-half, egg, and ¾ cup cheese. Stir in dry ingredients until combined. Pour batter into hot pan and sprinkle remaining ¼ cup cheese over top.

4. Bake 20 to 25 minutes, or until golden brown and toothpick inserted in center comes out clean. Serve warm. *Makes 6 servings/245 cals, 12g fat per serving*

Your Basic Biscuit . . .

Prep time: 15 minutes/Bake time: 15 minutes

As with most of the recipes in this book, these biscuits should be viewed as a mere jumping-off point for your creativity. See "Different Spins," at right, for suggestions.

You don't have to go out and buy a biscuit cutter: A drinking glass with a fairly thin rim about 2 inches in diameter will work just fine. To keep the dough from sticking to the glass, dip the rim of the glass in flour before making each cut.

2 cups flour

2 teaspoons baking powder

½ teaspoon baking soda

¾ teaspoon salt

4 tablespoons cold unsalted butter, cut up

2 tablespoons chilled solid vegetable shortening

¾ cup buttermilk (or soured milk; see "In a pinch," page 143)

1. Preheat oven to 400°F.

2. In large bowl, stir together flour, baking powder, baking soda, and salt. With pastry blender or 2 knives, cut in butter and shortening until mixture resembles coarse meal. Add buttermilk and stir in until dry ingredients are just moistened (mixture may be slightly lumpy).

3. Transfer dough to lightly floured surface and knead several times until it just holds together.

4. With lightly floured hands, pat dough out ½ inch thick. Flour 2-inch round biscuit cutter and cut out biscuits, placing them 2 inches apart on ungreased baking sheet. Gather up scraps, pat out again, and cut out more biscuits.

5. Bake 15 minutes, or until biscuits are lightly browned. Transfer to wire rack and serve warm or at room temperature. *Makes 12 biscuits/140 cals, 6g fat per biscuit*

Bacon-Cheddar Biscuits In 10-inch skillet, cook 5 slices bacon over medium heat 7 minutes, or until the bacon is crisp and the fat is melted. Transfer bacon to paper towels to drain; crumble. Reserve 2 tablespoons bacon fat in small bowl or cup, cover, and refrigerate until solid. Combine dry ingredients as directed in step 2 of basic biscuit recipe, but reduce salt to ½ teaspoon. Cut in reserved bacon fat and 3 tablespoons solid vegetable shortening; omit the butter. Stir in 1 cup shredded sharp Cheddar cheese (4 ounces) and crumbled bacon, then add buttermilk. Cut out and bake biscuits as directed above. *Makes 12 biscuits/180 cals, 10g fat per biscuit*

Different Spins

Here are some suggested add-ins for Your Basic Biscuit (use a total of about ½ cup): toasted sunflower or pumpkin seeds, minced country ham, minced sun-dried tomatoes, minced oil-cured black olives. You can also throw in a pinch or two of your favorite herb.

Muffins PLUS

Prep time: 15 minutes/Bake time: 20 minutes

The past few decades have seen an unprecedented muffin boom. And the more popular muffins became, the bigger, fattier, and sweeter they grew. A chocolate-chip muffin with fudge icing? Come on, you know that's really a cupcake! We vote for the return of the old-fashioned breakfast muffin—modestly sized, light in texture, and gently sweetened.

2 cups all-purpose flour

⅓ cup sugar

1½ teaspoons baking powder

½ teaspoon baking soda

¼ teaspoon salt

1 cup buttermilk (or soured milk, see "In a pinch," at right)

3 tablespoons unsalted butter, melted

1 large egg

1 teaspoon vanilla

1. Preheat oven to 375°F. Grease twelve 2½-inch muffin cups or line with paper muffin cup liners.

2. In large bowl, stir together flour, sugar, baking powder, baking soda, and salt.

3. In small bowl, whisk together buttermilk, butter, egg, and vanilla.

4. Make well in center of dry ingredients, pour in liquid ingredients, and stir just until dry ingredients are moistened (mixture may be slightly lumpy). Spoon batter into muffin cups, filling each three-quarters full.

5. Bake 17 to 20 minutes, or until golden brown and a toothpick inserted in center of a muffin comes out clean. Remove muffins from pan to wire rack to cool. Serve warm or at room temperature. *Makes 12 muffins/150 cals, 5g fat per muffin*

Fresh Fruit Muffins Stir 1 cup blueberries, raspberries, or finely chopped or shredded peeled apple or pear into basic batter and add 1 teaspoon grated lemon zest and ⅛ teaspoon each of ground allspice and freshly ground black pepper. Spoon into muffin cups as directed above and bake 21 to 22 minutes, or until toothpick inserted in center of a muffin comes out clean. *Makes 12 muffins/155 cals, 5g fat per muffin*

Dried Fruit & Nut Muffins Stir ⅛ teaspoon ground allspice into dry ingredients. Stir 1 cup dried cherries, cranberries, or diced dried strawberries, apricots, or prunes and ½ cup finely chopped toasted pecans or walnuts into basic batter. Bake muffins 17 to 20 minutes, or until toothpick inserted in center of a muffin comes out clean. *Makes 12 muffins/210 cals, 8g fat per muffin*

Health Muffins Substitute vegetable oil for melted butter and ½ cup whole wheat flour for ½ cup of the all-purpose flour in basic recipe. Add ⅓ cup toasted wheat germ to dry ingredients. Bake muffins 17 to 20 minutes, or until toothpick inserted in center of a muffin comes out clean. *Makes 12 muffins/155 cals, 5g fat per muffin*

◄ Home-baked muffins can't be beat, especially when fresh fruit is in season.

In a pinch

You don't taste the buttermilk in baked goods; it just gives them a uniquely tender texture. But if you don't like buttermilk and would rather not buy a quart of it, you can fake it by making "soured milk": Place 1 tablespoon of white vinegar or lemon juice in a glass measuring cup. Add enough regular milk to measure 1 cup. Stir and let stand for 5 minutes. You can also use plain yogurt in place of buttermilk.

KNOW HOW

Easy does it when you're mixing batter for muffins and other quick breads. If you beat the batter too long or too hard, the muffins will turn out tough and dense (in part because some of the leavening power is lost; see "Know How," page 144). So mix quick bread batter by hand, not with an electric mixer, and stir just long enough to moisten the dry ingredients—not until the batter is creamy-smooth. There will (and should be) lumps left in the batter.

Mango-Ginger Quick Bread

Prep time: 20 minutes/Bake time: 1 hour 5 minutes

Banana bread must have seemed exotic at some point, but we've all been there and done that. Time to move on. So try this moist quick bread made with mango puree and toasted coconut and studded with morsels of crystallized ginger. If mangoes haven't infiltrated your neighborhood yet, try one of the less-exotic variations that follow.

1½ pounds mangoes (1 large or 2 small)

½ cup sweetened coconut flakes

2 cups flour

1 teaspoon baking soda

½ teaspoon ground cinnamon

½ teaspoon salt

¼ teaspoon ground allspice

3 tablespoons finely chopped crystallized ginger

¾ cup packed light brown sugar

⅓ cup vegetable oil

2 large eggs

1½ teaspoons grated lime zest

1 tablespoon fresh lime juice

1. Cut flesh from mango pits (see technique, page 9), transfer to food processor, and process until smooth. (You need 1 cup puree to make the bread. A couple of tablespoons more than a cup won't hurt, but if you have quite a bit more, measure out 1 cup and save any remainder for another use).

2. Preheat oven to 375°F. Grease and flour 9 x 5 x 3-inch loaf pan.

3. Spread coconut on jelly-roll pan, and toast in oven, stirring occasionally, 5 minutes, or until golden. Cool to room temperature.

4. In large bowl, stir together flour, baking soda, cinnamon, salt, and allspice. Stir in ginger.

5. In another large bowl, with electric mixer on medium speed, beat brown sugar and oil until combined. Beat in eggs, 1 at a time, beating well after each addition, until light and creamy. Beat in lime zest and juice. Beat in mango puree and toasted coconut. Fold in dry ingredients until just combined. Spoon batter into loaf pan and smooth top.

6. Bake 55 to 65 minutes, or until toothpick inserted in center comes out clean. Cool in pan 10 minutes, unmold bread, and cool completely on wire rack. *Makes 1 loaf, 8 servings/380 cals, 13g fat per serving*

Apple-Raisin Quick Bread Follow recipe above with following changes: Use 1 cup applesauce instead of mango puree, raisins instead of coconut (omit toasting step), and lemon zest and lemon juice instead of lime zest and lime juice. *Makes 1 loaf, 8 servings/370 cals, 11g fat per serving*

Nectarine-Nut Quick Bread Follow recipe above with following changes: Use 1 cup pureed nectarines (from 3 large or 4 medium nectarines) instead of mango puree and chopped toasted almonds instead of coconut. Add ¼ teaspoon almond extract. Omit lime zest and crystallized ginger. *Makes 1 loaf, 8 servings/360 cals, 15g fat per serving*

pies cakes cookies & desserts

Riesling-Poached Pears

Prep time: 10 minutes/Cook time: 45 minutes/Chill time: at least 2 hours

Sometimes you want a light dinner and a rich dessert, sometimes just the opposite. These pretty poached pears, served chilled, are perfect after a substantial meal.

2½ cups Riesling or other fruity white wine

½ cup sugar

¼ teaspoon whole black peppercorns

1 whole vanilla bean, split lengthwise, or 1 teaspoon vanilla extract

4 firm-but-ripe Bartlett pears with stems (8 ounces each)

1. In 3-quart nonaluminum high-sided saucepan, stir together wine, sugar, pepper-corns, and vanilla bean (do not add extract here). Bring to a boil over medium heat.
2. Meanwhile, peel pears, leaving stems attached. With apple corer, core the pears from the bottom (you only have to go about halfway up; see how-to photo, page 8). Place pears in hot liquid, cover pan, and reduce heat to a simmer. Simmer 20 minutes, or until pears are tender but not falling apart when pierced with tip of knife. With slotted spoon, carefully transfer pears to medium bowl.
3. Bring poaching liquid to a boil over high heat; cook 25 minutes, or until reduced to a syrup. Let liquid cool and stir in extract, if using. Reserve vanilla bean if desired.
4. Pour syrup over pears in bowl, cover, and refrigerate, turning occasionally, at least 2 hours, or until well chilled. To serve, place 1 pear in each of 4 shallow bowls. Strain syrup and spoon over pears. *Makes 4 servings/230 cals, .8g fat per serving*

THE **RIGHT** STUFF

A vanilla bean is a slender pod filled with really tiny seeds (so that's what those little black flecks in vanilla ice cream are!). Vanilla beans are called for in recipes where you want to infuse a liquid (such as the pear-poaching liquid, at right, or the milk mixture for Panna Cotta, page 167) with vanilla flavor. After cooking with a vanilla bean, you can reuse it: Wipe it off and let it dry before storing. One way to store a vanilla bean is in a jar of granulated sugar, which has two benefits: It keeps the vanilla bean dry *and*, after about a week, you'll have vanilla-flavored sugar.

In a pinch

Another way to make the pear dessert that is not as pretty, but is a little easier to manage, is to poach pear halves instead of whole pears. (And you don't need pears with stems.) Peel the pears, halve them lengthwise, scoop out the cores, and cook the pears in the poaching liquid, but in a large skillet (not a high-sided saucepan). Test them for doneness after about 10 minutes. Pour the poaching liquid into a saucepan to reduce (see step 3).

Dried Fruit Compote

Prep time: 15 minutes/Cook time: 20 minutes

Dried fruit cooked in spiced wine is a casual, not-too-sweet dessert. Serve the compote with a scoop of vanilla ice cream or frozen yogurt. Offer some crisp cookies, such as our Almond-Orange Biscotti (page 162), on the side.

2 cups dry red wine

½ cup sugar

½ teaspoon ground cinnamon

½ teaspoon freshly ground black pepper

⅛ teaspoon ground allspice

8 ounces dried apples or peaches, coarsely chopped

8 ounces dried pears, coarsely chopped

6 ounces dried cherries or chopped dried apricots

½ teaspoon vanilla

In 2-quart nonaluminum saucepan, bring wine, sugar, cinnamon, pepper, and allspice to a boil over medium heat. Add apples, pears, and cherries, reduce heat to a simmer, and cover. Cook 15 minutes, or until fruit is tender and sauce is syrupy. Cool slightly and stir in vanilla extract. Serve warm, at room temperature, or chilled. *Makes 4 servings/580 cals, .5g fat per serving*

Decorate the Riesling-Poached Pears with faux pear leaves (we used small mint leaves). ▶

Plum-Berry Cobbler

Prep time: 20 minutes/Bake time: 25 minutes

Cobbler, crisp, slump, grunt, and pandowdy are all names of great old-fashioned American desserts. A cobbler—nobody seems to know for sure where the name comes from—consists of a deep pan of fresh fruit baked with a biscuit-like topping. And with only a flick of the wrist, this cobbler can become a crisp (see below).

Different Spins

Cobblers and crisps are accommodating recipes that you can (and should) vary with the seasons. Peaches or nectarines plus raspberries—or black-berries—make an extra-ordinary cobbler. In the fall, cut up apples and/or pears for a crisp, adding a few shakes of cinnamon and maybe a handful of toasted walnuts.

Filling:

¼ cup sugar

1 tablespoon flour

2 teaspoons grated lemon or orange zest

⅛ teaspoon salt

¾ pound red plums, cut into ¼-inch-thick wedges

2 medium Golden Delicious apples, peeled and cut into ¼-inch chunks

1 pint blueberries

Cobbler Topping:

1½ cups flour

2 tablespoons sugar

2½ teaspoons baking powder

¼ teaspoon salt

4 tablespoons cold unsalted butter, cut up

⅓ to ½ cup heavy or whipping cream

In a pinch

In a rush to get your cobbler into the oven? Instead of rolling out the biscuit dough and cutting it into rounds, just pinch off pieces of the dough and dot the top of the cobbler with them.

1. Preheat oven to 400°F.

2. Prepare Filling: In small bowl, combine sugar, flour, lemon zest, and salt. In large bowl, toss fruit with sugar mixture. Transfer to 7 x 11-inch glass baking dish.

3. Make Cobbler Topping: In large bowl, stir together flour, sugar, baking powder, and salt until well combined. With pastry blender or 2 knives, cut in butter until mixture resembles coarse crumbs. Make well in center of dry ingredients and stir in enough cream just to moisten mixture (start with ⅓ cup and add 2 or 3 more tablespoons if necessary to moisten dough). Transfer to lightly floured surface and knead dough 3 or 4 times, or just until it comes together.

4. With lightly floured hands, pat dough out ½ inch thick. With 2½-inch round biscuit cutter or floured water glass (see photo, page 141), cut out rounds and arrange them on fruit. Reroll scraps if necessary to get 8 rounds. Bake 20 to 25 minutes, or until biscuits are golden brown and fruit is piping hot and tender. Serve warm or at room temperature. *Makes 8 servings/280 cals, 11g fat per serving*

Plum-Berry Crisp Prepare Filling as for cobbler, above. But make a "crisp" topping instead of cobbler topping: In medium bowl, stir together ½ cup flour, ½ cup old-fashioned oats, ½ cup granulated sugar, and ¼ teaspoon salt until well combined. Add 3 tablespoons cold unsalted butter, cut up, and with fingertips blend until pebbly in texture. Sprinkle topping evenly over fruit mixture. Bake in preheated 400°F oven for 20 to 25 minutes or until topping is browned and juices are bubbling. *Makes 8 servings/225 cals, 5g fat per serving*

Killer Carrot Cake

Prep time: 30 minutes/Bake time: 35 minutes/Chill time: at least 1 hour

And now we come to the health-food portion of our desserts chapter. Not. Though carrots *are* good for you, what this cake is really about is the irresistible combination of a delicately moist, spicy cake and a lush, creamy, slightly tangy frosting. Currants and chopped nuts add yet another textural dimension. This makes a knockout birthday cake, by the way.

2 cups flour

2 teaspoons baking powder

1 teaspoon baking soda

1 teaspoon ground cinnamon

1 teaspoon ground ginger

1 teaspoon ground cardamom

½ teaspoon salt

2 cups sugar

⅔ cup vegetable or peanut oil

2 teaspoons grated orange zest

4 large eggs

6 large carrots, peeled and grated (3 cups)

⅔ cup dried currants or raisins

½ cup pecans, toasted and chopped

Cream Cheese Frosting (recipe follows)

KNOW HOW

Here's how to frost a cake without frosting the cake plate: Arrange four wide strips of wax paper under the edges of the cake to cover the plate. Just the edge of the cake should rest on the wax-paper strips; if the strips go too far underneath, they'll be hard to remove. Slather on the frosting, then carefully pull out the paper strips when you're done.

1. Preheat oven to 350°F. Grease two 9-inch round cake pans.

2. In large bowl, stir together flour, baking powder, baking soda, cinnamon, ginger, cardamom, and salt until well combined.

3. In another large bowl, with electric mixer on medium speed, beat sugar, oil, and orange zest until combined. Beat in eggs, 1 at a time, beating well after each addition. Stir in carrots, currants, and pecans. Stir in dry ingredients until blended.

4. Divide batter evenly between pans and smooth tops. Bake 35 minutes, or until toothpick inserted in centers comes out clean. Cool cakes in pans on wire racks 10 minutes. Run metal spatula around edge of each pan and invert cakes onto racks to cool completely.

5. Meanwhile, make Cream Cheese Frosting.

6. Place 1 cake layer, bottom side up, on cake plate or platter. Slide strips of wax paper under edges of cake to cover plate (see photo, at right). With large thin-bladed metal spatula, spread 1⅓ cups frosting evenly over top of layer, extending almost to edge. Place remaining layer, top side up, on filling. Spread remaining frosting evenly over sides of cake, then over top. Remove wax-paper strips.

7. Refrigerate cake at least 1 hour before serving. *Makes 16 servings/510 cals, 29g fat per serving*

Cream Cheese Frosting In large bowl, with electric mixer on medium speed, beat 1 pound softened cream cheese and 1 stick (8 tablespoons) softened unsalted butter until smooth. Beat in 2 cups confectioners' sugar and 1½ teaspoons vanilla until light and fluffy. *Makes 4½ cups/185cals, 14g fat per ¼ cup*

Strawberry Scone Cakes

Prep time: 10 minutes/Bake time: 25 minutes

KNOW HOW

You'll notice that while the scones are baking for the Strawberry Scone Cakes, you let the cut strawberries sit with sugar (and some strawberry jelly). The object of this process (called maceration) is to get the strawberries to create their own juices. Although cut strawberries sitting by themselves would eventually release some juice, adding sugar to the berries speeds the process.

The old-fashioned way (maybe the only way) to make shortcake is with freshly baked biscuits. We've gilded the lily by using warm, rich Cream Scones. Ideally, for this dessert they should be split horizontally in half to absorb the strawberry juices, but the scones are quite crumbly, so we've left them unsplit. Since it's just a cosmetic difference, you can do it either way. It'll probably depend on how fussy you think your audience is.

Cream Scones (page 140)

1 egg white beaten lightly with
   1 tablespoon water

5 tablespoons sugar

2 tablespoons strawberry jelly

2 pints strawberries, thinly sliced

1 cup well-chilled heavy or whipping
   cream

1 teaspoon vanilla

1. Preheat oven to 375°F.

2. Make Cream Scones dough through step 4, substituting dried strawberries for the dried cranberries if desired. Pat dough out into 12 x 6-inch rectangle. With sharp knife, cut into eight 3-inch squares. Transfer squares to ungreased baking sheet, brush

Don't let strawberry season pass you by without making this scone shortcake at least once. A small mint sprig makes a nice garnish.

with beaten egg white, and sprinkle with 1 tablespoon sugar. Bake 22 to 25 minutes, or until golden brown and set. Transfer squares to wire rack to cool completely.

3. Meanwhile, in medium bowl, stir together 2 tablespoons sugar and strawberry jelly. Add strawberries and toss gently to combine; set aside at room temperature.

4. In large bowl, with electric mixer on medium speed, beat cream to soft peaks. Gradually beat in remaining 2 tablespoons sugar, 1 tablespoon at a time, until cream is whipped to soft peaks. Beat in vanilla.

5. Spoon a couple of tablespoons of strawberry juice onto each dessert plate. Place a scone on each plate. With a fork, prick the tops of the scones in several places. Then top with strawberries and remaining juices. Top with dollop of whipped cream.
Makes 8 servings/510 cals, 29g fat per serving

Chocolate Truffle Cake

Prep time: 25 minutes/Bake time: 25 minutes

This is a cake that definitively proclaims a Very Festive Occasion—one for adults only. Vary the sophisticated deep-chocolate flavor by substituting an orange liqueur, such as Grand Marnier, for the rum.

2 ounces (2 squares) semisweet chocolate, chopped	1 tablespoon dark rum or bourbon
2 ounces (2 squares) unsweetened chocolate, chopped	3 large eggs, at room temperature
4 tablespoons unsalted butter, cut up	¼ cup sugar
¼ cup heavy or whipping cream	⅛ teaspoon salt
	Confectioners' sugar (optional)

1. Preheat oven to 375°F. Lightly grease bottom and sides of 8-inch round cake pan. Cut round of wax paper to fit bottom of pan, line with round, and grease paper. Place cake pan in larger baking pan.

2. In small saucepan, combine semisweet and unsweetened chocolates, butter, and cream and cook over low heat, stirring to combine, until chocolate melts and mixture is smooth. Remove pan from heat and cool mixture to room temperature. Stir in rum.

3. In large bowl, with electric mixer on high speed, beat eggs, sugar, and salt 5 to 7 minutes, or until very light and airy and the mixture falls in a ribbon when the beater is lifted. With rubber spatula, gently fold egg mixture into cooled chocolate mixture until thoroughly combined.

4. Pour batter into cake pan, then transfer baking pan to oven. Carefully pour boiling water into baking pan to come ½ inch up sides of cake pan. Bake cake 20 to 25 minutes, or until set and cake begins to pull away from sides of pan. Carefully remove cake pan from water and transfer to wire rack to cool for 5 minutes. Run a thin knife around inside of pan and invert cake onto cake plate. Remove wax paper and let cool.

5. Dust top of cake with confectioners' sugar if desired before serving. *Makes 12 servings/135 cals, 11g fat per serving*

The Chocolate Truffle Cake is re-e-e-a-lly delicious, but it's also kinda ugly. To help conceal this defect, we recommend that you dust the top of the cake with confectioners' sugar (or a combination of confectioners' sugar and cocoa). And, if the spirit moves you, you can either get a little fancy (see the simple decorating tip below) or a lot fancy: Use a paper doily as a stencil on top of the cake before sprinkling with sugar.

For a simple windowpane pattern, place paper strips on the cake before sifting sugar on top. When you're done, pick up the paper strips carefully, one at a time (don't exhale!).

Foolproof Chocolate Torte

Prep time: 20 minutes/Bake time: 25 minutes

In a classic torte, very finely chopped nuts and/or crumbs take the place of the flour. This lusciously moist chocolate torte with a hint of raspberry is made with hazelnuts *and* bread crumbs. To bring out the berry flavor, arrange a circle of fresh raspberries on top of the cake after the chocolate glaze has set.

1 cup hazelnuts	3 large eggs
1 tablespoon plus ¼ cup granulated sugar	1 tablespoon seedless raspberry jam
4 ounces (4 squares) semisweet chocolate, chopped	1 tablespoon Frangelico
1 stick (8 tablespoons) unsalted butter, at room temperature	¼ cup plain dry bread crumbs
¼ cup packed light brown sugar	Chocolate Glaze (recipe follows)

1. Preheat oven to 375°F. Lightly grease bottom and sides of 8-inch round cake pan. Cut round of wax paper to fit bottom of pan, line pan with round, and grease paper.
2. Spread hazelnuts on baking sheet and toast 7 to 10 minutes, or until skins begin to wrinkle and nuts are fragrant. With a kitchen towel, rub hazelnuts until skins come off. (Some bits of skin will remain even after rubbing.) Transfer nuts to food processor, add the 1 tablespoon granulated sugar, and process to a fine powder.
3. In small saucepan, melt chocolate over low heat, stirring, until smooth; cool slightly.
4. In large bowl, with electric mixer on medium speed, cream butter, brown sugar, and remaining ¼ cup granulated sugar until light and fluffy. Beat in eggs, 1 at a time, beating well after each addition. Beat in jam and Frangelico. Stir in bread crumbs, ground hazelnuts, and melted chocolate until combined.
5. Pour batter into pan and bake 25 minutes, or until toothpick inserted near center of cake comes out with a few crumbs clinging to it. Be careful not to overbake; the center should still be moist. Transfer to wire rack to cool completely.
6. Make Chocolate Glaze.
7. To glaze torte, run thin metal spatula around edge of pan and invert torte onto wire rack. Carefully peel off wax paper and invert torte top side up on rack. Slip sheet of clean wax paper under edges of cake rack. Pour chocolate glaze over top of torte and let it run down sides. With small metal spatula, spread glaze on any uncovered parts (you can also use some of the glaze that's dripped onto wax paper). Let torte stand at room temperature 30 minutes, or until glaze has set. With metal spatula, carefully slide torte onto cake plate. Serve at room temperature or slightly chilled.
Makes 12 servings/335 cals, 25g fat per serving

Chocolate Glaze In small saucepan, melt 4 ounces (4 squares) semisweet chocolate, chopped, over low heat, stirring until smooth. Remove pan from heat and whisk in 4 tablespoons unsalted butter, at room temperature, and 1 tablespoon honey. Whisk until glaze is thickened and smooth but still pourable. *Makes ¾ cup/85 cals, 7g fat per tablespoon*

THE **RIGHT** STUFF

Frangelico is a hazelnut-flavored liqueur. Other nut-flavored liqueurs include amaretto (almond), eau de noix (walnut), and crème de noyaux (which is made from apricot pits but tastes like almonds).

In a pinch

Although Frangelico nicely underlines the flavor of the hazelnuts in the torte, you can substitute another liqueur. In addition to the obvious choice of another nut liqueur (see above), you could also substitute a fruit-flavored liqueur such as triple sec (orange), crème de cassis (black currant), or crème d'abricots (apricot). Or take the torte in a different direction and use a coffee-flavored liqueur (Kahlúa or Tía Maria) or a chocolate-flavored one (crème de cacao).

Different Spins

This torte makes a perfect Passover dessert with one simple change: Use matzoh meal in place of the bread crumbs.

We'll Never *shh* Tell

Sometimes a dessert sauce is all you need to go from simple to spectacular. So we've come up with three superb sauces and some creative ways to use them. All three are wonderful over ice cream, of course; add other sundae fixings at will. Or, fold spoonfuls of sauce into softened ice cream for a "swirl" effect. Glorify angel food or pound cake with any of the sauces: For a dressy company dessert, "paint" the plate (see "Show Off" on page 167) with one of the sauces, add a slice of cake and top with ice cream or sorbet. The Dessert "Salsa" and Quick Cannoli Pudding are great last-minute desserts. Serve the "salsa" with ice cream and the pudding with cookies or fresh fruit. The ice cream sandwiches are a bonus treat—you'll probably be asked to make these more than once (try other cookies, too).

All-Purpose Dessert Sauces

Chocolate Sauce Supreme In medium saucepan, melt 2 ounces (2 squares) semisweet chocolate and 1 tablespoon unsalted butter over low heat, stirring, until smooth. Add ⅓ cup boiling water and stir until blended. Stir in ½ cup granulated sugar, ¼ cup packed light brown sugar, and 2 tablespoons light corn syrup and bring to a boil over medium heat. Cook, without stirring, for 7 or 8 minutes, or until thick. On heat, stir in ¼ cup heavy or whipping cream until blended. Serve hot. Makes 1 cup/115 cals, 6g fat per 2 tablespoons

Butterscotch Sauce In medium saucepan, combine ¾ cup packed light brown sugar, ¼ cup light corn syrup, 3 tablespoons unsalted butter, and ¼ teaspoon salt over medium heat. Bring to a boil and cook, stirring occasionally, 5 minutes, or until thick. Stir in ⅓ cup heavy or whipping cream and boil 2 minutes, or until well combined. Makes scant ¾ cup/240 cals, 11g fat per 2 tablespoons

Raspberry Sauce In food processor, puree 1 package (12 ounces) thawed frozen raspberries, 3 tablespoons sugar, and 2 tablespoons seedless raspberry jam. Push puree through fine-meshed sieve into small bowl, cover, and refrigerate until serving time. Makes about 1 cup/75 cals, .1g fat per 2 tablespoons

Dessert "Salsa"

In medium bowl, stir together 1 tablespoon each of honey and fresh lemon juice. Add 1 cup canned pineapple chunks, 1 cup sliced strawberries, and ½ cup raspberries and toss to combine. Serve chilled or at room temperature. Makes 2½ cups/60 cals, .2g fat per ½ cup

Quick Cannoli Pudding

In medium bowl, stir together 15-ounce container part-skim ricotta, 3 tablespoons sugar, 1 tablespoon orange juice, and 1½ teaspoons grated orange zest until well combined. Fold in ¼ cup mini chocolate chips. Makes 4 servings/235 cals, 11g fat per serving

Snappy Ice Cream Sandwiches

In medium bowl, stir together 1½ cups softened vanilla ice cream or frozen yogurt and ¼ cup finely chopped crystallized ginger. Using 16 gingersnaps (2¼-inch diameter), spread generous 3 tablespoons ice cream mixture onto half of gingersnaps; top with remaining cookies. Place on plate, loosely cover, and freeze until centers are solid, about 2 hours. Since these cookies improve with age (the ice cream begins to soften the cookies), you can also make them ahead of time (but wrap them tightly if you do). Makes 8 servings/190 cals, 6 g fat per serving

Pumpkin Cheesecake

Prep time: 15 minutes/Bake time: 1 hour 15 minutes
Chill time: at least 8 hours

Not everybody is a born pie baker, but that unavoidable craving for a pumpkin dessert after Thanksgiving dinner simply *must* be satisfied. The solution: Make this rich, spicy pumpkin cheesecake your holiday specialty. Some folks will be even more impressed than if you'd baked a pie (though the best secret of all is that cheesecake is easy to make!). The top of the cake will probably crack at some point during baking—it's something that cheesecakes often do. But after you've spread on the tangy sour-cream topping, no one will be the wiser.

9 ounces vanilla wafers (48 cookies)

4 tablespoons plus 1⅓ cups sugar

4 tablespoons unsalted butter, melted

3 packages (8 ounces each) cream cheese, at room temperature

1 can (15 ounces) unsweetened solid-pack pumpkin

1½ teaspoons vanilla

4 large eggs

1½ teaspoons ground cinnamon

1 teaspoon ground ginger

½ teaspoon ground nutmeg

¼ teaspoon ground allspice

¼ teaspoon salt

1 cup sour cream

1. Preheat oven to 375°F.

2. In food processor, process vanilla wafers and 2 tablespoons sugar until finely ground. Add butter and process until crumbs are thoroughly moistened. Press crumb mixture evenly over bottom and up sides of 9-inch springform pan. Bake crust 10 minutes. Transfer pan to wire rack to cool. Lower oven temperature to 300°F.

3. In large bowl, with electric mixer on medium speed, beat cream cheese and 1⅓ cups sugar until creamy. Beat in pumpkin and vanilla until smooth. Beat in eggs, 1 at a time, beating well after each addition. Beat in cinnamon, ginger, nutmeg, allspice, and salt until well combined. Pour batter into prepared shell.

4. Bake cake 1 hour and 15 minutes, or until set around edges (it will still be slightly wobbly in center). Leave oven on. Set cheesecake on wire rack to cool slightly while you make sour cream topping. (Cheesecake may crack slightly as it sits, but that's O.K.)

5. In small bowl, stir together sour cream and remaining 2 tablespoons sugar. Spread evenly over cheesecake and return to oven for 5 minutes. Set cheesecake on wire rack to cool to room temperature. When completely cool, cover cake and refrigerate at least 8 hours or up to 2 days. Remove sides of springform pan to serve. *Makes 12 servings/510 cals, 33g fat per serving*

True-Blue Berry Tart

Prep time: 30 minutes/Bake time: 35 minutes

Blueberries get sweeter when you cook them; still, it's a shame to lose the tart, sassy freshness of uncooked berries. The best of all possible blueberry desserts, then, will have some of each. This tart—a perfect example—is filled with cooked, sweetened, spiced blueberry filling (with fresh blueberries stirred in) and then topped with some more fresh berries.

Processor Tart Dough (recipe follows)

¾ cup sugar

3 tablespoons cornstarch

1 tablespoon fresh lemon juice

⅛ teaspoon freshly ground black pepper

⅛ teaspoon ground allspice

5½ cups blueberries

1. Preheat oven to 400°F.

2. Make Processor Tart Dough.

3. Transfer dough to 9-inch tart pan with removable bottom. Pinch off small pieces of dough and press them evenly onto sides of pan to form generous ¼-inch-thick edge. Press remaining dough in an even layer over bottom of pan. With fork, prick bottom and sides of tart shell. Line shell with aluminum foil, then fill foil with pie weights or dried beans. "Blind bake" shell 20 minutes (see "Know How," at right). Carefully remove weights or beans and foil and bake shell 10 to 12 minutes more, or until golden brown and set. If at any time edges start to overbrown, cover them lightly with strips of foil. Transfer pan to wire rack and cool shell in pan.

4. In 3-quart nonaluminum saucepan, stir together sugar, cornstarch, lemon juice, pepper, and allspice. Add 2 cups blueberries and cook over medium heat 5 to 7 minutes, or until berries are soft and mixture is thick. Remove pan from heat and stir in 2 cups of remaining berries. Cool filling until warm.

5. Spoon filling evenly into tart shell; top with remaining 1½ cups berries.

6. To serve, remove rim of tart pan (see "The Right Stuff," at right) and transfer tart to serving platter. The tart can also be served chilled. *Makes 8 servings/335 cals, 12g fat per serving*

Processor Tart Dough In food processor, combine 1½ cups flour, 1 tablespoon sugar, ¼ teaspoon salt, and 1 stick (8 tablespoons) cold unsalted butter, cut up, until mixture resembles coarse crumbs, 10 to 15 seconds. Drizzle in 1 to 3 tablespoons cold water and stir with a rubber spatula until dough just comes together; dough should not be wet. *Makes one 9-inch crust, 8 servings/195 cals, 12g fat per serving*

THE RIGHT STUFF

A tart pan with a removable bottom is a must for this recipe. The pan's thin, flat bottom fits neatly (but not tightly) into its rim. To remove the tart for serving, center the pan on a bowl or a can—something a few inches tall with a smaller diameter than the tart pan. Carefully separate the rim from the crust and let the rim fall to the counter.

KNOW HOW

Tart or pie shells are "blind baked" (baked unfilled) when the filling to go in them does not need to cook in the oven. To keep the pastry from puffing up as it blind bakes, the dough is first pricked with a fork, and then weighted down. You can use things called pie weights—aluminum or ceramic pebbles sold for this purpose—or you can use dried beans, or even rice. Once you've used the rice or beans, save them to use the next time you blind bake.

Lime Tarts with Raspberries

Prep time: 30 minutes/Chill time: 1 hour/Bake time: 20 minutes

Making homemade puff pastry is something to save for your next lifetime. But while you're waiting, frozen puff pastry from the supermarket will do fine. This recipe makes two tarts so that you can use up the whole package (two sheets of pastry) at once. If you'd rather make only one tart, save the extra Lime Curd for spreading on hot toast (a decadent breakfast), folding into whipped cream (instant lime mousse), or spooning onto a bowl of berries (sheer ecstasy). The Lime Curd keeps for a week in the refrigerator.

Lime Curd (recipe follows)

1 box (17¼ ounces) frozen puff pastry (2 sheets, about 9 x 10 inches each)

1 egg beaten with 1 teaspoon water

1 pint fresh raspberries

Use a ruler and a sharp knife to cut four ½-inch-wide strips from the pastry sheet.

1. Make Lime Curd and refrigerate until needed to assemble the tarts.

2. Preheat oven to 375°F. Line baking sheet with parchment paper.

3. Unfold the sheets of puff pastry. On lightly floured surface, using sharp knife and ruler, cut off 4 strips, ½ inch wide, from one long side of each puff pastry sheet. You should have two 7 x 10-inch rectangles. Place the rectangles side by side on a large baking sheet.

4. Make the borders of the tarts (see photos, at right): Moisten long edges of each pastry rectangle with water (use your finger; you only want to wet it a little). Place a strip of dough along each long edge and press lightly to adhere. Moisten short ends of rectangles and place strips along edges, overlapping the first set of strips, and overhanging an even amount on each side. Roll up the overhanging pieces (see bottom photo, at right) and secure with toothpicks. Brush the entire surface of the tarts with the beaten egg mixture (be careful not to let any drip down the sides of the dough or it will keep the dough from puffing).

Lightly moisten the edges of the pastry sheets and place the strips on them to form borders.

5. Bake 20 minutes, or until pastry is golden brown and crisp in the center. Check occasionally and prick any places that are puffing up. Transfer tart shells to wire racks to cool. (You can make the tart shells well ahead of time.)

6. Just before serving, fill each rectangle with Lime Curd, then arrange raspberries decoratively on top. With serrated knife, cut each tart crosswise into 4 rectangles. Serve at once. *Makes 2 tarts, 4 servings each/580 cals, 39g fat per serving*

Lime Curd In large bowl, combine 3 whole eggs, 3 egg yolks, 1 stick (8 tablespoons) unsalted butter, cut up, ⅔ cup sugar, 1 teaspoon grated lime zest, and ½ cup fresh lime juice. Set over pan of simmering water and cook, whisking constantly, 7 to 10 minutes, or until mixture is thick enough to heavily coat the back of a spoon. Remove bowl from pan and immediately transfer mixture to another large bowl (for a really smooth curd, pour it into bowl through a strainer). Cool mixture to room temperature. Store refrigerated; cover with sheet of plastic wrap pressed directly onto the surface to keep a skin from forming. *Makes 2 cups/220 cals, 15g fat per ¼ cup*

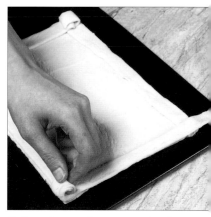

Roll up the overhanging ends of the strips of dough; they'll form decorative curls when baked.

◄ *A triple-whammy indulgence: fresh raspberries, rich lime curd, and buttery puff pastry.*

In a pinch

You don't have to stick with the apples listed in the pie recipe. There are lots of different apple varieties available these days, with a range of tartness and firmness. Experiment with different apples: If possible, use more than one type in the pie so you get some textural and sweetness differences.

THE **RIGHT** STUFF

These inexpensive baking accessories, often sold as a set, will help get you "rolling." The pastry cloth (you roll out the dough on it) is lightweight canvas. The slip-on rolling-pin cover is made of a stretchy mesh fabric called stockinette. When both are lightly floured, they do a good job of keeping the dough from sticking.

All-American Deep-Dish Apple Pie

Prep time: 30 minutes/Bake time: 1 hour

Three different kinds of apples give this pie unique appeal. The firm Granny Smith wedges hold their shape when baked; the Golden Delicious apple slices soften but don't break down; and the Macs practically turn into applesauce.

Two-Crust Pie Dough (recipe follows)

½ cup sugar

¼ cup flour

1 teaspoon ground cinnamon

3 large Granny Smith apples (about 1½ pounds)

3 large Golden Delicious apples (about 1¼ pounds)

3 large McIntosh apples (about 1 pound)

2 tablespoons fresh lemon juice

⅔ cup golden raisins

1. Make Two-Crust Pie Dough. Refrigerate as directed but remove dough from refrigerator to stand at room temperature 5 to 10 minutes before rolling.

2. Preheat oven to 425°F. Line baking sheet with aluminum foil.

3. Work with 1 disk of dough at a time. On lightly floured surface, with floured rolling pin, roll dough into 13-inch round. Fit dough into 9-inch deep-dish pie plate. With scissors, trim overhang to ¾ inch.

4. In small bowl, thoroughly blend sugar, flour, and cinnamon. Peel all the apples and cut them into 1-inch-thick wedges. Place wedges in large bowl and toss with lemon juice. Add sugar mixture and raisins and toss well. Arrange apple filling in pie plate, mounding apples in the center.

5. On lightly floured surface, with floured rolling pin, roll remaining dough disk into 13-inch round. Center round over apples in pie plate. With scissors, trim edge of top crust, leaving ¾-inch overhang. Turn edges of top and bottom crusts under to make them even with the edge of the pie plate. Decoratively crimp the pie edge to seal (see technique, page 17). With sharp knife, cut several slashes in middle of top crust to act as steam vents. Transfer pie to lined baking sheet.

6. Bake pie 15 minutes. Reduce oven heat to 375°F and bake pie 45 minutes more, or until crust is golden brown and apples are bubbly. (If the crust begins to over-brown, loosely tent with a piece of foil.) Transfer pie to wire rack. Let cool slightly before serving. *Makes 8 servings/530 cals, 21g fat per serving*

Two-Crust Pie Dough In large bowl, stir together 2¼ cups flour, 2 tablespoons sugar, and ¾ teaspoon salt. With pastry blender or 2 knives, cut in 1 stick (8 table-spoons) cold unsalted butter, cut up, and ⅓ cup chilled solid vegetable shortening until mixture resembles coarse crumbs. Sprinkle on ⅓ cup cold water and with fork toss until mixture just comes together and forms a ball. (Add additional water only if mixture is very dry and crumbly.) Divide dough in half and flatten each half into a disk. Wrap each disk in plastic wrap and refrigerate at least 1 hour or up to overnight. *Makes one 9-inch double crust, 8 servings/315 cals, 20g fat per serving*

Lemon Pudding Cakes

Prep time: 25 minutes/Bake time: 40 minutes

Doesn't the dessert world seem to divide into the chocoholics and the citrus addicts? Well, here's one for the lemon faction. As these rich cakelets bake, the batter magi-cally separates into two layers: A delicate cake layer rises to the top, and a rich, very lemony custard sauce forms on the bottom.

4 teaspoons unsalted butter, at room temperature	3 tablespoons flour
¾ cup sugar	1 cup milk
2 large eggs, separated	2 tablespoons sour cream
1 large egg yolk	1 teaspoon vanilla
1 teaspoon grated lemon zest	¼ teaspoon salt
⅓ cup fresh lemon juice	Confectioners' sugar (optional)

1. Preheat oven to 350°F. Grease six 6-ounce custard cups; transfer cups to a deep baking pan or small roasting pan.

2. In small bowl, with electric mixer on medium speed, cream butter and ½ cup sugar until well combined. Beat in the 3 egg yolks, lemon zest, lemon juice, and flour until smooth. Gradually beat in milk, sour cream, and vanilla until well combined.

3. In another small bowl, with electric mixer, beat egg whites and salt until foamy. (Be sure you use *clean* beaters for this, since any fat from the egg-yolk mixture will keep the egg whites from beating properly.) Gradually beat in remaining ¼ cup sugar until soft peaks form. Gently stir one-quarter of whites into lemon batter to lighten it; then, with rubber spatula, fold remaining whites into remaining lemon batter.

4. Divide batter among custard cups. Transfer pan to middle rack of oven and pour hot water into pan to come 1 inch up sides of cups. Bake 35 to 40 minutes, or until cakes have puffed and are golden brown on top (the bottom layer will look wet, because it's a sauce). Remove cups from water bath to wire rack to cool. Serve warm, at room temperature, or chilled.

5. Before serving, dust pudding cakes with confectioners' sugar if desired. *Makes 6 servings/230 cals, 10g fat per serving*

Lime Pudding Cakes Follow the above recipe but substitute lime juice and zest for the lemon juice and zest. *Makes 6 servings/230 cals, 10g fat per serving*

KNOW HOW

As you roll pie dough out, be sure to stop every once in a while and give the pastry round a quarter-turn. This not only helps in rolling out an even round, it also serves as a check that the dough is not sticking to the work surface.

KNOW HOW

Delicate desserts like custards (or these pudding cakes) are often baked in a water bath—called a *bain marie* in classical French cooking—which protects them from the uneven heat of the oven. The water diffuses the heat so that the desserts cook slowly and evenly. The best way to set up a water bath is to put the roasting pan (and custard cups) on the oven rack before you add the hot water. This way you don't have to carry a sloshing pan across the kitchen.

Mochaccino Mousse Pie

Prep time: 25 minutes/Cook time: 30 minutes/Chill time: 2 hours

The classic chocolate cream pie takes a trip to the espresso bar for a jolt of coffee in both the filling and the whipped-cream topping.

Chocolate Crumb Crust (recipe follows)

1⅔ cups milk

6 ounces (6 squares) semisweet chocolate, chopped

⅔ cup sugar

2 teaspoons instant espresso powder

¼ teaspoon salt

4 large egg yolks

1½ teaspoons unflavored gelatin

¾ cup well-chilled heavy or whipping cream

1 teaspoon vanilla

Espresso Whipped Cream (recipe follows)

1. Make Chocolate Crumb Crust; set aside.

2. In 2-quart saucepan, heat 1⅓ cups milk and chocolate over low heat, stirring until chocolate has melted.

3. In medium bowl, whisk together sugar, espresso powder, and salt. Whisk in egg yolks until well combined. Pour about ½ cup chocolate mixture into yolk mixture in bowl and whisk to combine. Pour yolk mixture into pan and whisk over medium-low heat 15 minutes, or until thick enough to coat back of spoon. Remove pan from heat.

4. In small bowl, sprinkle gelatin over remaining ⅓ cup milk; let stand 5 minutes, or until softened. Return saucepan to low heat, stir in softened gelatin, and whisk 2 minutes until gelatin has dissolved. Remove pan from heat and pour mixture into a medium bowl set in a larger bowl of ice water. Whisk occasionally until thickened to consistency of thick cake batter.

5. Meanwhile, with electric mixer, beat cream until stiff peaks form. Beat in vanilla. Fold whipped cream into semi-chilled mousse. Pour mousse into pie shell and smooth top. Refrigerate pie 2 hours, or until filling is set. Just before serving, make Espresso Whipped Cream. Spread over top of pie and serve chilled. *Makes 8 servings/650 cals, 44g fat per serving*

Chocolate Crumb Crust Preheat oven to 375°F. Grease 9-inch deep-dish pie plate. In food processor, process 1 box (9 ounces) chocolate wafers, 2 tablespoons sugar, and 1 teaspoon instant espresso powder until finely ground. Add 6 tablespoons melted unsalted butter and process until crumbs are thoroughly moistened. Press mixture evenly over bottom and up sides of pie plate. Bake crust 12 minutes. Cool on wire rack. *Makes one 9-inch crust, 8 servings/230 cals, 14g fat per serving*

Espresso Whipped Cream In cup or small bowl, dissolve 1½ teaspoons instant espresso powder in 1½ teaspoons hot water; let cool to room temperature. Add cooled coffee mixture to 1 cup well-chilled heavy or whipping cream and beat until soft peaks form. Beat in 2 tablespoons confectioners' sugar. *Makes 2 cups/30 cals/3g fat per tablespoon*

Let's have another cup of coffee—or better yet, another slice of this extravagant mocha cream pie.

Different Spins

Disassemble this pie and you have the beginnings of a bunch of other desserts: Make the crust and fill it with softened ice cream. Or make the whipped cream to go with brownies. Or make the mousse and spoon it into a dessert glass (O.K., maybe add some whipped cream).

KNOW HOW

Here's a neat way to form the cookie-crumb mixture into a perfect crust: Spread the crumbs more or less evenly around the bottom and sides of the pie plate. Then place a second pie plate on top, and press gently to make an even layer.

Almond-Orange Biscotti

Prep time: 20 minutes/Bake time: 50 minutes

Ultra-crisp Italian biscotti are enjoying a renaissance—maybe because they go so well with coffee, which has become an American mania! These double-baked cookies (*biscotti* means "twice-cooked") are meant to be dipped into hot or cold drinks, or, *alla Italiana,* into a glass of sweet dessert wine.

Form each portion of dough into a rough log on the baking sheet, then pat it out into a 3 x 11-inch "loaf."

2 cups flour	2 large eggs
½ teaspoon baking powder	2 teaspoons grated orange zest
½ teaspoon baking soda	1 tablespoon Cointreau, Grand Marnier, or other orange liqueur
¼ teaspoon salt	
1 stick (8 tablespoons) unsalted butter, at room temperature	¾ cup whole natural (unblanched) almonds
¾ cup sugar	

1. Preheat oven to 350°F. Grease and flour large cookie sheet.
2. In medium bowl, stir together flour, baking powder, baking soda, and salt.
3. In large bowl, with electric mixer on medium speed, cream butter and sugar until light and fluffy. Beat in eggs, 1 at a time, beating well after each addition. Beat in orange zest and Cointreau. Stir in flour mixture and almonds until dough comes together.
4. With floured hands, divide dough in half. Shape each half into a log roughly 11 inches long and place logs on baking sheet with 3 inches between them. Pat into 3-inch-wide loaves. Bake 30 minutes, or until dough is firm to touch. Transfer loaves to cutting board.
5. With serrated knife, cut each loaf crosswise on diagonal into ½-inch-thick slices. (There is no need to let logs cool.) Arrange slices in one layer on cookie sheet. Return to oven and bake for 10 minutes. Turn biscotti over and bake another 10 minutes. Transfer biscotti to wire racks to cool. Store in layers in airtight container.   *Makes 3 dozen biscotti/85 cals, 4g fat per biscotti*

After baking, while the loaves are still warm, cut each into ½-inch-thick diagonal slices. You'll get about 18 slices per loaf.

Banana-Chocolate Crunch

Prep time: 15 minutes/Bake time: 45 minutes

Ah, the incredible, edible, buttery, streusel-y crunch bar. Sigh. We wish we didn't like these so much, because if no one were looking we'd eat the whole batch.

1 cup old-fashioned oats	6 tablespoons cold unsalted butter, cut up
1 cup packed light brown sugar	
½ cup flour	½ cup chopped pecans
¼ teaspoon salt	2 bananas
	⅓ cup semisweet chocolate chips

These almond-studded biscotti are technically for dunking, but they're also perfect with ice cream or pudding.

1. Preheat oven to 350°F. Lightly grease 8-inch square metal baking pan.

2. In large bowl, combine oats, ⅔ cup brown sugar, flour, and salt. With pastry blender or 2 knives, cut in butter until mixture resembles coarse crumbs. Stir in pecans.

3. Spread half of crumb mixture evenly over bottom of baking pan, pressing it gently into corners. Dice bananas and scatter them and chocolate chips over crust. Sprinkle with remaining ⅓ cup brown sugar and top with remaining crumb mixture.

4. Bake 40 to 45 minutes, or until top is golden brown and begins to pull away from sides of pan. Transfer pan to rack to cool 20 minutes. Cut into 8 equal bars and serve while still warm. *Makes 8 bars/355 cals, 16g fat per bar*

Pineapple-Coconut Crunch Make crumb mixture and press it into pan as directed (through beginning of step 3). Omit bananas and chocolate chips and replace with 1 can (8 ounces) crushed pineapple in juice, well drained, and ¼ cup sweetened flaked coconut. Top pineapple-coconut layer with remaining sugar, then crumb mixture. Bake and cool as directed. *Makes 8 bars/325 cals, 15g fat per bar*

Different Spins

The crunch recipe is an easy one to play with. Just think of some other (not-too-wet) ingredients that would taste good sandwiched between layers of butter-pecan crumbs, such as: milk chocolate • chopped dried fruit (like apricots or pears) • fresh blueberries • chopped white chocolate • fresh cranberries • sliced apples or pears.

Pecan Shortbread

Prep time: 25 minutes/Bake time: 40 minutes

The cornstarch and confectioners' sugar ensure a smooth, melt-in-your-mouth shortbread. The dough is baked in a round pan and then cut into the long wedges traditionally called "petticoat tails." If you prefer shortbread bars to wedges, pat the dough into a 9-inch square pan and score it into squares or rectangles.

¾ cup flour

⅓ cup cornstarch

½ teaspoon salt

1 stick (8 tablespoons) unsalted butter, at room temperature

½ cup confectioners' sugar

1 teaspoon vanilla

½ cup pecans, finely chopped

1. Preheat oven to 325°F.
2. In medium bowl, stir together flour, cornstarch, and salt.
3. In large bowl, with electric mixer on medium speed, cream butter and sugar until light and fluffy. Beat in vanilla. Stir in pecans. Stir in dry ingredients just until combined (dough may still be crumbly).
4. Transfer dough to 9-inch round cake pan. Cover dough with piece of plastic wrap; with your fingers, press dough through plastic wrap into an even smooth layer, reaching to edges of pan. Score dough into 12 wedges, cutting all the way through. With fork, prick dough all over. Bake 40 minutes, or until pale golden and firm to the touch.
5. Transfer pan to wire rack to cool, but cut the scored shortbread into wedges while still warm. *Makes 12 servings/160 cals, 11g fat per serving*

Apricot-Topped Shortbread Bars Prepare Pecan Shortbread through step 4 with the following changes: Use a 9-inch square metal baking pan and do not score the dough. Bake for only 35 minutes. While the shortbread is baking, in small saucepan, bring 1 cup (6 ounces) dried apricots and 1¼ cups water to a boil over medium heat. Reduce to a simmer, cover, and cook 25 minutes, or until apricots are very tender. With wooden spoon (or an immersible blender), mash apricots until pureed. Stir in ½ cup firmly packed light brown sugar, 2 lightly beaten eggs, ¼ cup flour, ½ teaspoon baking powder, ¼ teaspoon salt, and ½ teaspoon vanilla until well combined. Spread apricot mixture evenly over baked shortbread. Increase oven temperature to 350°F, return shortbread to oven, and bake 35 minutes, or until topping is set. Cool in pan on a rack. Cut into 16 squares. *Makes 16 servings/190 cals, 9g fat per serving*

Different Spins

Here's a variation that's sometimes called Millionaire's Shortbread because it's s-o-o-o-o rich! When the shortbread is baked and still warm, cover the top with squares of milk or dark chocolate (from thin chocolate bars). When they melt, spread the chocolate into a smooth layer. Cool until the chocolate has set, then cut the shortbread into wedges.

THE **RIGHT** STUFF

Shortbread's predominant flavor comes from the generous amount of butter that goes into it. So be sure to use unsalted butter, preferred by bakers for its fresh, sweet flavor. (And for heaven's sake, don't substitute margarine or vegetable shortening in this recipe!) If you stock up when butter is on sale—a wise move— remember that it readily picks up flavors from other foods: Refrigerate or freeze the sticks in their original box, overwrapped in foil or a tightly sealed plastic bag.

Chocolate-Chip Saucer Cookies

Prep time: 25 minutes/Chill time: 3 hours/Bake time: 30 minutes

One to a customer, please! At 5 inches across, one of these mega-cookies makes a generous dessert (especially if you top it with a scoop of ice cream and a drizzle of Chocolate Sauce Supreme or Butterscotch Sauce, both on page 153). They make great gifts, too, individually wrapped in colored cellophane and tied with ribbons. Maybe you could include a jar of one of the dessert sauces while you're at it.

1⅔ cups flour

¾ teaspoon baking powder

½ teaspoon baking soda

¼ teaspoon salt

1 stick (8 tablespoons) unsalted butter, at room temperature

⅓ cup chunky peanut butter

½ cup firmly packed light brown sugar

½ cup granulated sugar

2 large eggs

1½ teaspoons vanilla

1 package (12 ounces) semisweet chocolate chips

1 cup coarsely chopped salted peanuts

1. In medium bowl, stir together flour, baking powder, baking soda, and salt.

2. In large bowl, with electric mixer on medium speed, cream butter, peanut butter, brown sugar, and granulated sugar until light and fluffy. Beat in eggs, 1 at a time, beating well after each addition. Beat in vanilla.

3. With mixer on low speed, beat in dry ingredients. Stir in chocolate chips and peanuts. Wrap dough in plastic wrap and refrigerate about 3 hours or up to overnight, until well chilled.

4. Preheat oven to 350°F. Line 2 large cookie sheets with aluminum foil. Grease and flour foil.

5. Measure out dough in ½ cupfuls (see "Know How," at right) and place on cookie sheets, leaving 2 inches between them. Flatten dough into 4-inch rounds. You'll be able to fit about 5 cookies on each cookie sheet.

6. Bake 15 minutes. Reverse cookie sheets on oven racks, moving top sheet to bottom and bottom sheet to top. Bake 10 to 15 minutes longer, or until cookies are firm to touch and browned around edges. Cool 5 minutes on baking sheets, then with large metal spatula, transfer to wire racks to cool completely. *Makes 10 cookies/550 cals, 31g fat per cookie*

Different Spins

You probably came up with some variations on our saucer cookies in the time it took to read the recipe. If not, ponder the following alternative "add-ins": walnuts, pecans, hazelnuts, or macadamias; mini, maxi, mint, milk chocolate, peanut butter, or butterscotch chips; chopped chocolate bars or peanut-butter cups; raisins. And sure, make the cookies smaller if you must!

KNOW HOW

Here's how to measure perfect ½-cup amounts of cookie dough. Line a ½-cup measure with plastic wrap. Fill cup with dough, packing it in. Then drop it onto the baking pan and peel off the plastic. (Flatten the mound of dough out as directed.) This works for smaller cookies, too; just change the size of the measuring cup used (duh).

Mango Mousse

Prep time: 20 minutes/Cook time: 5 minutes/Chill time: at least 3 hours

In a pinch

Peaches or nectarines—perfectly ripe ones, of course—can stand in for the mangoes. You'll need about 1½ pounds of fruit (3 large or 4 medium) to make 2 cups of puree. If you use peaches, you'll have to peel them first. Use the same blanching technique as for peeling tomatoes (see page 12).

In our humble opinion, many exotic tropical fruits are just sweet and nothing more. But the mango is an exception. It is tart-sweet, with a lush texture and a flavor reminiscent of . . . of . . . mango. There's nothing like it.

2½ pounds mangoes (2 large or 3 medium)

¼ cup honey

3 tablespoons fresh lemon juice

1 envelope unflavored gelatin

⅓ cup well-chilled heavy or whipping cream

2 teaspoons sugar

½ teaspoon vanilla

Whipped cream, mango cubes, and mint leaves for garnish (optional)

1. Cut flesh from mango pits (see technique, page 9). Transfer to food processor or blender, add honey and lemon juice, and puree until smooth.

2. In small heatproof cup, sprinkle gelatin over ¼ cup water; let stand 5 minutes until softened. Set cup in small pan with enough simmering water to come 1 inch up sides of cup and heat gently about 3 minutes, or until gelatin has dissolved. Add gelatin to mango puree and process until well combined. Transfer puree to large bowl.

Serve Mango Mousse in high style with a cloud of whipped cream, bright cubes of mango, a crisp cookie, and a jaunty mint leaf.

3. In small bowl, with electric mixer on medium speed, beat cream until foamy. Add and beat to soft peaks. Beat in vanilla. Fold whipped cream into mango puree. Divide mousse among 4 goblets or wineglasses, cover, and refrigerate at least 3 hours, or until set and well chilled.

4. At serving time, garnish with whipped cream, mango cubes, and mint leaves if desired. *Makes 4 servings/305 cals, 12g fat per serving*

Panna Cotta

Prep time: 10 minutes/Cook time: 10 minutes/Chill time: at least 4 hours

This Italian classic is called "cooked cream," but we've lightened it up a little by using mostly milk. Serve these molded custards with fresh fruit, a sauce, or both. And if you're really feeling ambitious, make crisp cookies (like the Almond-Orange Biscotti on page 162) to go with it.

4 cups milk	1 whole vanilla bean, split lengthwise, or 2 teaspoons vanilla extract
2 cups heavy or whipping cream	
1 cup sugar	⅛ teaspoon salt
4 strips (2 x ½ inch each) orange zest	2 envelopes unflavored gelatin
4 strips (2 x ½ inch each) lemon zest	

1. In 3-quart saucepan, stir together 2 cups milk, cream, sugar, orange and lemon zests, vanilla bean (do not add extract here), and salt and bring to gentle simmer over low heat. Remove from heat, cover, and let steep 15 minutes.

2. Meanwhile, pour remaining 2 cups milk into small bowl. Sprinkle gelatin over milk and let stand 5 minutes, until softened.

3. Stir softened gelatin into cream mixture and bring to a boil over medium heat, stirring, until gelatin is dissolved. Strain mixture through fine-meshed sieve into pitcher or large glass measuring cup with spout. Stir in extract here, if using. Reserve vanilla bean if desired (see "The Right Stuff," page 146). Pour mixture into eight 6-ounce custard cups (or ramekins). Cover and refrigerate until chilled and firmed up, at least 4 hours.

4. Serve in custard cups or run knife around edge of each cup and invert panna cotta onto dessert plates. *Makes 8 servings/385 cals, 26g fat per serving*

Chocolate Panna Cotta Omit lemon zest. Add 4 ounces (4 squares) semisweet chocolate (or ¾ cup semisweet chocolate chips) to cream mixture in step 1. Cook over low heat, whisking, until chocolate is melted. Proceed with recipe as directed. *Makes 8 servings/455 cals, 30g fat per serving*

Espresso Panna Cotta After adding softened gelatin to cream mixture in step 3, stir in 2 tablespoons instant espresso powder; whisk until dissolved. Proceed with recipe as directed. *Makes 8 servings/390 cals, 26g fat per serving*

Show Off

Choose a Dessert Sauce (page 153), grab a squeeze bottle, and paint that plate! Mix and match flavors: plain (vanilla) Panna Cotta with Butterscotch Sauce, Chocolate Panna Cotta with Raspberry Sauce, Espresso Panna Cotta with Chocolate.

Pour the sauce into a squeeze bottle like the ones used for mustard or ketchup. Scribble, swirl, or sketch a pattern.

Turn the chilled panna cotta out onto the painted plate and garnish with fresh berries.

Ice Cream Puffs

Although a pastry bag is definitely a useful tool, it is not an absolute necessity for piping large things like cream puffs. You can use a heavy-duty plastic bag instead (see bottom photo).

Use a pastry bag with no tip to squeeze 2-inch dollops of dough onto the pan.

A heavy-duty plastic freezer bag can serve as a pastry bag. Cut off enough of one of the corners to leave a ½-inch-diameter opening, then pipe the dough through the opening.

Prep time: 25 minutes/Bake time: 50 minutes/Freeze time: 2 hours

There are two kinds of pastry that "puff," and this one, you'll be glad to know, is the easy kind, the one the French call *pâte à choux* (pronounced "pot-a-shoe"). It is the dough used to make éclairs, cream puffs, and mini cream puffs (also called profiteroles). Cream puff dough is put together in a most unusual way. You begin by heating butter and water in a saucepan and dumping flour into the pan all at once. Then you add eggs, which instantly change the dough into a slithery mess (if we didn't warn you, you might think you'd made a horrible mistake at this point). But rest assured, it all eventually comes together. And when the baked puffs "puff," as they are supposed to, you will have earned major bragging rights.

¼ teaspoon salt

1 stick (8 tablespoons) unsalted butter, cut up

1 cup flour

4 large eggs

1½ pints coffee ice cream, softened

Chocolate Sauce Supreme (page 153)

½ cup sliced almonds, toasted

1. Preheat oven to 425°F. Line 2 large cookie sheets with aluminum foil or parchment paper.

2. In 2-quart saucepan, bring 1 cup water and salt to a boil over medium heat. Add butter and heat until melted. Remove pan from heat and add flour all at once, stirring to combine. Return pan to heat and cook, stirring, until dough forms a ball and leaves sides of pan.

3. Remove pan from heat. Add eggs, 1 at a time, beating vigorously with a wooden spoon to incorporate each egg. (Do not add another egg until previous one is well incorporated.) Beat in final egg and continue to beat until mixture is smooth.

4. Spoon half the dough into large pastry bag that is not fitted with a tip. Pipe 2-inch mounds, 2 inches apart, onto one cookie sheet. (You will have 12 mounds.) Pipe 12 more mounds with remaining dough onto second cookie sheet.

5. Bake 20 minutes. Reverse cookie sheets on oven racks, moving top sheet to bottom and bottom sheet to top. Reduce heat to 350°F and bake 20 minutes longer. Without removing cookie sheets from oven, with a small paring knife, poke a hole in the side of each puff. Bake 5 minutes more. Remove sheets from oven, transfer them to wire racks, and cool puffs completely.

6. With serrated knife, cut top third off each puff. Remove and discard any soft dough inside, leaving a hollow shell. Spoon 2 tablespoons ice cream into bottom of each puff and replace tops. Transfer filled puffs to a cookie sheet and freeze until ice cream is firm, about 2 hours.

7. Make Chocolate Sauce Supreme and keep warm. To serve, place 3 cream puffs on each plate, drizzle with warm chocolate sauce, and garnish with almonds. *Makes 8 servings/440 cals, 29g fat per serving*

appendix & glossary

EMERGENCY SUBSTITUTIONS

Ingredient	Emergency Substitution
ANCHOVY FILLET, 1	1 teaspoon anchovy paste
BAKING POWDER, 1 TEASPOON	¼ teaspoon baking soda plus a scant ¾ teaspoon cream of tartar
BREAD CRUMBS, DRY, 1 CUP	¾ cup finely ground cracker crumbs
BUTTERMILK, 1 CUP	1 cup plain yogurt or 1 tablespoon white vinegar or lemon juice stirred into 1 cup whole milk and left to stand 5 minutes until curdled
BROTH (CHICKEN OR BEEF), 1 CUP	1 bouillon cube dissolved in 1 cup boiling water
CHILI SAUCE	Ketchup with a dash of hot pepper sauce or chili powder
CHILIES, MILD, CANNED	Sautéed green bell pepper plus a dash of chili powder or cayenne pepper
CHOCOLATE, SEMISWEET, 1 OUNCE (FOR BAKING)	½ ounce unsweetened chocolate plus 1 tablespoon granulated sugar
CHOCOLATE, UNSWEETENED, 1 OUNCE	3 tablespoons unsweetened cocoa powder plus 1 tablespoon butter
CORNSTARCH, 1 TABLESPOON (FOR THICKENING)	2 tablespoons flour
CREAM, HEAVY, 1 CUP (NOT FOR WHIPPING)	¾ cup whole milk plus ⅓ cup melted butter
CREAM, SOUR, 1 CUP (FOR BAKING)	1 cup plain yogurt plus ⅓ cup butter, melted and cooled
EGGS, WHOLE, 2 (FOR LOW-FAT OMELETS)	1 whole egg plus 2 egg whites
FLOUR, CAKE (SIFTED), 1 CUP	1 cup minus 2 tablespoons sifted all-purpose flour
FLOUR, 2 TABLESPOONS (FOR THICKENING)	1 tablespoon cornstarch
GARLIC CLOVE, 1 SMALL	⅛ teaspoon garlic powder
HERBS, FRESH, 1 TABLESPOON MINCED	1 scant teaspoon dried
HONEY, 1 CUP	1¼ cups sugar plus ¼ cup water
LEMON JUICE, 1 TEASPOON	½ teaspoon vinegar
MILK, WHOLE, 1 CUP (FOR BAKING)	1 cup skim milk plus 2 tablespoons melted butter
MUSTARD, DRY, 1 TEASPOON	1 tablespoon prepared mustard
SUGAR, CONFECTIONERS', 1 CUP	2 cups granulated white sugar ground to a powder in a food processor
SUGAR, LIGHT BROWN, 1 CUP	½ cup dark brown sugar plus ½ cup granulated sugar
SUGAR, GRANULATED, 1 CUP	1¾ cups confectioners' sugar or 1 cup packed light brown sugar
TOMATO SAUCE, 1 CUP	½ cup tomato paste plus ½ cup water
TOMATOES, 1 CAN (16 OUNCES)	2½ cups chopped peeled fresh tomatoes simmered for 10 minutes
VANILLA BEAN, 1	1 teaspoon vanilla extract

Vegetable Cooking Chart

The simplest way to serve most cooked vegetables is to top them with a little butter and/or a squeeze of fresh lemon juice, along with salt and freshly ground pepper. Or, try a splash of good extra-virgin olive oil. Should you feel like something fancier, any one of the sauces and dressings at right works very nicely, too.

Vegetable Sauces

VEGETABLE	AMOUNT & PREP	METHOD
ARTICHOKES	4 medium, trimmed & tough stems removed, lower leaves removed	**To Boil:** 20–40 minutes, until artichoke heart can be easily pierced with knife
ASPARAGUS	1 lb, ends trimmed & peeled (optional)	**To Boil:** 3–5 minutes, depending on size of stalk, until tender, in skillet of boiling water **To Grill:** 4 minutes, in hinged basket or on grill topper over moderate heat **To Steam:** 3–4 minutes, until tender
BEANS (GREEN & WAX)	1 lb, trimmed	**To Boil:** 3–5 minutes, depending on size, until crisp-tender **To Steam:** 3–5 minutes, until crisp-tender
BEETS	1 bunch, tops removed, leaving 1-inch stem, scrubbed well	**To Boil:** 30–40 minutes, until fork-tender; cool & peel before serving **To Roast:** 1½–2 hours, until fork-tender, on baking sheet in preheated 400°F oven; peel and slice
BROCCOLI	1 head (1½ lbs), cut into florets	**To Boil:** 5–8 minutes, until crisp-tender **To Steam:** 5–7 minutes, until crisp-tender
BRUSSELS SPROUTS	1 lb, stem end & tough outer leaves removed, if necessary	**To Boil:** 7–10 minutes, just until tender
CABBAGE	1 head (1 lb), cored & quartered	**To Boil:** 10–15 minutes, until tender **To Steam:** 10–15 minutes, until tender
CARROTS	1 lb, peeled & sliced ¼ inch thick	**To Boil:** 3–4 minutes, until tender **To Steam:** 3–4 minutes, until tender
CAULIFLOWER	1 head (1½ lbs), cut into florets	**To Boil:** 3–6 minutes, until crisp-tender **To Steam:** 3–5 minutes, until crisp-tender
CELERY	1 whole head, trimmed and separated into stalks	**To Braise:** Cook in 2 tablespoons melted butter, covered, 10–15 minutes, or until tender

VEGETABLE	AMOUNT & PREP	METHOD
CORN	4 ears, husks removed	To Grill: 8–15 minutes, turning until tender To Boil: Place ears in large pot of boiling water. Cover pot, bring water back to boil and turn off heat. Let corn stand 5 minutes, then remove
EGGPLANT	1 lb (ends removed), sliced ½ inch thick	To Grill: 4–6 minutes per side, until tender, in hinged grill basket or on grill topper over moderate heat
ENDIVE	8 small heads, core ends removed	To Braise: Sauté in 2 tablespoons melted butter, covered, 15 minutes, or until tender
FENNEL	1 bulb (1 lb), trimmed & quartered	To Roast: 20 minutes, turning, until crisp-tender, in preheated 400°F oven
GREENS (BEET, COLLARD, MUSTARD & TURNIP)	1 lb, trimmed & very well rinsed; chopped if large	To Boil: 10–15 minutes, until tender
LEEKS	4 medium, root ends removed, split lengthwise & rinsed well	To Boil: 10–15 minutes, until just tender, in large skillet of boiling water To Grill: 5–10 minutes, turning, until tender, in hinged grill basket or on grill topper, over moderate heat
MUSHROOMS (BUTTON)	1 package (10 oz), stemmed & wiped clean	To Sauté: 3–5 minutes in 2 tablespoons oil or butter, until softened and liquid has evaporated
MUSHROOMS (PORTOBELLO)	4, stemmed & wiped clean	To Grill: 5 minutes per side, brushing with olive oil, until tender, in hinged grill basket or on grill topper over moderate heat
ONIONS (YELLOW & RED)	2 lbs, peeled & sliced ¼ inch thick	To Grill: 4–8 minutes per side, until tender, in hinged grill basket or on grill topper over moderate heat
ONIONS (SMALL WHITE)	1 lb, peeled	To Boil: 10–35 minutes (depending on size), until tender
PARSNIPS	1 lb, peeled & sliced ½ inch thick	To Roast: 20–30 minutes, until tender, on baking sheet in preheated 350°F oven
PEAS (GREEN)	1 lb, shelled	To Boil: 3–5 minutes, until just tender, in saucepan of boiling water; drain well before serving
PEAS (SNOW PEAS)	1 lb, strings removed	To Steam: 2–3 minutes, until crisp-tender
PEAS (SUGAR SNAP)	1 lb, strings removed	To Steam: 2–3 minutes, until crisp-tender
PEPPERS (BELL)	4 whole, cut lengthwise into wide pieces, seeds removed	To Grill: 6–8 minutes per side, until tender, over moderate heat
POTATOES (ALL-PURPOSE)	2 lbs, peeled (optional) & quartered	To Bake: 20–30 minutes, until tender, in preheated 350°F oven To Boil: 20 minutes, until fork-tender
POTATOES (BOILING)	2 lbs, peeled (optional) & quartered	To Roast: 20–30 minutes, tossed in olive oil, on baking sheet in preheated 375°F oven.

VEGETABLE	AMOUNT & PREP	METHOD
POTATOES (BOILING, cont'd)	2 lbs, peeled (optional) & quartered	**To Boil:** 20 minutes, until fork-tender
POTATOES (BAKING)	4 whole, scrubbed and pricked with fork	**To Bake:** 50–60 minutes until tender, in preheated 400°F oven.
PUMPKIN (SUGAR)	1 small, halved, seeds & strings removed	**To Bake:** 40–45 minutes, until tender, on baking sheet in preheated 350°F oven; scrape flesh from shell & mash
RUTABAGA	1½ lbs, peeled & sliced	**To Boil:** 7–10 minutes, until tender; drain, then mash
SCALLIONS	1 bunch (6 to 8 medium), root ends trimmed	**To Grill:** 5 minutes, until tender, tossed with olive oil, in hinged basket or on grill topper over moderate heat
SPAGHETTI SQUASH	1 medium, halved, seeds & strings removed	**To Bake:** 40–45 minutes, until tender, on baking sheet in preheated 350°F oven; scrape flesh from shell and mash
SPINACH	2 lbs, well washed & stems removed	**To Cook:** 2–3 minutes, until wilted, in large pan. Do not use any additional water, only water that clings to leaves after rinsing
SWEET POTATOES	2 lbs, peeled & thickly sliced	**To Boil:** 10–15 minutes, until tender
	4 whole large, scrubbed & pricked with fork	**To Bake:** 30–60 minutes, until fork-tender, in preheated 400°F oven
SUMMER SQUASH (YELLOW & ZUCCHINI)	1 lb (ends trimmed), sliced ¼ inch thick	**To Sauté:** 3–6 minutes, until crisp-tender, in olive oil with salt & pepper
	1 lb (ends trimmed), quartered	**To Grill:** 5–7 minutes, in hinged basket or on grill topper over moderate heat
SWISS CHARD	3 lbs, very well washed, stemmed; leaves & stems chopped into 1-inch pieces	**To Boil:** 5–8 minutes, until leaves are wilted & stems are tender
TOMATOES	6 large, cored & halved crosswise	**To Roast:** 20 minutes, until charred, in preheated 400°F oven
WHITE TURNIPS	1 lb, peeled & quartered	**To Roast:** 30–45 minutes, until tender, on baking sheet in preheated 350°F oven
	1 lb, peeled & diced	**To Boil:** 8–10 minutes, until tender; drain, then mash
WINTER SQUASH (ACORN, BUTTERNUT & HUBBARD)	2 lbs, halved, seeds & strings removed	**To Bake:** 40–45 minutes, until tender, on baking sheet in preheated 350°F oven
	2 lbs, peeled & diced	**To Boil:** 5 minutes, until tender; drain, then mash
	2 lbs, cut into ½-inch slices	**To Grill:** 5–10 minutes per side, turning, in hinged basket or on grill topper over moderate heat

POULTRY ROASTING CHART

Cut & Weight	Oven Temperature	Total Cooking Time	Temperature* on Meat Thermometer
CHICKEN, WHOLE, UNSTUFFED			
3–5 LBS	350°F	1¼–1½ hours	180°F
6–8 LBS	350°F	2–2¼ hours	180°F
CHICKEN PARTS			
BREAST (BONE IN), 6–8 OZ	350°F	30–40 minutes	170°F
BREAST (BONELESS), 4 OZ	350°F	20–30 minutes	160°F
LEGS (BONE IN), 8 OZ	350°F	40–50 minutes	170°F
THIGHS (BONE IN), 5–7 OZ	350°F	30–40 minutes	170°F
THIGHS (BONELESS), 3 OZ	350°F	20–30 minutes	160°F
TURKEY, WHOLE, UNSTUFFED			
8–12 LBS	325°F	2¾–3 hours	170°F in breast; 180°F in thigh
14–18 LBS	325°F	3¾–4¼ hours	170°F in breast; 180°F in thigh
20–24 LBS	325°F	4½–5 hours	170°F in breast; 180°F in thigh
TURKEY, WHOLE, STUFFED			
8–12 LBS	325°F	3–3½ hours	170°F in breast; 180°F in thigh
14–18 LBS	325°F	4–4¼ hours	170°F in breast; 180°F in thigh
20–24 LBS	325°F	4¾–5¼ hours	170°F in breast; 180°F in thigh
TURKEY BREAST, UNSTUFFED			
4–6 LBS	325°F	1½–2¼ hours	170°F in thickest part
6–8 LBS	325°F	2¼–3¼ hours	170°F in thickest part

SOURCES: National Broiler Council and National Turkey Federation

BEEF ROASTING CHART

Cut & Weight	Oven Temperature	Total Cooking Time	Temperature* on Meat Thermometer
EYE ROUND ROAST, 2–3 LBS	325°F	1½–1¾ hours	145°F for medium-rare
ROUND TIP ROAST			
3–4 LBS	325°F	1¾–2 hours	150°F for medium-rare
		2¼–2½ hours	165°F for medium
4–6 LBS	325°F	2–2½ hours	150°F for medium-rare
		2½–3 hours	165°F for medium
6–8 LBS	325°F	2½–3 hours	150°F for medium-rare
		3–3½ hours	165°F for medium
TENDERLOIN, WELL TRIMMED			
2–3 LBS (CENTER CUT)	425°F	35–40 minutes	145°F for medium-rare
		45–50 minutes	160°F for medium
4–5 LBS (WHOLE)	425°F	50–60 minutes	145°F for medium-rare
		60–70 minutes	160°F for medium
TRI-TIP ROAST (BOTTOM SIRLOIN) 1½–2 LBS	425°F	30–40 minutes	145°F for medium-rare
		40–45 minutes	160°F for medium

BEEF ROASTING CHART (continued)

Cut & Weight	Oven Temperature	Total Cooking Time	Temperature* on Meat Thermometer
RIB ROAST (CHINE BONE REMOVED)			
2 RIBS, 4–6 LBS	350°F	1¾–2¼ hours 2¼–2¾ hours	145°F for medium-rare 160°F for medium
2–4 RIBS, 6–8 LBS	350°F	2¼–2½ hours 2¾–3 hours	145°F for medium-rare 160°F for medium
4–5 RIBS, 8–10 LBS	350°F	2½–3 hours 3–3½ hours	145°F for medium-rare 160°F for medium

SOURCE: National Cattlemen's Beef Association

PORK ROASTING CHART

Cut & Weight	Oven Temperature	Cooking Time Per Pound	Temperature* on Meat Thermometer
RIB ROAST (BONELESS), 2–4 LBS	350°F	20 minutes	160°F
LOIN ROAST (BONE IN), 3–5 LBS	350°F	20 minutes	160°F
TENDERLOIN, 8 OZ–1 LB	450°F	20 minutes	160°F

SOURCE: National Pork Producers Council

LAMB ROASTING CHART

Cut & Weight	Oven Temperature	Cooking Time Per Pound	Temperature* on Meat Thermometer
BONELESS LEG (ROLLED & TIED) 4–7 LBS	325°F	20 minutes 25 minutes	145°F–150°F for medium-rare 160°F for medium
LEG OF LAMB (BONE IN)			
5–7 LBS	325°F	15 minutes 20 minutes	145°F–150°F for medium-rare 160°F for medium
7–9 LBS	325°F	20 minutes 25 minutes	145°F–150°F for medium-rare 160°F for medium
SIRLOIN ROAST (BONELESS) 1¼–1¾ LBS	325°F	45 minutes 55 minutes	145°F–150°F for medium-rare 160°F for medium
RIB ROAST, RACK 1½–2½ LBS	375°F	30 minutes 35 minutes	145°F–150°F for medium-rare 160°F for medium
CROWN ROAST, UNSTUFFED 2–3 LBS	375°F	25 minutes 30 minutes	145°F–150°F for medium-rare 160°F for medium

SOURCE: The American Lamb Council

*Meat and poultry should be removed from the oven when the internal temperature measures 10°F below the recommended temperature for doneness. This is because the temperature will rise another 10° after the meat sits for 10 to 15 minutes.

ADOBO SAUCE

A thick, chili-based Mexican sauce used as a cooking ingredient and condiment. Canned chipotle chilies (see *Chili Peppers*) come packed in it; you can use the adobo from the can as a seasoning.

ALLSPICE

Not a spice blend, this is just one spice that tastes like a blend of cinnamon, cloves, and nutmeg. Dried allspice berries are sold whole and ground.

ALMONDS

Almonds are sold in the shell, shelled whole, slivered, and sliced. "Natural" means that the brown skin has been left on; skinned almonds are labeled "blanched."

ANCHOVY PASTE

Anchovies are tiny Mediterranean fish most often seen in their cured, canned form. When pureed and blended with vinegar and spices, they become anchovy paste, which is sold in tubes. Keep some on hand to add intense, savory flavor to sauces and salad dressings.

APPLES

What kind of apple you prefer to eat fresh is up to you, and the same goes for cooking—although some apples are better than others for certain recipes. If you're stuck in a Delicious-and-McIntosh rut, you owe it to yourself to try some others. Like them tart? Try a Northern Spy, Winesap, Gravenstein, Baldwin, or Granny Smith. For sweeter apples, sample Jonagolds, Galas, Macouns, Fujis, Empires, and Paula Reds. To keep apples at their crispest and juiciest, always refrigerate them.

ARBORIO RICE

Grown in Italy's Po Valley, Arborio is preferred for risotto, because when it is cooked, the rice's starchy exterior becomes creamy, while the center remains slightly firm. Arborio is sold in gourmet and Italian food shops and some supermarkets.

ARTICHOKES

Artichokes are the buds of a thistle-like plant. The fleshy bottom, or heart, of the artichoke is the most delectable part; the bases of the leaves are tasty, too, but the leaf tips and fuzzy "choke" are inedible. Choose heavy artichokes with fleshy-looking, tightly closed leaves.

ARUGULA

A favorite Italian salad green, arugula has a peppery, slightly bitter flavor. Unlike lettuce, arugula doesn't form a head, but grows as individual leaves that look something like dandelion leaves. Wash arugula thoroughly—it's often sandy.

AVOCADOS

The avocado grows like a fruit but "eats" like a vegetable. It's deliciously nutlike in flavor, with a velvety texture. The black, pebbly-skinned Hass avocado has a richer texture and taste than the smooth-skinned green Fuerte variety. If the avocado you buy is slightly underripe, store it in a paper bag at room temperature for a few days. When it's ripe, a toothpick should slide easily through the skin into the flesh.

BAIN MARIE

Delicate foods, such as custards, that need to be protected from direct heat are sometimes cooked in a water bath, called a *bain marie* in French. The pan or baking dish of food is placed in a larger, shallower pan containing hot water. This pan then goes in the oven or on the stovetop.

BAKING POWDER

This baking ingredient leavens batters and doughs by releasing carbon dioxide. Double-acting baking powder, the most common form, releases some CO_2 when it's moistened; the oven's heat produces a second release. Baking powder must be fresh; if it's more than 3 months old (check the date on the can), test its potency: Stir 1 teaspoon of the powder into ⅓ cup of hot water. If it fizzes furiously, it's fine. If not, buy a new can.

BAKING SHEET
see Cookie Sheet

BAKING SODA

Baking soda is bicarbonate of soda, a chemical compound that releases CO_2 when combined with an acid ingredient such as buttermilk. Baking soda gives off its gas as soon as it's moistened, and unlike baking powder, does not have a second reaction in the oven, so it's important to get the batter into the oven quickly, before the baking soda "uses up" its raising power.

BALSAMIC VINEGAR
see Vinegar

BAMBOO SHOOTS

Cream-colored, ribbonlike sliced bamboo shoots are sold in cans in the Asian ingredients section of most supermarkets. These crisp, pleasantly fibrous shoots are often used in stir-fries.

BASIL

Best known as an Italian ingredient, but also common in French, Thai, and other cuisines, basil is a deliciously fragrant herb that is often used in combination with garlic. Fresh basil is widely available. Store it in a container of water, with a plastic bag loosely pulled over the leaves.

BAY LEAF

This culinary herb is the thick, dark-green leaf of a type of laurel bush. California bay leaves are most common, but Turkish bay leaves have a milder, more pleasing flavor. Since the leaves are tough and sharp, and don't soften much in cooking, remove them before serving.

BEAN SPROUTS

Bean sprouts are adzuki, mung, soy, or other beans that have sprouted. The tender shoots have a great fresh flavor. Fresh sprouts (sold in the produce sections of many supermarkets in little plastic boxes) are preferable to canned sprouts, which invariably have a "tinny" flavor.

BEANS, DRIED & CANNED

Canned beans are convenient, and you can get many varieties, including pinto, black, kidney, and chick-peas, in this form. Rinse and drain them well before using, and they're fine for most purposes. But dried beans you cook yourself turn out firmer and fresher-tasting, and they're not hard to prepare (see "Bean There, Done That," page 96). *See also Lima Beans.*

BLANCHING

A brief, partial cooking in boiling water that softens vegetables slightly but leaves them crisp-tender. Blanching also loosens the skins of foods like tomatoes and peaches, making them easy to peel. To blanch, drop the food into a pot of boiling water. When it's done, drain immediately and cool in ice water so that it does not overcook.

BLENDER, IMMERSION

This hand-held appliance consists of a rotary blade on a shaft; the shaft is attached to an upright handle, which contains a small motor. An immersion blender lets you blend food right in the pot it was cooked in, and there's no blender container to wash.

BLUE CHEESE

Cheeses treated with special molds during manufacturing develop streaky blue or green "veins"—and rather pungent flavors. The best-known blues are French Roquefort, Italian Gorgonzola, and English Stilton. Blue cheeses are also made elsewhere in Europe and in the U. S.

BOK CHOY

Perhaps the most familiar type of Chinese cabbage, bok choy has crisp, white stalks and dark green, ruffly leaves. It has a milder flavor than regular green cabbage and is often used in stir-fries. Because the leaves are much more delicate than the stalks, add the cut stalks to the pan and let them cook for a while before adding the leaves.

BRAISING

In braising, food is first sautéed to brown it, then cooked slowly in a little liquid in a tightly covered pan. You can braise on the stove or in the oven. Pot roast is an example of braising, which is a good way to tenderize tougher cuts of meat.

BULGHUR

This Near Eastern ingredient (also spelled bulgur) consists of wheat kernels that have been steamed, dried, and then cracked. This makes the wheat cook quickly—in fact, it can be "cooked" by simply steeping it in water, rather than simmering it on the stove.

BUTTERMILK

Buttermilk is made by culturing nonfat or low-fat milk, which turns the milk tangy and slightly thicker. Because of its acidity, buttermilk makes baked goods more tender. To fake buttermilk, see Emergency Substitutions, page 170.

CANOLA OIL
see Oils, Cooking

CAPERS

Capers are the flower buds of a Mediterranean shrub. When pickled in salted vinegar, capers develop a strong, piquant flavor. The tiny French capers (near right) labeled "nonpareil" are usually superior in flavor to the larger Spanish capers (far right).

CARDAMOM

This spice, related to ginger, is sold as whole, seed-filled pods, or ground to a powder. Richly aromatic, cardamom is a component of curry powder; it is also used in sweet baking, especially in Scandinavian recipes.

CAYENNE PEPPER

Also called "ground red pepper," cayenne is dried red chilies in powdered form. Cayenne is fiery hot, and it's advisable to start with less than the recipe calls for if you're wary of spicy food.

CHALLAH

This traditional Jewish bread, served on the Sabbath and holidays, is a fine-textured, eggy yeast bread with a soft, nut-brown crust. The loaves are usually shaped into large, tapered braids.

CHILI PASTE, ASIAN

The base of this condiment and cooking ingredient is fermented beans. In addition to chilies, there may be garlic in it, too. Use chili paste to "hot up" Asian-style dishes and stews, but use it sparingly at first; some brands can be searingly hot.

CHILI PEPPERS

These fiery cousins of the sweet bell pepper add lively heat to foods. Several types of chilies—fresh, dried, and/or canned—are available at supermarkets.

Most of the chili pepper's "heat" comes from compounds concentrated in the membranes (ribs) and seeds: Remove these to tame the heat. These compounds can burn your eyes and irritate your skin, so wear rubber gloves when handling chilies. If you don't have gloves, wash your hands thoroughly with soap when you're done preparing the peppers. Here are some of the more common chili peppers: *Jalapeño* A thumb-sized green or red chili that's pretty tame in its pickled (canned) form, but can be fiery when fresh. Fresh jalapeños are unpredictable in their heat levels, so taste a bit and adjust the recipe as necessary. *Chipotle* A dried, smoked jalapeño sold as is, or roasted and canned in adobo sauce. *Poblano* A dark green, sort of triangular chili of low to moderate hotness. Poblanos can be used almost like sweet bell peppers; they're often served stuffed with cheese. *Mild green chilies* are pickled chili peppers and come in cans, whole or chopped. Their heat level is mild to medium.

CHILI POWDER

This seasoning blend contains powdered dried red chilies spiked with some or all of the following: oregano, cumin, garlic, salt, allspice, cloves, and coriander. Chili powder is sold in mild, medium, and hot strengths. Although supermarket brands do not carry a heat strength on the label, they are almost always mild to medium.

CHIPOTLE PEPPERS
see Chili Peppers

CHIVES

The slender, grasslike shoots of a type of onion, with a delicate oniony taste. Used as an herb, they're sold in small bunches.

CHOCOLATE

We hardly need to tell you what chocolate is, but to clarify what's what for cooking: *Unsweetened chocolate* has no sugar added. It comes in a box, in individually wrapped

1-ounce squares. *Semisweet chocolate* has added cocoa butter and sugar. It's sold in bars and individually wrapped squares for cooking. *Bittersweet chocolate* contains slightly less sugar but can be substituted for semisweet in most recipes. *Sweet cooking chocolate* is a dark but sweet chocolate that comes in bars. Store chocolate in a cool, dry place, tightly wrapped.

CHUTNEY

A piquant relish from India, used as a condiment and in cooking. Traditional chutneys contain fruits and/or vegetables, chilies, herbs, spices, and vinegar, and are often made fresh. The chutneys sold in jars are usually sweet-and-spicy fruit-based mixtures, of which the best known is Major Grey's, a mango chutney.

CILANTRO

Also called fresh coriander or Chinese parsley, this herb resembles Italian flat-leaf parsley. To tell the difference, rub a leaf between your fingers and sniff the distinctive, sharp fragrance. You can buy fresh cilantro in most supermarkets. Store it in a container of water, like a bouquet. If the roots are attached, save them: Scrubbed and minced, they can be used as a seasoning and actually have a stronger flavor than the leaves.

CLAMS, HARDSHELL

Canned clams can't touch fresh ones for delicate sweetness, and the smallest fresh clams are the tastiest. Two diminutive varieties—both called "littlenecks" but technically unrelated—are harvested on the Atlantic and Pacific coasts. Another hardshell clam, Eastern cherrystones, are slightly bigger than littlenecks. Buy clams the day you plan to use them, and make sure they're alive: If a clam shell isn't tightly closed, tap the clam—it should snap shut. Pass up any clams that don't.

COCONUT MILK

Coconut milk is used in Southeast Asian cooking for creamy richness. It is made by steeping coconut meat in water, then straining the resulting liquid. Don't confuse canned coconut milk with "cream of coconut" or *crema de coco*, which is the sweet stuff used in piña coladas.

COMPOUND BUTTER

A mixture of butter and flavorings, such as herbs, spices, garlic, or citrus zest. A pat of compound butter can serve as a sauce atop hot food. Compound butters can be frozen for two months. (See recipes, page 58.)

COOKIE SHEET

A cookie sheet (or baking sheet) is a flat, rectangular pan with no sides, so it's easy to remove cookies from the pan after baking. Sometimes one end of a sheet is slightly turned up to serve as a handle. *See also Jelly-roll pan.*

CORIANDER

The seed of the cilantro plant, coriander is an important spice in Mexican, Indian, and Near Eastern cuisines. The seeds taste nothing like the leaves: They are very aromatic, with a citrusy edge. You can buy coriander seeds whole or ground.

COURT BOUILLON

A seasoned broth used for poaching, court bouillon is flavored with aromatic vegetables and herbs, and wine or vinegar. Court bouillon is most frequently used for cooking fish and seafood.

COUSCOUS

This North African pasta is made by rolling semolina (a coarse wheat flour) into  tiny beads. Couscous is traditionally steamed over a pot of stew; the pasta and stew are served together. The packaged couscous you buy in boxes in the supermarket is quick cooking ("instant"), and requires just steeping in boiling water or broth.

CREAM

The rich, fatty portion of milk that naturally rises to the top of unhomogenized milk if left to sit (nowadays cream is separated from the milk by centrifuge). *Heavy, or whipping, cream* is the richest, with at least 36 percent milk fat. *Light cream,* also called "coffee cream" or "table cream," contains between 30 and 36 percent milk fat. It cannot be whipped like heavy cream. *Half-and-half* is a mixture of milk and cream that contains between 10.5 and 18 percent milk fat. It cannot be whipped.

CREAM CHEESE

This slightly tangy, spreadable cheese is made from a mixture of cream and milk. It comes in full-fat and low-fat (light) versions. Neufchâtel cheese, also called reduced-fat cream cheese, has about one third less fat than regular cream cheese. There is also nonfat cream cheese but it's not recommended for cooking.

CREMINI
see Mushrooms

CUCUMBERS

Instead of seeding regular cucumbers (below, bottom), you might use a European cucumber—also called "hothouse," "English," or "burpless" (below, top), which is unwaxed, so you can eat the skin, and has almost nonexistent seeds. You could also try small, crisp Kirby cucumbers, which are used for pickling. They, too, are unwaxed and seedless, though they can be hard to find.

CUMIN

Often partnered with coriander, cumin is a pungent spice used in Middle Eastern, Asian, Mexican, and Mediterranean recipes. If you've ever eaten curries or chili, you'll know cumin's unique flavor.

CURRANTS

These tiny raisins are made from small black grapes. They can be used like regular raisins (and vice versa), but some British and European baked goods, such as scones, need currants to be authentic.

CURRY POWDER

A mixture of spices used in Indian cooking to season and color curries and other dishes. While Indian cooks prepare different seasoning blends for different dishes, most supermarkets carry a more-or-less standard curry powder. Turmeric is a major ingredient; curry powder may also contain fenugreek, ginger, cardamom, cloves, cumin, coriander, and cayenne pepper. "Madras" curry powder is hotter than other packaged types.

CUSTARD CUPS/RAMEKINS

These ovenproof glass or ceramic baking cups have a capacity of about 6 ounces. They're used for custards and other individual desserts, such as mini-soufflés.

DILL

This feathery-leaved herb and its small, hard seeds are used as an herb and a spice. Dillweed and dill seeds are popular in Scandinavian and Eastern European cooking, and are often used with fish, cucumbers, and in creamy sauces.

DRIED FRUIT

When fresh fruits are dried, they turn into sweet, chewy treats. In addition to such standbys as raisins, prunes, dates, figs, and apricots, you can also buy dried cherries, cranberries, apples, pears, strawberries, pineapple, and papaya. Dried fruit keeps for a long time if refrigerated in an airtight container. See also *Currants; Raisins*

DUTCH OVEN

This versatile cooking pot is large (at least 4 quarts), with a close-fitting cover and two side handles. It is designed for use on top of the stove as well as in the oven; the handles and lid handle are ovenproof. A Dutch oven is useful for soups, stews, braises, and casseroles.

EGGPLANT

This more-or-less egg-shaped vegetable has fairly bland, porous flesh under a thin, glossy skin. Italian eggplants are the large, purple kind; Japanese eggplants are long and slender, and may be paler purple in color. Other Asian eggplants are small, white, and do look like giant eggs. Use eggplants within a few days of purchase; if stored too long, they can become bitter.

EGGS

Eggs are a crucial ingredient in cakes, cookies, quick breads, custards, and soufflés. The fresher an egg, the better it will taste—and the better it will function in cooking—so check the date on the carton. (Store the eggs in the carton, too—not in the refrigerator door.) After 5 weeks, eggs are technically still usable, but you're better off discarding them. All baking recipes in this book (and in most cookbooks) specify large eggs, and the results may be disappointing if you substitute a different size.

EMULSION SAUCE

A sauce in which two liquids that do not readily combine—such as melted butter and milk, or oil and vinegar—are blended so that tiny droplets of one liquid remain suspended in the other. Mayonnaise, hollandaise, and vinaigrette are all emulsion sauces. Mayonnaise is a permanent emulsion (which stays blended), while vinaigrette is a temporary emulsion (it will separate if you let it stand).

FENNEL, FRESH

This vegetable looks like a flattened, bulbous head of celery; its long stalks (which are often cut off before the fennel is marketed) are topped with feathery fronds. Fennel has a subtle licorice-like flavor. You can eat fennel raw or cooked; the chopped fronds can be used as an herb. If you can't find fennel in the supermarket, look for it in an Italian grocery store.

FENNEL SEEDS

With their mildly sweet, licorice-like taste, fennel seeds supply the predominant flavor in Italian sausages. Fennel seeds are also a popular seasoning for seafood, and are used in some types of rye bread.

FETA CHEESE

Tangy and salty, soft yet crumbly, feta is the best-known Greek cheese. Feta is traditionally made from sheep's or goat's milk; the fetas imported to the United States today are made from sheep's milk, while American-made versions are made from cow's milk. Feta is sometimes sold packed in brine; rinse the cheese before using to reduce the saltiness.

FLANK STEAK

One of the leanest cuts of beef, flank steak comes from the belly of the steer. Flavorful and tender if properly cooked, flank will become tough if overcooked. It benefits from marinating, and should be carved across the grain into thin slices (see technique, page 40).

FLOUR

Wheat flour comes in different "styles" for different types of baking. *All-purpose flour* is a refined flour (the bran and germ have been removed), usually a blend of hard and soft wheats. It is suitable for most basic baking as well as for sauce-making and other general cooking uses. Some all-purpose flour is bleached to whiten it. *Cake flour* is a bleached, refined flour made solely from soft wheat. It produces a light, fine-textured, tender cake. It's best to use cake flour when it's called for (see Emergency Substitutions, page 170). *Whole wheat flour* is milled from the whole wheat kernel, including its germ and bran. This yields a more nutritious flour that can be used in breads, muffins, and other sturdy baked goods (but not delicate ones). Whole wheat flour is usually used in combination with white flour to keep baked goods from being too heavy. *Bread flour* is ground from hard wheat and has a high protein content. This flour forms a strong structure that maintains the volume of the yeast-raised dough. *Self-rising flour* already has leavening (and salt) added. Use only when specifically called for.

GAETA OLIVES
see Olives

GELATIN, UNFLAVORED

Unflavored gelatin is a base for jelly-like fruit desserts and is also used in some cheesecakes, pie fillings, puddings, and glazes. Gelatin also stabilizes whipped cream. Some fresh fruits—pineapple, figs, kiwi, and papaya—contain an enzyme that prevents gelatin from jelling; don't use these in gelatin-based desserts (canned pineapple, however, is fine).

GINGER

Fresh ginger is the fleshy underground stem of a semitropical plant. It looks something like a chubby hand with knobby "fingers," and has a spicy-hot flavor and a sharp, fresh aroma. *Ground ginger* is a pale golden powder made by pulverizing dried ginger. It has some of the warm-sweet pungency of fresh ginger, but is not really a good substitute for fresh. Ground ginger is used in baked goods and fruit desserts. *Crystallized (or candied) ginger* is a candy-like treat made by cooking fresh ginger in syrup and then coating it with granulated sugar. Chopped or diced crystallized ginger is used in baked goods, chutneys, and sauces. You can find crystallized ginger in the supermarket spice aisle, but it's a lot cheaper when purchased in bulk at a candy store, gourmet shop, or Asian grocery.

GOAT CHEESE

Goat's milk cheese, or *chèvre,* is imported from France and also made in the United States. Goat cheese has a characteristic tangy tartness, and the longer the cheese is aged, the sharper the flavor. A mild, young cheese is suitable for most cooking purposes. Montrachet, sold in small logs, is among the mildest; Bucheron (a larger log, sold by the slice) and Ste. Maure (an 8-ounce log) are a little stronger. Domestic cheeses have different names, but come in similar styles. Ask about them at a good cheese shop.

HAM

Ham is a cut of fresh pork (from the hind leg), but the word more commonly refers to this cut after it's been cured and smoked. Hams are either dry-cured (by rubbing them with salt and spices) or brine-cured in a strong salt solution. Some are then smoked over a hardwood fire for a rich, smoky flavor. Hams may be "fully cooked"—most canned hams, and boiled or baked hams sold at the deli counter, fall into this category—or they may need to be cooked before eating. Country-style hams, like Smithfield, need to be cooked. Be sure to check the label to see which kind you're buying. *See also Prosciutto.*

HAZELNUTS

Also called filberts, these sweet, rich-tasting nuts are a favorite dessert ingredient. They're particularly good when combined with chocolate. See page 18 for how to remove the skin from shelled hazelnuts.

HOISIN SAUCE

This Chinese condiment and cooking ingredient is a thick spicy-sweet sauce. Based on fermented soybeans, hoisin is seasoned with chilies, garlic, and spices.

HOMINY

Hominy is dried corn kernels that have had their hull (outer coating) and germ (the central part of the grain) removed. Hominy is sold dry, but it's most commonly available reconstituted, in cans.

HORSERADISH

This pungently hot root vegetable is used as a seasoning and condiment. Grated horseradish is sold in jars, sometimes with beet juice added for color. Grated fresh horse-radish is very strong; use it judiciously. *Wasabi* is a Japanese green horseradish that's particularly fiery. It's served with sushi and sashimi. It comes as a powder that you mix with water to make a paste, or you can buy the premixed paste in a tube.

HOT SAUCES

Although there is a bewildering variety of hot sauces available, the most common hot sauces, such as the Tabasco brand, from Louisiana, are made from vinegar, salt, and chilies. The two main styles are red (made from tabasco chilies) and green (made from jalapeños). If you love hot food, try one of the other hot sauces out there (such as Tex-Mex, Cajun, or Caribbean), though often their heat levels make them unsuitable for cooking.

JELLY-ROLL PAN

A shallow rectangular baking pan about 10 x 15 inches and 1 inch deep (top pan shown; bottom pan is a cookie sheet). A jelly-roll pan is used for baking thin sheet cakes (such as those that are made into jelly rolls) and can also serve as a broiler pan.

KALAMATA OLIVES
see Olives

LEEKS

Leeks look like oversized scallions, and are similarly mild-flavored members of the onion family. Leeks are eaten cooked, either as a vegetable in themselves or as an ingredient in soups and braises. Usually just the white part and the pale green parts of the leaves are used, and the coarse, dark green leaf tops are cut off and discarded. Autumn is peak season for leeks. See page 11 for how to clean leeks.

LETTUCE

Different lettuces are suitable for different salads, and it helps to know which is which. *Iceberg*, the familiar cabbage-shaped, mild-flavored lettuce, is notable for its crunchy, refreshing texture. Iceberg is best served shredded or in chunks. *Bibb* is a "butterhead" lettuce with soft, velvety leaves that form small cup shapes. Bibb is mild in flavor, and works best with other delicate ingredients and a dressing that's not overpowering. *Romaine* (also called cos) is a sturdy, versatile lettuce with long leaves that branch out from a thick white base. The inner leaves are sweeter and paler than the outer ones. Use romaine with thick, zesty dressings and in combination with other robust salad fixings.

LIMA BEANS

These flat, pale green, kidney-shaped beans come in two varieties: Fordhooks and baby limas. The "babies" are smaller and tastier. Frozen lima beans are widely available all year round.

LIQUEUR

Liqueurs are sweet alcoholic beverages infused with the flavors of fruit, herbs, spices, nuts, seeds, flowers—even chocolate or coffee. Liqueurs are usually served as after-dinner drinks, but they're also great cooking ingredients. Try these: Frangelico (hazelnut); Sambuca (anise); Cointreau or Triple Sec (orange); Amaretto di Saronno (bitter almond); Kahlúa (coffee); Sabra (chocolate-orange).

LIQUID SMOKE

This "barbecue in a bottle" is a flavoring ingredient made by infusing a fluid base with real smoke. A few drops give food a rich barbecued or smoked flavor.

LOBSTER

The big lobster with the meaty claws and tail is an American lobster (as opposed to the spiny lobster, which has no claws). Lobsters are sold live, and you should choose one that fights back when it's pulled out of the tank; its tail should curl tightly underneath it. The lobster should feel heavy for its size. Buy the lobster the same day you plan to cook it; if you have to keep it for a few hours, put it in the refrigerator, wrapped in a wet cloth (don't immerse it in fresh water or it will die).

MANCHEGO CHEESE

A semi-firm Spanish sheep's milk cheese with a hard yellow rind. The cheese has a rich, tangy flavor.

MANGO

This once-exotic tropical fruit is now widely available in American markets. A mango's deep-orange flesh is juicy and fragrant, a little like a peach but much more lush and flowery. A ripe mango's yellow-orange skin has a reddish blush. For how to peel a mango, see page 9.

MATCHSTICKS

Often called julienne, matchsticks are small, thin strips of food. Matchstick pieces are square in cross-section (think of a wooden match) and up to about 3 inches long.

MEAT POUNDER

A mallet-like metal or wood implement for flattening cutlets into scaloppine and tenderizing meat. Meat pounders may have flat surfaces, or they may be ridged or toothed. A rolling pin or a small, heavy skillet can stand in for a meat pounder.

MELONS

Two of the most popular varieties of these sweet, juicy summer fruits are cantaloupe and honeydew. *Cantaloupe* is an orange-fleshed melon; its yellowish-green rind is covered with a raised, mesh-like "netting." A ripe cantaloupe will have a sweet aroma. *Honeydews* are larger melons with pale green flesh and a smooth, cream-colored rind. Choose a honeydew with a velvety "bloom" on the rind. If a melon has been picked at just the right time, it will have a slight indentation at the stem end, showing that the stem parted easily from the fruit.

MINI FOOD PROCESSOR

With a work-bowl capacity of about 2½ cups, this junior model of a favorite kitchen appliance is perfect for small jobs, such as chopping onions, garlic, herbs, or nuts or grating a chunk of Parmesan.

MINT

The cool flavor of mint (spearmint and peppermint are the most popular) is a delicious accent to fruit desserts; mint is also traditional with lamb, and is used in savory dishes in some Asian cuisines.

MOLASSES

Molasses is a thick, sweet liquid created during the refining of sugarcane. Molasses is boiled to produce various intensities of flavor. *Light molasses* is quite sweet, with a mild flavor. *Dark molasses* has a more robust flavor but is less sweet. Both are used in cooking, pretty much interchangeably. *Blackstrap molasses* is boiled down still further, until it's very dark and hardly sweet at all. Blackstrap molasses is sold in health-food stores and is rarely used in cooking.

MONKFISH

This lean saltwater fish is also called anglerfish or goosefish. It's a large creature, with a particularly ugly head that rarely appears at the market (monkfish is almost never sold whole). In fact, only the monkfish's meaty tail is eaten. This fish is dense and firm, with a delicate sweetness sometimes likened to lobster.

MONTEREY JACK CHEESE

First made in Monterey, California, this mild cheese—similar to Muenster—is now produced elsewhere as well. Monterey Jack melts well and is often used in Tex-Mex dishes. Aged Jack is hard, like Parmesan, and is used as a grating cheese.

MORTAR & PESTLE

This two-part kitchen tool consists of a heavy, deep bowl and a grinding instrument shaped like a baseball bat. Mortars and pestles are often made of stoneware or porcelain; they may also be of heavy glass, metal, stone, or wood. Use a mortar and pestle to crush whole spices and to blend seasoning pastes.

MOZZARELLA CHEESE

This mild, milky-flavored Italian cheese is famous as a melting cheese. Supermarket mozzarella is available in whole-milk, part-skim, and fat-free versions. Either whole-milk or part-skim is fine for cooking (fat-free can be a little rubbery). Fresh mozzarella is moister, more tender, and far fresher-tasting than the prepackaged cheese; it's sold packed in whey at gourmet shops and some supermarkets.

MUSHROOMS

The familiar white mushrooms at the supermarket, called "common" or "button" mushrooms, have a very mild flavor that's intensified by cooking. Check out some of the more "exotic" (and tastier) fresh mushrooms. *Cremini* are small, tan button mushrooms that are a fuller-flavored substitute for white mushrooms. Cremini are actually small portobellos (see below). *Porcini* is the Italian name for the delicious, broad-capped mushroom called *cèpe* in French. The smooth brown caps of these highly prized mushrooms have a pale, spongy underside; the stems are thick and meaty. Fresh porcini are scarce and pricey, but dried porcini are sold in many supermarkets. Combine a small amount of reconstituted dried porcini with fresh button mushrooms to imitate the flavor of fresh porcini. *Shiitake* is a Japanese mushroom with an intensely meaty flavor. Fresh shiitakes have wide, dark-brown caps and tough stems that are not usually eaten. Dried shiitakes are an even more powerful flavoring; look for them in Asian grocery stores. *Portobellos* are large mushrooms (often 6 inches in diameter) with a beefy texture and flavor. Portobellos are often grilled and cut into thick slices, like steak.

MUSSELS

These small mollusks have narrow, oblong shells and delicately sweet meat. Mussels are sold in-shell; be sure they're alive (i.e., tightly closed) when you buy them. Mussels are most often cooked in their shells, steamed in broth.

MUSTARD

The pungent seeds of the mustard plant are used whole as a spice; in the form of a fine powder; or ground and blended with liquid to make a spreadable condiment. Dijon mustard, which originated in Dijon, France, is a fairly hot mustard made with dry white wine. Dijon comes in smooth and grainy versions (the grainy type has coarsely ground mustard seeds in it).

NUTMEG

This spice is a fragrant enhancement to pumpkin pie, cakes and cookies, winter squash, and cooked green vegetables. Most cooks buy ground nutmeg, but freshly grated nutmeg is worth a try. A whole nutmeg is a hard, olive-sized brown seed. Miniature graters are made especially for nutmeg, but you can also use the fine side of an ordinary grater.

OATS

This nutritious grain comes in several forms. **Old-fashioned rolled oats** are whole oat kernels that have been steamed and then flattened between rollers. For **quick-cooking oats**, the kernels are cut into small pieces before rolling, so the flakes are thinner and more delicate. **Instant oats** are rolled still thinner. Old-fashioned oats hold their shape and texture in baked goods; quick-cooking oats may be substituted in some recipes, but instant oats should not be.

OILS, COOKING

These liquid fats have many uses, from frying to baking to vinaigrette making. Sometimes you want a tasteless oil (for greasing cake pans, for example), and sometimes you want a flavorful oil that adds something to the food. Cooking oils have different smoke points—that is, some can be cooked at higher temperatures without breaking down, and so they're better for frying. Here are some of the more common cooking oils: **Canola oil** is actually rapeseed oil, but Canadian producers of this oil wisely changed the name (Can+ola= "Canadian oil"), and this oil has become very popular. Canola oil is bland in flavor, and a healthful choice because it's lower in saturated fat than any other oil, and high in monounsaturates, which may lower blood cholesterol. **Olive oil**, which has similar health benefits, now comes in "Light" and "Extra-Light" forms that are as bland as regular vegetable oils (you can even use them for baking).

When you *do* want to taste the oil, choose the right one: For uncooked dishes (salads, for instance) or when adding the oil to already-cooked food, use extra-virgin olive oil, which has the lowest acidity and the fruitiest flavor. For general cooking, "virgin" or "fine" olive oil is appropriate. "Pure" olive oil is the standard supermarket grade. Olive oil has a fairly low smoke point and should not be used in high-heat cooking. **Peanut oil** imparts a slight peanut flavor, which works well in stir-fries. It can also be used for sautéing and deep-frying, and in salad dressings and baked goods. **Other vegetable oils** include corn, safflower, sunflower, and soybean. Corn, safflower, and soybean have high smoke points. *See also Sesame oil.*

OIL SPRAYER

A do-it-yourself version of nonstick cooking spray, this gadget lets you use your own oil to lightly coat foods and cooking utensils. The sprayer dispenses a very fine mist, so it's great for greasing pans and spritzing vegetables before grilling.

OLIVES

Olives have an earthy tang that complements many dishes. Green olives are unripe, while black olives are fully ripe. Both are cured to make them palatable—they are too bitter to eat straight off the tree. Some olives are cured in brine, some in lye, and some dry-cured in salt. After curing, olives are packed in liquid or rubbed with oil; sometimes herbs or other flavorings are added. **Kalamatas** are slit, brine-cured Greek black olives packed in vinegar. Canned Kalamatas are sold in many supermarkets. Salt-cured Italian **Gaetas** are wrinkly black olives with an intense flavor. Look for Gaetas at Italian groceries and gourmet shops. Lye-cured **pimiento-stuffed green olives** are packed in brine and filled with bits of sweet red pepper.

ONIONS

There's hardly a savory dish that's not improved by the addition of some type of onion. But which type? **Yellow globe onions** are the standard cooking onion, with an assertive pungency. **Red onions** are usually bigger; they have purplish skins and a milder flavor. **Spanish onions** and **Bermuda onions** are other large, mild onions. **White boiling onions** are the little mild-flavored ones used whole in side dishes and stews. **Sweet onions** include Vidalia, Walla Walla, and Maui onions, all of which have a high sugar content and are delicious raw. Store dry-skinned onions in a cool, dry place; sweet onions are more perishable and should be kept in the refrigerator. *See also Chives; Leeks; Scallions; Shallots.*

ORZO

Used in many Greek dishes, this pasta shape resembles large grains of rice (although its name means "barley").

OYSTER SAUCE

A Chinese ingredient made from soy sauce and flavored with oysters, this thick brown sauce is often used in stir-fries.

PAPILLOTE

The French term for a parchment-paper packet in which food is oven-steamed. Fish is often cooked *en papillote*, which entails enclosing the food in a sheet of parchment and sealing the edges.

PAPRIKA

Mild dried red peppers are ground to produce this spice. Paprika gives food a bold, brick-red color and a peppery sweetness. Imported Hungarian paprika comes in hot and sweet (mild) forms.

PARCHMENT PAPER

This sturdy greaseproof paper has many kitchen uses, from lining pans to forming *papillotes* (cooking packets).

PARMESAN CHEESE

A well-aged Parmesan, freshly grated, is a must for pasta, risotto, and other Italian (and non-Italian) dishes. The best Parmesan, stamped "Parmigiano-Reggiano," is made in a single region of Italy and usually aged for about two years. It's a very hard, straw-colored cheese with a sweet, nutlike flavor.

PARSNIPS

This winter root vegetable looks like a knobby beige carrot. When cooked in a soup or stew (which they often are), parsnips develop a gentle, sweet flavor.

PASTA

We no longer "call it macaroni" but we eat more than we ever have of this most versatile food. The best pasta (both imported and domestic) is made from semolina, a coarsely ground hard wheat flour that helps keeps the pasta from getting mushy when cooked. Pasta comes in hundreds of shapes, and although there are traditional preferences for combining pasta and sauce, you can pretty much make your own choices as long as the sauce doesn't overwhelm the pasta.

PASTRY BLENDER

This utensil consists of a horizontal handle fitted with several parallel U-shaped tines or wires. Used with a chopping motion, it incorporates chilled fat into flour evenly and quickly (see technique, page 16).

PASTRY BRUSH

A small, soft-bristled "paintbrush" for glazing pastry, greasing pans, and brushing crumbs off a cake before icing. A small, new nylon paintbrush works fine.

PEARS

Sweet and juicy, pears go into some classic desserts. Some of the best cooking pears are: *Bartlett*, fragrant, flavorful, and fine-textured; *Bosc*, a tall, sweet russet-skinned pear that holds its shape well when cooked; and *Comice*, a squat brownish-green pear that's a great baker. Pears are almost always picked before they're ripe, because when ripe, they are so tender that they won't survive shipping. So buy pears a few days ahead of time and let them ripen at room temperature.

PEPPERCORNS

Peppercorns are the dried berries of a tropical vine. Black peppercorns are picked unripe, then sun-dried; white peppercorns are picked ripe, and hulled. White has a gentler flavor, and doesn't show up as dark specks in light-colored dishes. Do invest in a pepper grinder and a small package of peppercorns; the taste of pre-ground pepper is totally flat by comparison.

PIE PLATES

A standard pie plate is a round metal, glass, or ceramic dish 9 inches in diameter, with flared sides. A deep-dish pie plate is the same diameter but about ½ inch deeper.

PINE NUTS

Also known as pignoli, these sweet, oily little "nuts" are the seeds of a Mediterranean stone pine tree. Pine nuts are a main ingredient in pesto (see recipe, page 118) and are also used in cookies and desserts.

POACHING

Delicate foods such as fish, fruit, or eggs are the ones most often poached—cooked in liquid that's just barely at a simmer.

POBLANO PEPPERS
see Chili Peppers

PORCINI
see Mushrooms

PORTOBELLOS
see Mushrooms

POTATOES

The kind of potatoes you buy depends on how you plan to cook them. Large, starchy, thick-skinned potatoes, such as *Russets*, are best for baking. Russets are commonly labeled Idaho potatoes, though they come from a number of other states. Glossy-skinned, waxy-fleshed potatoes are best for boiling. These include the small, thin-skinned, red or white *new potatoes*, which are sent to market soon after they're harvested, without having been stored. If you want to buy a single bag of potatoes that will work for both boiling and baking, choose **all-purpose potatoes**, such as long whites or round whites.

PROSCIUTTO

Traditionally made in and around Parma, Italy, prosciutto is a dense, richly flavored, salt-cured, air-dried ham. The finest is the imported ham labeled "Prosciutto di Parma." Prosciutto is often served as part of an antipasto course.

PUFF PASTRY

A rich pastry made by enfolding bits of butter in layers of dough. When baked, the pastry rises into flaky layers. It's tricky to make, but you can buy ready-to-use puff pastry in the supermarket.

RAISINS

It's hard to believe these are just dried grapes—they're so much sweeter. Both dark and golden raisins are made from white grapes, but the dark raisins are sun-dried, while the golden are oven-dried and specially treated to preserve their light color. Use either kind, as you prefer; golden raisins are usually softer. *See Currants.*

REDUCTION SAUCE

A sauce made by rapidly boiling a liquid such as broth or wine until the sauce thickens through evaporation.

RICE

We tend to take rice for granted, but there are a few basics you should know. **Long-grain white rice** is a kitchen staple; its grains remains light and separate when properly cooked. **Converted rice** has been pressure-steamed to preserve certain nutrients; it takes longer to cook than other white rice. Brown rice has its bran layer left on; it's high in fiber, with a robust flavor, and cooks in about 45

minutes. **Instant** or **quick rice** is bland and mushy, and hardly worth eating. *See also Arborio rice; Wild rice.*

ROSEMARY

Rosemary leaves resemble pine needles and have a strong evergreen-citrus flavor. Don't use too much, or the herb will overpower the dish. Crush or chop fresh or dried rosemary leaves with a mortar and pestle or a chef's knife before adding to a recipe.

RUTABAGA

This softball-sized root vegetable (below, left) is a relative of the turnip (below, right). A rutabaga has a thick tan-to-purple skin and deep-yellow flesh. They resemble turnips in flavor. The skin of rutabagas is heavily waxed; pare the wax and skin with a sharp knife before using. *See also Turnips.*

SAGE

The velvety gray-green leaves of this herb have a pleasantly musty mint taste. Dried sage is sold as whole leaves, ground, and in a "rubbed" version. If you can't buy fresh sage, the next best thing is dried whole leaves that you crush yourself.

SAKE

A slightly sweet Japanese wine made from fermented rice. It's drunk warm, and is also used in cooking.

SALAD SPINNER

The quickest way to dry washed greens is with this device, a rotating basket that fits

into a plastic tub. A crank handle or pull cord sets the basket spinning, throwing off the moisture.

SCALLIONS

Some people call these green onions or spring onions. They're immature onions (or a particular type of onion that doesn't develop a bulb) with a mild, slightly sweet flavor. Scallions are tasty raw or cooked.

SCALLOPS

Scallops grow in handsome shells, but are almost always sold shucked—pristine rounds of pale, tender flesh. Quick-cooking and versatile, they're great for fast, festive meals. Sea scallops are about 1½ inches across; bay scallops, sweeter and more expensive, are only about ½ inch in diameter. Buy scallops that look translucent and smell ocean-fresh.

SESAME OIL

This sable brown Asian oil is used in small amounts as a flavoring, rather than as a cooking medium. It's made from toasted sesame seeds and has a rich, nutlike flavor. There are also untoasted sesame oils; they are light in color, very mildly flavored, and mostly available in health-food stores.

SESAME SEEDS

These tiny seeds come from a plant native to Indonesia and East Africa. White sesame seeds are the most familiar, although you'll also find black sesame seeds in Indian grocery stores. Bring out the nutlike flavor by toasting the seeds in a dry skillet until they start to pop.

SHALLOTS

A gentle-flavored member of the onion family, shallots are prized for cooking. They grow in clusters; each shallot looks like a large, tan-skinned garlic clove. Store shallots in a cool, dry place.

SHIITAKES
see Mushrooms

SHRIMP
Deservedly America's most popular seafood, shrimp have sweet, tender flesh. They're marketed in a range of sizes. The most common sizes are medium (about 30 to the pound), large (about 25), and jumbo (about 15). Shrimp are sold in-shell and shelled, fresh or frozen. See page 13 for how to shell and devein shrimp.

SOY SAUCE
This indispensable Asian ingredient is made from fermented soybeans and wheat or barley. (Some poor-quality soy sauces are made from hydrolized soy protein; avoid them.) Japanese soy sauce tends to be lighter and less salty than Chinese.

SPATULAS
Every kitchen needs both flexible rubber spatulas (for folding batters and scraping bowls), and a few different sizes of metal spatulas (pancake turners) for flipping and moving food in a skillet. If you sauté in a nonstick pan, use a heatproof plastic or nylon spatula.

SPRINGFORM PAN
The sides of this deep, round baking pan are separate from the bottom, and expand so that you can remove the sides of the pan from the cake. The sides are held together with a strong clamp. Springform pans are used for cheesecakes and tortes.

SQUASH
The great divide in squashes is between the winter and summer varieties. *Summer squashes*—zucchini, pattypan, and yellow crookneck, for instance—are mild flavored and thin skinned, with a high water content. They're usually sautéed. Winter squashes, such as butternut, acorn, hubbard, and pumpkin, are hard-shelled, dense, and starchy. They are far more flavorful and sweet than summer squash, and are often baked. Summer squashes will keep for 4 to 5 days in the refrigerator; hard-shelled winter squashes can be stored in a cool, dry place for up to 2 months.

STEAMING
Cooking food over—or in a very small amount of—boiling water. It's a choice method for delicate foods, and preserves the nutrients in vegetables. See page 15.

STOCKPOT
A tall, narrow pot that holds at least 8 quarts. You want a stockpot with a heavy bottom and a tight-fitting lid.

SUGAR
The three standard sugars in the American kitchen are granulated, brown, and confectioners'. *Granulated sugar* is white sugar that has been processed to form fine, crystalline particles; when a recipe doesn't specify, use granulated sugar. *Brown sugar* (dark or light) is granulated white sugar mixed with molasses; it's soft and moist, with a caramelized flavor. *Confectioners' (powdered) sugar* is white sugar that has been crushed to a fine, flourlike powder. It's used where smoothness is a virtue, as in icings.

SUN-DRIED TOMATOES
Whether it's really done by the sun or in a slow oven, drying turns tomatoes chewy and sweet, like dried fruit (which they are). Dried tomatoes are sold packed in oil or "dry" (loose or in packages). The dry ones have to be soaked to soften them.

THERMOMETERS
Correct temperature is important for proper cooking, so thermometers are a kitchen requirement. An *instant-reading thermometer*—shown here with analog (left) and digital (right) dials—is a big improvement on the old-fashioned kind. You poke its slender metal shaft into the food (or liquid) and it registers within 30 seconds, reading up to 220°F. Another important thermometer to have around is an *oven thermometer* (not shown): Because oven thermostats can be inaccurate, set or hang an oven thermometer on the middle rack, and adjust your oven settings accordingly.

TOFU
Bean curd, or tofu, is a mainstay of Asian cuisines. It's a creamy white soybean product that can be sliced, cubed, mashed, or pureed. Recipes may call for extra-firm tofu (this usually comes in a small pillow shape), firm tofu, or soft (or silken) tofu. There are full-fat and low-fat tofus available.

TORTILLAS
These Mexican flatbreads are made from cornmeal or wheat flour. Corn tortillas contain no shortening; somewhat stiff, they are usually about 6 inches across. Flour tortillas are made with fat and are thinner and more flexible. They come in much larger sizes (up to 12 inches) for making burritos and sandwich wraps. Either kind should be warmed before serving.

TURMERIC

Powdered turmeric, a vivid yellow spice, is used to flavor and color curries and rice dishes. Its flavor is slightly bitter, so don't overdo it.

TURNIPS

This winter vegetable goes into a lot of soups and stews. A globe-shaped root with a white-and-purple skin, the turnip has the slightly bitter flavor of all cabbage-family vegetables, but a mild sweetness as well. *See also Rutabaga.*

VANILLA

One of America's favorite flavors, vanilla is made from the slender seed pod of a type of orchid. Most often used in the form of an alcohol-based extract, vanilla is also available as a whole pod, or "bean." The whole bean can be simmered in liquids; or you can split the bean and scrape the seeds into the food you want to flavor. If using the whole bean, you can rinse it, blot it dry, and reuse it.

VEGETABLE OIL
see Oils, cooking

VINEGAR

Vinegar is made by fermenting various liquids, such as fruit juice, wine, or grain alcohol. Your culinary vinegar collection should include basic **distilled white vinegar** and tangy **cider vinegar**. Add good-quality **wine vinegars**, red and white, as well as **Balsamic vinegar**, which is made from the unfermented juice of wine grapes and aged in wooden casks. A good balsamic vinegar is sweet and mellow. **Rice vinegar** is a white, rice-based vinegar that's very mild; use it in Asian-style dishes and in salad dressings. **Sherry** and **champagne vinegars** are two other wine-based products to try, and you can also buy vinegars flavored with herbs, such as tarragon.

WASABI
see Horseradish

WATER CHESTNUTS

This crunchy Asian tuber often turns up in Chinese stir-fries. It has the texture of a very firm apple and a neutral flavor. Whole and sliced water chestnuts are sold canned; they should be rinsed and drained before using.

WHISK

A pear-shaped "cage" formed of wire loops attached to a wooden or metal handle, this kitchen tool is made for blending and beating, especially when you want to incorporate air into the food. The word "whisk" is also a verb, meaning to beat with a gentle but rapid motion.

WILD RICE

Not a true rice, this native American foodstuff is the seed of a type of marsh grass. The long, slender, brown kernels are chewy, with a smoky, nutlike flavor. Wild rice is expensive, so it's often combined with white or brown rice to "stretch" it.

WORCESTERSHIRE SAUCE

This tangy, savory condiment and cooking ingredient is a thin brown sauce made from vinegar, molasses, garlic, anchovies, tamarind, and onion.

YEAST

This microscopic single-celled organism feeds on carbohydrates and produces carbon dioxide gas—which is what makes dough rise. Yeast comes in several forms: **Active dry yeast** is a dry granular yeast that comes in individual packets. **Quick-rising yeast** is special dry yeast that works faster than regular yeast. **Compressed yeast** comes in moist little cakes, individually wrapped. See page 18 for how to "proof" yeast (see if it's still active).

YOGURT

This delicately tart cultured milk product may be made from whole, low-fat, or skim milk. Whole-milk yogurt, naturally, has the best texture and flavor. Plain yogurt can be used in dressings, dips, and marinades; it can also stand in for buttermilk in baking.

ZEST

The thin, bright-colored outermost layer of the rind of citrus fruits. Zest contains powerfully aromatic oils and is used as a flavoring. The white pith under the zest layer is bitter, so be careful not to remove it when peeling zest from fruit. See page 8 for how to grate citrus zest.